Commonly known as the 'Queen o̶f̶ ̶ has become one of Australia's favou̶r̶i̶t̶e̶ ̶p̶a̶r̶e̶n̶t̶i̶n̶g̶ authors and educators, with a particular interest in the early years, adolescence and resilience.

Maggie's experience includes teaching, counselling and working in palliative care/funeral services and suicide prevention. Maggie is an advocate for the healthy, common-sense raising of children in order to strengthen families and communities. She is a passionate, positive voice for children of all ages.

Now an in-demand writer and speaker, Maggie is a regular contributor to Fairfax's Essential Kids website and she can often be heard on ABC and commercial radio around the country, including Nova 93.7. She also appears on national TV programs. Maggie is the host of the ABC's *Parental As Anything* podcast.

She is the author of six books, including her bestselling 2018 release *Mothering Our Boys*. Maggie has also authored several e-books and is a prolific creator of resources for parents, adolescents, teachers, educators and others who are interested in quietly improving their lives.

Maggie is the proud mother of four wonderful sons, and an enthusiastic and grateful grandmother. She lives in the South Coast region of NSW with her good bloke Steve Mountain and their dear little dog, Mr Hugo Walter Dent.

MAGGIE DENT

from boys to men

MACMILLAN
Pan Macmillan Australia

First published 2020 in Macmillan by Pan Macmillan Australia Pty Ltd
1 Market Street, Sydney, New South Wales, Australia, 2000

Reprinted 2020 (five times)

A catalogue record for this
book is available from the
National Library of Australia

Typeset in 10.5/16 pt Sabon by Midland Typesetters, Australia
Printed by IVE
Cover design by MDCN Creative
Cover image and model used for illustrative purposes only

Extract from *Teen Brain* by David Gillespie reprinted by permission of
Pan Macmillan Australia Pty Ltd. Copyright © David Gillespie, 2019.
Extract from *The Grown-Up's Guide to Teenage Humans* by Josh Shipp
reprinted by permission of HarperCollins Publishers.
Copyright © Brilliant Partners, 2017.

The paper in this book is FSC® certified.
FSC® promotes environmentally responsible,
socially beneficial and economically viable
management of the world's forests.

In the author's note, I write about Matthew – a boy whom I had the honour of teaching in 1977.

I dedicate this book to Matthew and all the other Matthews in our world who find themselves in middle school or high school with a wounded heart or a broken spirit, low literacy and/or learning challenges or special needs, and who struggle every single day. Also, to all the Matthews whom we have missed and who have slipped through the cracks.

May we strive to stop punishing them by still using outdated behaviour management programs. Instead, may we find them the caring adult allies they need to thrive. May we offer these boys support to identify their needs and meet those needs while also recognising and celebrating their unique strengths.

Every boy matters.

Contents

I wish to acknowledge and pay my respects to Australia's first peoples and to the traditional custodians of this amazing land. I especially pay my humble respects to the Noongar peoples of South West Australia, the custodians of my homeland, the country of my childhood, which I carry deeply within my heart every day of my life.

The ancient knowledge and wisdom that our Indigenous elders have known and shared for thousands of years still has value for our modern world. May we all find ways to walk gently and compassionately on these ancient lands, and come to a place where every child ever born is respected, valued and has a strong sense of belonging.

Breakout Key

Keep an eye out for the following breakout boxes throughout this book. They each mean something different:

> ### MEN'S SURVEY
> This box contains a quote from a survey of adult men reflecting on their teen and tween years, conducted online in 2019.

> ### TEEN'S SURVEY
> This box contains a quote from a survey of current teen boys, conducted online in 2019.

> ### MAGGIE TIP
> This box contains a relevant tip from the Queen of Common Sense.

> ### INFO BOX
> This box contains scientific or other information relevant to the topic at hand.

Foreword

by Dr Michael Gurian

Our boys need us now more than ever. While some boys succeed and thrive, many do not, and every parent of a boy is on the front lines of a collective distress in modern culture around how to be a healthy boy and loving, wise and successful man.

Maggie Dent knows a lot about boys! She has raised boys herself, and her research and teaching is popular and profound. To raise boys the 'Maggie Dent way' is to advocate for and raise girls well, too. The lives of boys and girls, and women and men, and everyone across every spectrum are vastly interconnected. What we do for one, we do for all.

As a child advocate and author in the United States, I've long admired Maggie's work not just for her unmistakable wit but also her insights and practical strategies that resonate with both brain science and common sense. Maggie understands the spontaneity of the parent–child relationship, which is the mark of a good writer and communicator. When Maggie speaks, I love to listen!

In this book you will learn how to:

- raise healthy boys in a complex and challenging digital age
- manage adolescent brain and social changes that impact choices and behaviours
- build resilience in boys, no matter the obstacles they will face
- best communicate with your sons (and even your husbands!)
- navigate under-motivation and potential high school disengagement among boys
- help your sons build networks of good people to guide them.

Boys have always been raised by many people – women, men, elders, peers, siblings, mentors, coaches, teachers. The only requirement we need have for one another is that all of us *understand boys*. Maggie understands boys and I join her in congratulating all of you in what you have done already in 'son-raising'. We are in this journey together.

Dr Michael Gurian, *New York Times* bestselling author, including *Saving Our Sons* and *The Stone Boys*

Author's note

It was important to me to have the voices and views of both teen boys and men in this book. I am enormously grateful to the 1672 men over 30 and the 957 boys aged 12–18 years who took the time to complete our 2019 online surveys. I have included many of their authentic responses (unedited out of respect for their voices).

The survey for men received responses from around the world, not just Australia but from the US, the UK, New Zealand, Canada, Singapore, South Africa, India, Thailand and several countries in Europe. I asked these questions:

1. Looking back, who helped you most as a teen?
2. What did you most enjoy doing for fun as a teen?
3. What was your most challenging experience when you were a teen?
4. What advice do you have for teen boys today?
5. If you had your teen years over again, what would you change?
6. What do you wish your parents had done differently when you were a teenager?

In a way these voices, looking back across the bridge, validated many of my own views about supporting teen boys and they also changed the shape of my intended book.

This is how I will display the men's responses throughout the book.

IF YOU HAD YOUR TEEN YEARS OVER AGAIN, WHAT WOULD YOU CHANGE?

Show more respect to my parents. They are there to help you and will always do what they can to protect you even if I didn't realise it at the time.

I was blown away by the teen boys' honesty. Being anonymous can allow for such expressions of truth without fear of judgement. Their responses really show the wide range of concerns they have and what they believe can help them.

The questions I asked the boys were the following:

1. What is the best thing about being a teen boy today?
2. What annoys you most as a teen boy?
3. What worries you most about growing up?
4. What do you most enjoy doing for fun as a teen?
5. Who is your 'lighthouse' – significant adult ally – not your parents?
6. Do you have access to good men in your life?

This is an example of how I will be displaying the teen boy answers throughout the book.

WHAT WORRIES YOU MOST ABOUT GROWING UP?

When I have kids will this planet still be alive or will it be dying, is there any point in having kids anymore is it too late?

I will be sharing many true stories throughout the book, and out of my deep respect for the boys and men whose stories I will share,

I am going to give them pseudonyms. So all the boys will be known as Oliver and all the men will be known as Gary. I may or may not include their age in brackets.

The only exception to this is my first story because I have shared this story about Matthew many times. Matthew and his story have shaped me as a teacher, a counsellor and a mum.

This is Matthew's story

In my first year of teaching as a high school English teacher, I met a wise 'teacher' in one of my classes. His name was Matthew. He was 13 and he was illiterate. I can still clearly remember his cheeky, smiling face and the most beautiful brown eyes peering out from under his long fringe. Matthew was always restless and found it hard to sit still in class and to concentrate. Not once during my university degree to become an English teacher had anyone mentioned I may have students who could not read or write in my classrooms!

One afternoon after helping him with some work, I offered to drop him home as it was really hot. We lived in a large country town and so this was not seen as an unusual thing to do back in 1978. When I arrived at his home, he asked if I would like a cup of tea. His manners and his courtesy took me by surprise. In class, all I had heard were the typical boy responses 'yep' or 'nup' or more commonly 'dunno!'.

Once inside, he turned the kettle on and excused himself for a few minutes and soon returned with the washing off the line all neatly folded. Anyone who has sons will know this is pretty unusual. Washing brought off the line usually still has the pegs attached!

Then Matthew said, 'I am home first and so I help Mum get things done as this is her late day and Paul, my brother, has basketball training. I just have to put a chicken in the oven and then I will make your tea. Is that all right with you?'

I watched as this capable young lad took a chicken out of the refrigerator and put it into the oven for his sole-parent mum and obviously much-loved brother. Then we had a cup of tea made with a teapot and a strainer. We chatted about many things, from friends to pets to his favourite foods. It was a very comfortable experience and I felt I was in the company of someone much older – someone I had never met before. Someone who had taken off his teen mask!

The following week, I showed the class a video that was an introduction to a topic on tolerance. It was a symbolic presentation that simply showed different coloured dots that moved around with background music. When it had finished, I asked the class what the video was about. There were many confused faces in the room and even my highest achieving students had no idea what the video was about.

Matthew put up his hand and said, 'Miss, it's easy. The video is about colour prejudice and shows how some people think they are better than other people because of the colour of their skin – and that's not true. We are all the same really. We are all one.'

The class was stunned and so was I. Here was the boy who couldn't read and could only write a few words showing us that wisdom, true wisdom, cannot be measured by grades or assessment. Matthew showed me that day something that all teachers need to know. Students cannot be judged by their academic performance, their dress, their hair or the way they behave. What is important is that we believe in the inherent goodness and wisdom that lie within, maybe dormant, but still present nevertheless. It's the character and humanity that quietly develops within us all as we progress through life that are really significant. My perception that illiterate students may be in some way dumb or less intelligent than those more literate students was shattered forever – thankfully!

From that day on, Matthew was respected in our class and that meant the world to him. He felt he belonged and that people cared. His behaviour was never a problem and the other students helped him with his literacy tasks and always turned to him to listen to how he viewed the world.

Unfortunately having poor literacy skills meant that life outside of school was much tougher for Matthew. It was almost impossible for him to get a driver's licence or fill in job applications, as this was before today's technology. Without a supportive network other than his loving mum and brother, who loved and cared for him, Matthew struggled in life and numbed the pain of believing he was dumb and useless with drugs and alcohol.

This journey took him into mental illness and deep depression and Matthew took his own life when he was 23 years of age.

I hold Matthew as one of the wisest teachers I ever met. The world lost a bright light when he died. Matthew helped me become a better human being and I owe it to him and all the other Matthews in our schooling systems to help them find a way to be supported to discover their place in our world.

Matthew's story showed how often boys' authentic selves are hidden deep under a mask and this is why I asked teen boys to share their views and opinions. The most powerful part of the survey was the advice that men gave the teen boys today. It is hard to believe that these men were also once – a long time ago – confused, moody boys struggling with all the things that come with changing from being a boy into a man. Check out some of the profound messages, and then it's time to dive into the book.

WHAT ADVICE DO YOU HAVE FOR TEEN BOYS TODAY?

- Stay true to who you are. Focus on your goals and strive to achieve. Be good to all people.
- Just be yourself and you will find people/friends or they will find you! Stand up for yourself, even if you're scared.
- Be confident and follow your own dreams and interests. Don't be influenced by your peers to be someone you are not.
- Sometimes you have to back yourself. Be your own backup; learn from mistakes and double check what you do. Make it easier to trust yourself so you can back yourself.

- Do whatever you have to, take whatever actions you need to, to find out who you really are and be that regardless of those around you. If you can't do/be that, go find somewhere where you can. And, find out the things YOU, your heart, really wants to do.
- Look out for those around you. If you see someone being bullied, or who looks lonely, or is struggling, step up and help them. Be the man you want to grow into. Because when you are a man and you look back on it, you'll cringe and wish you could go back, do more, and be better.
- You're not alone. It gets easier. There is always someone who wants the best for you. Sometimes you just need help finding who that is.
- You're at the start of a long journey, many men have been here before, learn from them as much as you can. Now is the time in your life to start understanding who you are and have fun trying things out. You won't always get it right and nobody expects you to, but be aware of what you're learning and ask for help.
- And . . . get off your f@cking phones!
- Don't get caught up in trying to be the macho, stereotypical male because you can do and gain a lot more in life in the future being a strong but caring and nurturing person.
- True 'alpha males' are like Hugh Jackman; they are in touch with their whole emotional spectrum; they love their wife and children; they seek to better themselves for the benefit of their family. Shirt-off posturing is not alpha. Be a true gentleman.
- It's not a sign of weakness or lack of manliness to want to talk through issues, to have self-doubt or to become emotional. However, you do need to express your emotions respectfully.
- We don't care whatever has happened, we love you and we would love to know stuff that's going on with you so we can help you. We only want to help you get through shit . . .
- Less screen time, more engaging with other people. It makes me so sad to see so many young people stuck into their smartphones, and they spend too much time gaming. Luckily, this wasn't an issue for me. Nowadays, far too much of their lives are lived virtually.

Introduction

> What worries me is that we are not looking after our planet and that we prepare so much for our future lives, but we don't even know if we will have one because we might destroy the planet before then. I'd like to have kids but is it moral to bring people into the world where their world is going to be destroyed? However, at the same time we don't want to sacrifice anything that we already have especially technology which is one of the biggest contributors to the destruction of our planet.

Every boy is a unique one-off. There is no-one else on this earth who sees the world as he sees it. No-one else who has his unique set of genomes in his DNA with invisible codes of strengths and challenges. No-one else feels things the way he does. His experience of the world is valid and coming to understand it will help you be the teacher and guide he needs as he travels from being a boy over the long bridge to becoming an independent, mature man.

So please be mindful as you read this book that some things will resonate with your son or a boy you work with, and some things won't.

This would also apply to religious and cultural differences. I will write often 'not all boys', however, I am talking about a statistically significant number of boys. Fortunately, throughout this book you will hear the voices of teen boys and men who remember being a teen boy and they bring such truth and insight to my work of over 40 years exploring how boys experience life and the world around them.

Let's be honest.

The world has changed in many unhelpful ways. Parents are much more fearful about letting their children have freedom to explore their neighbourhoods, local creeks and streams, or even to climb trees and build cubbies with their friends. This constriction of children's wild freedom to roam has seen a massive shift in boyhood in particular, and it has come at a cost that I will explore later. Rather than explore and experience life in the real world through their senses and experiences, many boys now explore the world through a screen. This shift in societal norms is especially damaging for our boys, who are still biologically wired to learn through experience – through testing themselves with real challenges with other people while learning to negotiate, construct, create and destroy! Remember that moment of jumping on top of a sandcastle that took all day to build? Now that's a moment to remember.

For most of today's tween and teen boys, boyhood has not given them a strong foundation to negotiate the massive shifts in testosterone, physical growth or brain changes that occur in adolescence. Nor has it given them the social and emotional awareness to manage the complex, ever-changing school environment. The 'schoolification' of early years care and education, and the growth in benchmark testing across the Western world has put a strong overemphasis on marks, grades and how they compare nationally. Allegedly this approach was introduced to revolutionise education and was intended to improve the academic outcomes of all students. Sadly, it has done the reverse. Literacy and numeracy rates have not improved. In Australia, there has been a huge increase in the number of four- to five-year-old children being suspended and even expelled, mostly boys. In many ways, we are punishing boys who are not developmentally ready for a curriculum that has been pushed downwards. Many of the scars from the early years follow our boys into late primary and middle school and the negative attitudes and mindsets make it really difficult to optimise engagement.

Masculinity has been attacked in recent times as being problematic but it is a very small percentage of men who are toxic and hurtful. Growing up under this dark cloud must be another challenge for today's boys. The world is full of fabulous men who are wonderful partners, fathers, uncles, coaches, educators, businessmen, academics, scientists, chefs, doctors, nurses, tradesmen, farmers, musicians and artists. The list is endless.

However, despite all the good men, history has seen horrific, disgusting and cruel things happen to women in every generation, every culture, and in every country in the world. In his challenging book *Women, Men and the Whole Damn Thing*, David Leser explores the darkest underbelly of unhealthy patriarchy. The world needed the #MeToo movement to shine a light on all the women who have stayed silent out of fear. This light has led many men, like Leser, to really question much of the conditioning that lie deep in the unconscious of the male psyche. Sadly, much of this abuse of women still exists in our world today. Of course, women have been conditioned in so many unhelpful ways too and so to really transform the way that men and women walk in our world, both genders need to question what is untrue and unconstructive. It would be wonderful to come to a place where everyone, regardless of gender, can be seen as potentially equally healthy and valued.

Statistically our boys are struggling right now – especially our boys on the adolescent journey to adulthood, from 12 to 25 plus.

More and more of our boys are choosing to end their lives – in every town in every country in the Western world. It's not just those lads who have experienced trauma, serious deprivation and abuse; many of our brightest and most capable boys are also choosing to leave this world and the people they love.

Why?

This is a simple question, however, the answers are complex and multi-dimensional. My purpose in writing this book is to help firstly parents, then other significant people – the 'lighthouses' – in our boys' lives better understand the intricacies of this turbulent time in a boy's life so we can better support them when things get tough.

Do you have any of these questions about your tween, teen or almost-man boy?

- Why has he stopped talking to me?
- Why is he so moody and unpredictable?
- Why isn't he putting the milk back in the fridge after he uses it?
- Why is he so hungry all the time?
- Why does he sometimes kick the furniture?
- Why is he so angry about nearly everything?
- Why doesn't he listen more?
- Why doesn't he wear deodorant because he stinks?
- How can I stop him gaming so much?
- Why is he just coasting with his schoolwork?
- Why has he stopped playing sport?
- When do I need to worry?
- How do I talk to him about pornography?
- What do I do when he speaks to me so rudely?
- Why doesn't he want to spend as much time with his family anymore?
- Why is he always hurting himself accidentally?
- How can I help my son who is exercising excessively?
- Why doesn't he shower every day like he used to?
- Why is he being so mean to his siblings?
- Why is he so damn grumpy and moody?

I promise I will answer all of these questions and more.

Dr Vanessa Lapointe, a well-respected Canadian psychologist and mamma of two boys herself, kindly wrote the foreword for my best-selling book *Mothering Our Boys: A guide for mums of sons.*

She shared the typical experience of so many boys who visit her psychology practice, who are struggling from years of being misunderstood.

However, in a world where the typical developmental patterns of girls have been preferred over those of boys, and where classroom environments often cater to the same, he became a normal boy who was very misunderstood. The more misunderstood he was, the more protective he had to become. And so defiance and acting out behaviours increased while quietly, on the inside, so too did his questioning of his own self-worth.

Now imagine this toxic brew of misunderstanding as the daily environment in which your precious boy is marinated. It is perhaps little wonder then that when you fast forward seven or so years, he will be much more vulnerable to becoming anxious, depressed, and/or so full of shame that he considers his only option that of ending his own life. This is what I see playing out in my clinic.

This is what brings us to our knees.

Not only are many boys struggling with feeling anxious and depressed, many also struggle with serious school disengagement, life-threatening risky behaviour, irrational anger, aggression and violence, chronic apathy, dysfunctional relationships with friends and family and self-harm behaviours, and sadly too many are still ending their lives. Boys of colour and Indigenous boys around the world are ending their lives at higher rates by far. Boys who are gay, bisexual or transgender are most at risk of dying by their own hands. Sad but true.

From the first time I stepped into a classroom, I have cared about the boys, especially the misunderstood teenage boy. Many tween and teen boys came into my room when I was a full-time counsellor and I found giving them an understanding of the things that were most confusing them could make such a huge difference. They were misunderstanding so many things that were going on around them. Confusion creates stress, anxiety and a sense of being out of control, and this then triggers a deep and profound sense of self-loathing and worthlessness that they try to escape from with so many of the problematic behaviours that sometimes have fatal consequences.

Managing conflict, especially interpersonal conflict, is something many boys and indeed men struggle with and we need to build an awareness of how to find ways to improve this. Boys and men yearn for love and affection exactly the same as girls and women. They also feel just as deeply but often struggle to articulate and express big emotions, especially spontaneously.

We cannot leave the transition from boyhood to manhood to chance anymore. All boys are at risk no matter where you live or how well-educated your son may be! We must step forward as families and communities and surround our boys with as many committed, caring adults as possible. This 'boy-tribe' needs to be capable of enormous patience, unconditional love, never-ending support and encouragement despite lots of challenging moments. The tribe needs to have the time to spend with our precious boys so that they always know they have a safe base to land when things get tough, as they will.

We can turn the awful statistics around – and we need to start now. We can only do this by learning better ways *to understand our boys on so many levels.*

Thank you for picking up this book and sharing this journey with me. You will not regret reaching out to a boy on the bridge even if he only grunts back at you. Any time you make a tween or teen boy feel noticed and that they matter, even if it's just a tiny bit, you are changing how they see themselves and how they feel about themselves. Every bit of light in the form of kindness and compassion does make a difference.

Years later men remember who was or wasn't there for them. The voices from the survey of over 1600 men show this strongly. They certainly remember and appreciate those who shone a light on that path for them. We simply need to make sure every boy on the cusp of puberty has someone beside them whom they can lean on when they need support and guidance. YouTube is not going to cut the mustard in this ancient awakening process that starts when the first pube appears. They need real people – and they need them now.

Within our communities we need to see that our boys are *our boys* – as they do in traditional kinship communities. There is no them and us, it is quite simply 'we'.

Maggie Dent
Passionate 'boy champion' who also likes girls,
August 2020

1

Help – someone has stolen my son!

Beginning the bridge to manhood

I have received many desperate emails from parents (mainly mums) asking me what could have possibly happened to their beautiful boy, even considering the possibility that he's been stolen by an alien and replaced! Many parents ask, 'Where did I go wrong? How can I fix this?' Often, they express concerns that unless their son starts to apply himself at school, he will ruin his life forever. I have certainly heard some serious catastrophising about this stage of boys' lives.

During adolescence, it can seem like an alien has stolen your beautiful boy as he becomes more forgetful, more disorganised, moodier, grumpier and seemingly insensitive to the world around him. All of this is completely normal, however, and it is well beyond his control to 'snap out of it' or to 'be more thoughtful!' Or worse still, 'grow up'.

I have some good news for a tiny percentage of you: there are some boys who stay delightful, cheerful and who change very little in this window. I have met some over the last 42 years since I first stepped into the classroom. Let's hope you have one of these as it really is so much of an easier ride. They will still make really poor choices though and possibly still struggle to notice they smell, but their communication capacity is not compromised in any way!

In my many years as a secondary English teacher and then as a lucky mum of four lads, I met so many 12- to 14-year-old boys who fit the description above. They were so forgetful. They had no idea where they had left their sports shoes, computers, phones or bags, and left all manner of things behind wherever they went. They were often disorganised, not remembering when assessments were due (even when I reminded them!) or being able to find their files or biros. Compounding this, they became increasingly difficult to understand as they mumbled and offered up monosyllabic responses. As a mum, I had to deal with their endless hunger, badly behaved penises (especially at breakfast) and every excuse under the sun for avoiding chores and being generally slovenly.

So often lads of this age seem like they can't be bothered with anything but perhaps there is more to it than teen laziness.

Adolescence is a completely confusing journey of change and up to age 15 is a time of incredible vulnerability for our boys, mainly because they have been conditioned not to share their vulnerable emotions and fears with anyone. These few years can be really tough on mums and dads who had a great relationship with their pre-teen boy. You can really miss him.

He will *gradually* start reconnecting to you around 16–17 as the later stages of puberty kick in. It may seem like an incredibly long time for you to feel there is a void between you and your son. Know that you are both doing the best you can with this challenging window and that seriously, it will pass. Please try to avoid endlessly wondering what you have done wrong in parenting him through his boyhood!

It really helps to create a tribe with other parents raising teen boys as well, because a village that is committed to the wellbeing of every boy is exactly what they need. Be compassionately patient and know that he will come back to you.

Today's parents and teens: the generation chasm

Further to the challenges of parenting a grumpy, smelly, monosyllabic boy is the inevitable gap between your own experience as a teen and the vastly different and challenging world your teen boy lives in. There has always been a generation gap between parents and teens. Things change from one generation to the next and this is perfectly normal. It seems, however, that in our global, fast-paced digital world the generation gap has become more like a chasm – and one which seems to keep widening almost day-by-day!

It is worth considering just how *very* different your son's world and experience are from your own as a means of stepping back and grasping the reality of the situation. It is like we are on different planets now.

> When my dad tells me stories from when he was a kid I can't believe he didn't have a mobile, a PlayStation or even internet for YouTube videos so maybe the best thing is we have these things now to talk to and play with our friends whenever we want and even if Mum makes me get off sometimes I'm not bored and don't leave the house to hang out with friends looking for something to do like my dad used to do.

How different is it for teens today?

1. **The developmental hunger to be accepted** used to take place within the family and community. It now seems to take place digitally and in the public eye (even better if you receive exposure across the world). Going viral is now a life goal!
2. **Privacy is no longer respected or valued** as it was when parents were teens. The days when it was accepted to value modesty or to be a little discreet (especially around our private parts, both in our homes and in public) have almost disappeared. Many argue that this shift in social norms has to do with the influence of pornography.

3. **Sexting images** of breasts, penises and vaginas is seen by some, however thankfully not the majority of teens, as fun and a part of courtship. An Australian survey of 600 girls aged 15–19 found 51 per cent believed that girls were pressured into sending sexy images. This pressure came from boys. We have some work to do as this was not even on the horizon when today's parents were teens!

4. **Children are being marinated in sexualised images** from a young age from so many different places: billboards, advertising, online, social media, TV shows and films. Body-image pressures are impacting both our boys and girls in such unhealthy ways and it is so much worse than in the previous generation.

5. **For many teens, sex has become just something physical** – not something to be savoured with someone you have feelings for. It is just something you can do if you want, to have fun, to fit in and to hopefully have someone notice you. Both boys and girls have been watching pornography and by the mid-teens they have been conditioned by it in ways that would horrify most parents.

6. **Violence is now prevalent** in so many forms, from our 24/7 news channels, to videos of beheadings on YouTube, violence in online games, the sharing of fight videos from school grounds, and the endless, senseless violence of films that (despite adult ratings) are viewed so easily by teens in illegal downloads or on mum and dad's Netflix or Plex or other streaming apps.

7. **The internet has become like the proverbial rabbit hole** that most of our teens have disappeared into. They are mainly defined by their relationship with their online world; it is irreparably connected to who they are. We cannot cut them from this world because that is how they stay connected. Yet this is also where teens connect with sexual predators, bullies and trolls who cause so much suffering. Helping them to navigate this world safely is a huge, necessary responsibility. See my 10 agreements for gaming in chapter 18.

8. **Teens today can solve most problems via Google.** Instead of needing adult guidance most teens know there will be a video on

YouTube that can teach them anything! They also expect they will always have wi-fi and their phone, which can be a dubious reality for many when they need to find that solution, as fake sites and fake news is rife.

9. **Digital abandonment by parents**. Many of today's teens have had parents who have been significantly distracted by their phones and this means they are less connected BEFORE they push back from their parents as puberty happens.

10. **Mental illness** has increased among 12- to 24-year-olds. Mission Australia's 2018 Youth Survey reports that 22.8 per cent of Australians aged 15 to 19 exhibited symptoms of a serious psychological issue, up from 18.7 per cent in 2011.

Hopefully as a parent you can now appreciate why the generation gap has become a chasm. A chasm that our teens need help to bridge.

What else has changed for teen boys?

In our survey we asked men over 30 what they had done for fun as a teenage boy.

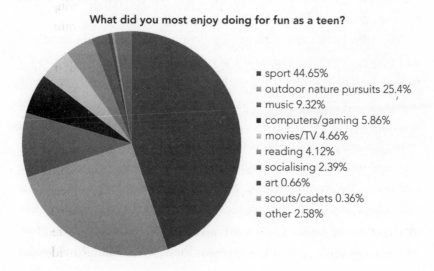

What did you most enjoy doing for fun as a teen?

- sport 44.65%
- outdoor nature pursuits 25.4%
- music 9.32%
- computers/gaming 5.86%
- movies/TV 4.66%
- reading 4.12%
- socialising 2.39%
- art 0.66%
- scouts/cadets 0.36%
- other 2.58%

We also asked teen boys what they most enjoy doing for fun as a teen today.

What do you most enjoy doing for fun as a teen?

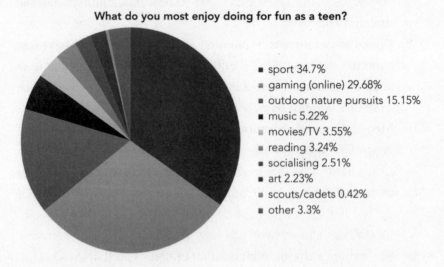

- sport 34.7%
- gaming (online) 29.68%
- outdoor nature pursuits 15.15%
- music 5.22%
- movies/TV 3.55%
- reading 3.24%
- socialising 2.51%
- art 2.23%
- scouts/cadets 0.42%
- other 3.3%

The survey results show very clearly how the pastimes of teen boys have changed. The most significant shift is from outdoor to indoor activities. The men's survey showed that as teens these men now over 30 had spent around 70 per cent of their time on sport and outdoor pursuits, and around 18 per cent on indoor pursuits such as music, reading, watching TV and movies.

The teen boys' survey showed a drop in the time spent outdoors and playing sport of around 20 per cent. The time spent indoors for today's teen boys represented in the survey is almost 42 per cent, with nearly 30 per cent gaming. It is interesting to see that the time spent reading has only dropped less than 1 per cent and that the time spent on music has only dropped by roughly 4 per cent.

Combined numbers around the arts, music, reading and watching movies or TV have increased. One of the good things today is that technology has allowed more teen boys to teach themselves to play music, compose music, record music and to use technology to explore and expand their love of whatever floats their boat. Multimedia options such as making videos can be incredibly creative and educational too, and just plain fun!

Another interesting statistic showed that exactly the same number of boys and men have enjoyed skating/skateboarding as a teen boy.

But while the landscape may have changed, teens still have the same basic needs they always have. With the help of this book, you can navigate these choppy waters together with your teen and see him grow into a responsible, mature, compassionate adult.

I want to share two letters that I think capture a powerful message – that no matter how tough the going gets, our teens need us. The first letter is an extract from a longer blog post by psychologist and author of *Journey Through Trauma*, Gretchen Schmelzer, and is published at gretchenschmelzer.com. I think it perfectly sums up what a teen might say from the middle of the bridge – and they are words we all need to hear.

Letter Your Teenager Can't Write You

. . . I need this fight and I need to see that no matter how bad or big my feelings are – they won't destroy you or me. I need you to love me even at my worst, even when it looks like I don't love you. I need you to love yourself and me for the both of us right now. I know it sucks to be disliked and labeled the bad guy. I feel the same way on the inside, but I need you to tolerate it and get other grownups to help you. Because I can't right now. If you want to get all of your grown up friends together and have a 'surviving-your-teenager-support-group-rage-fest' that's fine with me. Or talk about me behind my back – I don't care. Just don't give up on me. Don't give up on this fight. I need it.

This is the fight that will teach me that my shadow is not bigger than my light. This is the fight that will teach me that bad feelings don't mean the end of a relationship. This is the fight that will teach me how to listen to myself, even when it might disappoint others.

And this particular fight will end. Like any storm, it will blow over. And I will forget and you will forget. And then it will come back. And I will need you to hang on to the rope again. I will need this over and over for years.

I know there is nothing inherently satisfying in this job for you. I know I will likely never thank you for it or even acknowledge your side of it. In fact I will probably criticize you for all this hard work. It will seem like nothing you do will be enough. And yet, I am relying entirely on your ability to stay in this fight. No matter how much I argue. No matter how much I sulk. No matter how silent I get.

Please hang on to the other end of the rope. And know that you are doing the most important job that anyone could possibly be doing for me right now.

Love, Your Teenager

Please don't let go of the rope, parents – no matter how much you are challenged.

After a weekend when I read too much negativity aimed at teens in both print media and online I felt moved to write this letter to all teens, not just teen boys.

A letter to a 21st century teen: 10 things I want you to know

Dear Teen,

There are so many doomsayers and negative voices speaking despairingly about what's wrong with being you (a teen) today. That's why I'm writing this letter: to reassure you that even though the world has changed a lot over the last 20 years, what you need to thrive and grow hasn't really changed at all.

However, the statistics are pretty clear that more and more children and teens are struggling with anxiety, depression and a deep sense of apathy about the world that we grown-ups have created for you to inherit. I am really sorry about that.

So I am writing this letter to all of you who are on this bumpy ride to adulthood. I'm going to explore for you some key concepts and ideas that may help you when things get wobbly, as they often do during this incredibly tumultuous time of your life.

There are 10 things I'd like to share with you.

1. Change triggers stress

From around 10 years old, you will have been experiencing invisible changes that have caused you stress. These are changes you did not ask to happen and they are changes that are biologically woven into our DNA to ensure that each child transforms into an adult. This is why this stage is called 'adolescence' – it is a time of major change that transitions you from being a child to being an adult and it can make things pretty bumpy from the ages of around 12 to 25.

Invisible changes are happening to your hormones, your physical body, your emotional world and most importantly and completely invisibly, in your brain. On top of these invisible changes, you will experience other forms of change that will definitely make you feel very wobbly. New schools, new teachers, new classrooms, new time-tables, peer and friendship conflicts, weight gain, weight loss, lost phones, broken hearts, failed tests, physical injuries that prevent you doing things you love, online nastiness, exhaustion from lack of sleep, poor choices that end up with more conflict in your life, clashes with parents around your need for independence and autonomy, increased disorganisation, highly volatile emotional states, moods that are really hard to change, struggles to avoid using technology like gaming or social media in harmful ways, and even a global pandemic.

When we feel we have a sense of control over our lives, we often feel calmer. With the list I have just written is it any wonder that you have some days when you feel incredibly stressed, scared, confused and really unsure about how to make yourself feel better?

This is normal. This happened to all the grown-ups who
are on our planet at the moment. This happened to me.
This happened to your mum and dad. It will pass just
not for a while.

HOT TIPS

1. Not everyone will agree with you. That's OK.
2. Not everyone will like you. That's OK.
3. Not everyone will be friendly. That's OK.
4. Not everyone will see the world like you. That's OK.
5. Not everything will go the way you want. That's OK.

2. How your adolescent brain can get you in trouble

During adolescence, your brain's changes are mainly responsible for an increased intensity of emotions – both good and bad – a hunger for risk-taking behaviour, and a tendency to make impulsive choices that lack thought and consideration. This means you will make some really poor decisions.

So please keep in mind that if you make a poor decision that you deeply regret, *you are not dumb or stupid or flawed*. You have an incomplete adolescent brain that is prone to making impulsive, poor choices, especially in the heat of the moment.

The prefrontal cortex in your brain, which helps you make much better decisions, does not finish developing until sometime in your mid-twenties. So if you have a friend or a sibling who makes a poor choice, especially one that causes physical pain, know that they will struggle for some time after the event. Step forward and be a good friend as it really will make a difference to how quickly and how much better they will recover. Remember every teen's worst enemy is themselves.

3. Feeling stressed and anxious is not always a bad thing

You are meant to feel anxious when you start a new school, you have to do an oral presentation in class, perform in front of the school or you have an exam or test or when something awful happens.

A certain amount of anxiety can be beneficial to increase your capacity to focus. However, when it is flooding you, and paralyses you from going to school, or from having a go, it has become problematic.

Learning ways to calm anxiety and stress are an important part of managing our own wellbeing.

There are many ways to build positive neurochemicals that can counteract the stress neurochemicals and you need to learn what they are as soon as you can. For some it's music; for others it's physical activity; for some it's spending time in nature and that might mean fishing, mountain biking, surfing or just walking the dog.

You can take charge of whether stress takes charge of you or not.

Every now and then, give yourself an opportunity to stretch yourself – choose a new goal, take up a new hobby, set a different PB – stretching builds courage and confidence.

4. Please don't listen to your inner critic voice

The mindless thoughts that flood through your head really get stronger in adolescence. Small things can easily become big things and I explain this as being an ANT attack. ANT stands for automatic negative thoughts, and if they are allowed to run wild in your mind, you can get stuck in some really dark places.

Hiding deep inside your mind is also the voice of your 'higher self' or your inner compass. This voice is much quieter than the inner critic and can be really hard to hear in a teen's brain. If you can learn to practise some mindfulness or calming strategies, you will begin to hear the incredible wisdom that it holds for you. The more stressed you are, the less you will hear this wise voice. Before you make a quick decision, pause, take a few deep breaths and imagine you are asking your heart if this is a good idea. Better still, sleep on any decision that is really important and ask yourself the question again in the morning.

Some of our craziest behaviours are often an attempt to end an ANT attack because they tend to trigger more stress, more of the stress hormone cortisol and it feels really lousy.

Pleasurable activities – both real and imagined – can help you feel better in your inner and outer world.

Remember everything begins with a thought and keeping an eye on your thoughts will help you to clear negative ones when they appear.

So kind thoughts, grateful thoughts or thoughts about how to help or encourage others always make positive brain chemicals and act like ANT poison!

5. Find your real life 'spark' and prioritise it in your life

No matter what it is – being an environmental warrior, a climate activist, being competent and passionate about horse riding, painting, dancing, cooking, music, outdoor education, fishing, footy, watching other people play games on YouTube, breeding ducks, chatting with your friends, mountain-bike riding, rock-wall climbing, yoga – find the thing that makes you 'spark' and do it often. This will improve your mood, give you energy and basically improve your life.

6. Find your lighthouse

Every teen needs to have a significant adult ally who is not their mum and dad; I call them 'lighthouses'. Sometimes it can be a teacher or a coach, an aunt or uncle, a neighbour, a family friend, a friend's mum or dad – you just need to have somebody who genuinely cares about you and believes in you.

What is interesting is that so often teens who have had a wonderful lighthouse, automatically want to be a lighthouse for another teen in the future.

7. Be a good friend

Watching out for your friends will help you become a more caring human being. Tell your friends that you care about them often and that you have got their back.

When teens feel emotionally flat they can stop connecting with their friends and the outside world and this can be a very dark place for them to be. It's always OK to ask your friend 'are you OK?' and the simple act of just listening, being there and letting them cry with you is often enough. Remember, though, if you fear for a friend's safety, you may need to seek help from a trusted adult (and please check out many of the online support services that are available for adolescents).

8. Embrace the gifts that failure can give

No, seriously, failure really can be a gift! If you fail a significant test at school, this will tell you that you were not prepared enough, or that you did not have the required level of understanding and you can go and ask a teacher for help. On another level, the failure might be suggesting to you that this won't be something you will pursue for the rest of your life.

Yup, it feels awful when we fail and if we can support our friends when they fail, that can be really helpful. So many elite athletes and famous people have failed big time in their lives before they brushed the dust off, got back up and had another go.

Failure is not always pleasant, and it is not a true indicator of who you are or the depth of your character. It is just something that happens and it will happen when you're a grown-up too.

What's that saying? 'If you're not failing then you're not even trying.' That is so true.

9. Your parents really love you

No, really, they do!

There will be times that you will have significant conflict with your parents and you may even shout at each other and slam doors.

The push and pull of independence is as ancient as the beginning of time.

Parents want to keep you safe and away from harm and you want to spread your wings and fly away.

I believe every parent is doing the best job they can with the skills they have and parenting is a really difficult task in a world that is constantly changing . . . and they really love you.

Seriously, your parents really do love you no matter how tough the going gets. If you are struggling, please ask for their help. Please. And if for whatever reason you can't go to your parent/s, please ask another adult you can trust. We all want you to get through to adulthood.

10. You are not your grades

There are a lot of grown-ups who put pressure on teens about their school grades and what they are planning to do with their lives, especially what career pathway they are planning to choose.

For so many of you getting through tomorrow is often your number one goal. For those of you who have a dream – hold onto it tightly and don't let any grown-up steal it or crush it!

For those of you who aren't sure, I am going to give you another suggestion about what to do with your life to keep in the back of your mind. Quite simply aim to make the world a better place in some small way. See what you can do in order to do that every day.

You could pick up some litter, you could help an elderly person with their shopping, you could initiate a recycling program in your school, or make your mum a cup of tea or you could stop teasing your little sister just for a day.

Every time you do something to help someone else or to help our planet, you will make yourself feel better and more worthwhile. It is actually that simple.

So dear teen, these years of transformation and change will have many wobbly times where you will find yourself confused and a bit lost.

It's really important to know that bad things happen to good people. Everything is not your fault. With no rhyme or reason, life can just deliver some very hard things to us sometimes.

You are not alone. It's happening to so many on this bumpy ride – and to all of your friends! Search for the good grown-ups who understand and who can hold a safe base for you to fall upon.

As your brain matures, you'll see there are far more good grown-ups in the world than you might believe. Again, I want to emphasise if you're worried about a friend be bold and speak to a lighthouse because sometimes teens can be really struggling not just wobbling, and seeking help may save their lives.

Things will gradually get better as you get closer to 20 and by 25 so much of the internal angst you may feel now will have settled and you'll be making fantastic choices about your own life in a responsible way.

Be mindful of ignoring the negative messages about being a teenager from those who have a poor understanding of the unique potential for goodness and hope that lies within every teenager's heart.

Spread those wings and fly. You've got this.

PART 1

WHAT'S GOING ON WITH OUR BOYS?

2

The bridge of adolescence and the biological drivers towards manhood

For a long time, people have used the metaphor of a bridge to describe the journey from childhood to adulthood. It is a rather simple but perfect way to explain adolescence, which in this book will refer to the journey across the bridge from boyhood to manhood. Adolescence can be a stage or time of life that shapes the rest of an individual's life, either positively or negatively. Each boy has his own blueprint for when he will begin and complete adolescence and the unique challenges he will meet during his time on the bridge. Puberty is just one part of adolescence; there is so much more to it than those often very visible physical changes.

Adolescence in the past

Evolutionary biologists have explored how traditional cultures of thousands of years ago took the bridge to manhood, and indeed womanhood, very seriously. Sometimes from as early as 10 boys were removed from the safe nurturing circle of women to spend time with men. Gradually, day by day boys were mentored and taught how to become healthy, capable and respected men. They were not only taught important life skills, they were taught how to make choices that were in alignment with the values of their community. They also experienced strong bonding activities through rituals with men such as song, dance, craftwork, making tools, musical instruments and ornaments, cooking and storytelling. There were plenty of times for fun and laughter and the strong sense of shared purpose held each boy in a safe sense of community.

To be finally recognised as a man, boys needed to go through a rite of passage and again this was something they needed to earn. It was not simply a consequence of a boy turning 18 or 21.

Adolescence today

Mentoring in real-time has almost disappeared today, and I believe this is contributing to the loss of many of our young lads. Overcrowded curriculums and an excessive focus on accountability and testing has stolen much of the precious time where passionate teachers stepped forward as mentors to our boys during the most vulnerable years of adolescence.

Even just one hundred years ago, puberty tended to begin later (around 14) whereas nowadays puberty is beginning earlier and earlier and girls are menstruating earlier and earlier.

Today, both boys and girls are finishing adolescence much later, usually sometime in the mid-twenties, and for boys it is more towards the late twenties. So, the bridge to adulthood is now much longer than it was traditionally and that could explain why we have so many confused, frazzled and stressed parents. Heck, five years of parenting an adolescent sure looks like a better option than 10 to 15 years!

Teens still need their parents and other good grown-ups to help them navigate this incredibly confusing, unpredictable, sometimes chaotic and always fascinating time of change. Indeed, part of the message of this book is not to leave your parenting job because you think they are now mature and don't need you. It can be hard to see your six-foot son at age 14 and not think that he has matured early. Let me reassure you his body may have matured but his brain certainly hasn't. In a way it's a bit like driving a Porsche without brakes. Avoid listening to all the doomsayers who complain about our teen boys and who think that they are all bumbling, incompetent beings. Your son needs to cross the bridge to manhood by walking on his own two feet. He definitely needs his parents just like you need the railings on the bridge. Even though there is a part of him yearning to be free to be a man, there is also a small boy inside him yearning to be back in his boyhood.

From boy to man

Essentially, as a boy crosses the bridge to manhood he moves from 'boy psychology' to 'man psychology'. This is how Dr Arne Rubinstein describes this process in his book, *The Making of Men*, a great read for parents on helping your son to develop a healthy personal identity in adolescence. At some point, a boy needs to be called upon to grow up and leave his boyhood behind and accept the responsibility and the unique gifts of being a mature man. For this change to occur, a boy needs to have a well-developed prefrontal cortex, which he will not form until the end of adolescence. Developmentally, it can be difficult for our emerging future men to always act respectfully and conscientiously. It's much like how toddlers act out developmentally as toddlers are meant to. Thankfully, both these phases do pass, however, we need to keep expectations in alignment with reality. Frankly, we need to learn to love what is, not just what could be.

Boy psychology
- I seek acknowledgement
- I want it all for me
- Power is for my benefit

- I am the centre of the universe
- I believe I am immortal
- I take no responsibility for my actions
- I want a mother.

Healthy man psychology

- I seek that which I believe in
- I share with my community
- Power is for the good of all
- I am just part of the universe
- I know I am mortal
- I take full responsibility for my actions
- I want a relationship with a partner.

– Dr Arne Rubinstein, *The Making of Men* (2013)

Main developmental drivers in adolescence
Seeking autonomy and independence

As soon as our teens' bodies start changing as adolescence begins, they need to slowly be given more choices so we can empower them to be able to stand on their own two feet. This isn't to say we just allow them to make all their own decisions and do as they like. Autonomy should emerge gradually, and we must be mindful that mistakes and poor choices are quite normal, indeed inevitable, during adolescence. The big take-away message from this driver is that every choice will have a consequence of some kind – sometimes positive, and sometimes negative and painful. The role of good parenting or mentoring is to help them explore how to make choices with an understanding that decisions may have far-reaching consequences. When parents threaten, for example, to ground an adolescent for two years over a broken curfew or lying about where they've been, they may not be helping the adolescent learn from the experience. The teen may just become really angry and resentful, and that tends to make them rebellious. Remember, every experience will have a learning opportunity – especially the failures, the disasters and the muck-ups! There are some helpful tips in chapter 10.

In our fear-driven world, many well-intentioned and loving parents have practised a form of overprotection. I deliberately choose not to employ any of the names that are often used in the media to explain this tendency because to me it is still driven by love. Every parent wants to protect their child from pain and suffering, however, the evidence is quite strong that children learn many ways to become resilient through play in the natural world with lots of other children. They are biologically wired to interact with the world and make sense of it. They cannot work out that a footpath is too hot for their feet and could potentially burn them if they have never played in nature without their shoes, for example.

The less independence and autonomy our children have, especially from 5 to 12, the more likely they are going to struggle to push you back from the bridge so that they can make their own choices. Allowing our children to dress themselves, and to play outside on a cold day without a jumper are small examples of how autonomy can look. There are many mums who despair every day because their young son refuses to wear warm clothes on cold days! It seems that the muscle layer in our boys, which is thicker than it is in our girls, gives them more protection from the cold. This is one battle I encourage all mums to give up early with their sons. Put a jumper in their bag and let them go. They will work it out themselves.

When I was counselling full-time, I would regularly have a mum insist that her often-angry son come to see me so we could figure out what was wrong with him. Quite frequently the son revealed that what he really needed was for mum to step back a little, to allow him to make more choices and to give him some more space. This need is often both a conscious and an unconscious reaction from our boys, however, they are responding to the biological and hormonal changes happening within them. Many boys find this drive difficult to articulate and just get angrier at their mum over small and benign things.

Commanding, demanding, nagging and yelling will always inflame a teen boy who is trying to find his own form of autonomy, sense of self and independence.

Identity searching

The search for 'Who am I?' is a huge part of the bridge to adulthood. Some want to follow the tribe at any cost, and others want to follow no-one!

Part of the search for identity may be expressed in appearance and clothing choices. For many teen boys, they seem to think that wearing their jeans low on their hips so you can see their underpants is a way to express themselves! Teen boys often have a favourite shirt or pair of jeans and will only wear that, even if it hasn't been washed for weeks! Commonly, teen boys can struggle with school uniforms. Many deliberately try to break the rules around uniforms partly as an expression of their identity and partly as a pushback against figures of authority. It is helpful to remember that things they do with their hair, no matter how bad they look, will grow out one day.

> **MAGGIE TIP**
>
> The louder you complain about their hair, their clothes or their choice of footwear, the longer it will stay. If your son walks in and he has some piece of metal implanted into his eyebrow, take a few deep breaths and don't overreact. If you overreact and insist it comes out, there will probably be an extra piece of metal in his eyebrow tomorrow and you could very well cause serious damage to your relationship with your son.

The fundamental need to belong

As a child morphs into an adolescent on the way to adulthood, the biological drive to survive as a species becomes very strong. In order to really maximise our chances of survival, we need to have other people around us, and in adolescence this means our need to have friends becomes stronger. Teens do have a deep need to 'just hang' together without necessarily having a purpose. If you want to still do family things like trips away or visiting old family haunts, it may pay to have your adolescent bring a friend. They simply need to be with other young people as you basically become more boring to them. So, if you have a teen boy at home, consider creating a space where he can bring his friends so they can hang out in real time. A pool table; a table-tennis table; a fire pit; the second living room/rumpus room, if you have it; or the garage can make good boy hang-out spaces.

Sometimes our boys' poor choices are driven by a hunger for connection and love. Even though most boys don't look sensitive and in need of love, affection and tenderness, they are. Steve Biddulph writes about this sensitivity around feeling unloved and abandoned, especially in young boys. Ensuring your son's connection cup is full needs to be done in small ways and often – it's even better when done without words and more with actions. Kicking, hitting and fighting with siblings more than usual may be a sign your boy needs more connection. *Sometimes negative connection seems better than no connection.* Notice I use the word connection and not attention because many grown-ups still use the term 'attention seeking' and I believe that is incorrect and disrespectful in many ways.

Boys want to gain status

For a boy to feel better about himself and to be seen as 'better' in the eyes of the tribe, he will often do things to gain credibility and status. This is where some of the most risky behaviours come from: jumping from a taller branch or higher rock, or throwing rocks at windows or streetlights. This can be a real issue for boys during adolescence – so be warned and remember impulse control needs a level of maturity that he still does not have. There is seldom an evil intention behind their impulsive choices!

> Tween and teen boys tend to behave much better towards their siblings and their parents when they have a friend around.

Having positive friendships is a major protective factor for teens. However, making, maintaining and sometimes repairing friendships is something many boys can struggle with.

There is no question that many teens are feeling even more connected in the digital world than the real world. This is not all bad. Teens who can struggle socially, particularly those who are neuro divergent, have a disability or have social anxiety for example, find they can feel more connected than ever before.

It is important to note that these drivers are biological, and they occur for adolescents everywhere – even for those with special needs – and they occur according to each individual's unique inner-programming. Our teens do not ask for these changes to happen, however, they do need to happen in order to allow a child to begin the changes necessary to become an adult in the future. Interestingly boys have always liked structure, predictability and boundaries. Yes, they will push up against those boundaries, but knowing that there are boundaries and people who are creating structures to keep them safe does really matter. These are the railings on the bridge to manhood – and our boys need to know they are there.

The inner warrior

Let's explore the notion of the inner warrior: the invisible instinctual drive that makes boys and men want to stretch themselves in some way.

In days gone by, as in my father's generation, boys had the freedom to roam unsupervised on adventures. These adventures allowed them to be massively engaged in pursuits that helped them learn and grow using life's greatest teacher – experience. It was not unusual for boys to ride their bikes up to 10 kilometres to go fishing by themselves or with a group of other lads. In his book *Free to Learn*, well-respected American researcher, scholar and professor of psychology at Boston College, Dr Peter Gray explores the negative impacts of the diminishment of free play in the natural world. Nowadays, boys of the same age as my father was when he went fishing with his mates would be driven by their parents to the water and an adult would probably be present for the whole experience – perhaps even putting bait on the hooks in case their son accidentally hurt himself.

> Our boys need enough parental guidance to keep them alive versus enough freedom to allow them to seize authentic moments of joy and delight that makes them glad to be alive.
>
> – Maggie Dent, *Mothering Our Boys* (2018)

Biologically driven instincts and roles

Our modern-day phobia that the world is unsafe is creating an environment where boys are finding it more and more difficult to find that place of self-worth through external moments of potency and success, and this may be contributing to creating a generation of frustrated and angry young men. There seem to be a couple of traditional roles of mature men that have their biological beginnings inside the DNA of every little boy ever born. I wish to acknowledge and respect the work of Alison Armstrong, as several of these terms come from her excellent work.

1. The mammoth-hunter role

The first biologically driven role of mature men is to ensure the safety and protection of the tribe or community, especially those more vulnerable members of the group. This drive exists to ensure the continuation of the tribe/species. Essentially, when there was any threat to the tribe's safety and wellbeing, whether that be a rampaging mammoth or another hostile tribe, men took up arms and went to destroy the enemy. This meant the men needed to know how to kill and annihilate the threat whether with clubs, axes, arrows or other means. In order to be really competent at using weapons, when there was no threat to the tribe men spent their days practising using weapons (which is a bit like the role of sport in our modern world).

In traditional communities, men worked closely together as a collective to achieve a very valuable purpose or outcome. Even the older men would have a sense of purpose mainly as mentors and teachers for the younger lads.

This traditional drive of men working together to achieve a valuable purpose may also be in play when boys are engaged in eSport online as they do play in teams at times. This purposeful activity is fundamentally important in building a collective sense of purpose as well as an individual sense of worth. These activities fill a hunger for boys and men to belong somewhere – a great antidote to loneliness.

Evolutionary biologists claim that the *biological drive to protect and defend* is still fundamentally strong inside today's men. It is also present in our teen boys and is one of the reasons why some of the risk-taking behaviours during adolescence can frighten the heck out of parents. Seeking to feel brave and strong in a world where there are fewer collective opportunities to do that than there were in the past makes things interesting for all of us. There are still modern-day mammoth killing tasks that men feel driven to conquer. Sport, mountain climbing and surfing all create these opportunities in a healthy way, most of the time. Men have shared with me that the main reason they play in a local football team is because of their hunger for camaraderie. To be able to belong to a group that is striving for a common goal is largely innate. Our number one biological need is to belong, and it is equally important for girls as well as boys.

We see mammoth hunters among us even now, as good blokes step up during disasters, for example, and are driven to help conquer fire, flood or whatever Mother Nature is serving up by working hard to restore order from chaos. Often, they do this in extremely challenging conditions and it requires bravery and tenacity. We could consider getting our teen boys involved in these efforts in some way, through joining the local SES or Rural Fire Brigade for example. When they're able to see that collective of men working for a greater good, especially when it's potentially dangerous, there is an excellent learning opportunity for them. Of course, women work alongside the men too but I'm talking about male role models here. There are many other ways in which men pursue mammoths in our modern world: taking a risk on a business startup; building a house; travelling; racing cars or motorbikes; working in high-risk jobs like firefighters, police, sea rescue; working on scaffolding; deep-sea diving or serving in the defence force. These are all worthwhile pursuits that, if successful, give men a strong sense of their own self-worth and value. Yes, many of them are potentially risky, however, to deny boys these opportunities may be to deny them something really important in terms of their mental wellbeing.

Mammoth hunting is really about striving and stretching oneself, conquering challenge, removing threat and creating certainty. It also brings a sense of achievement, self-respect and that incredibly important thing – self-worth. It is easy to understand how some of our teen boys today who have had limited opportunity to do these mammoth-hunting activities as boys can put themselves in seriously dangerous situations without enough thought. Taking selfies in incredibly dangerous places, or attempting some of the 'Jackass' antics that they see on social media are just two examples of how boys are trying to be mammoth hunters in the modern world.

Sadly, in our world today there is still a strong individualistic, competitive pressure to win at all costs. There has been a rise in narcissistic-type behaviour among a large percentage of men that may have a quietly disturbing negative impact on our boys. Rather than the collective striving for the greater good that happened in prehistoric times, individual success seems to have taken priority.

Today, benchmark testing, some online gaming and even body-image concerns are putting undue pressure on our boys to be better than others. This means those boys who have an additional challenge, like being neuro divergent, or who have ADHD or dyslexia or maybe struggle with anxiety, often see themselves in a far darker light than just being 'different'. Feeling bad or a failure creates a mindset that can shape how a boy sees himself for life.

Young mammoth hunters, boys under eight, are hungry for experiences that give them the opportunity to conquer, win, overcome or succeed, whether that's in sport, climbing a tree, building a cubby or a den, play fighting, playing an online game or having a power play with mum. When we deny boys competitive moments in childhood, how are they supposed to feel good about themselves if they are wired to need external evidence of their ability to win? I am deeply concerned how we have sanitised play in Australia, Canada, the US and the UK.

2. The deer-hunter role

If the primary role of protecting the women and children was taken care of and there was no imminent threat, then the secondary role of men in traditional communities was to hunt meat for food, hence the metaphor of the deer hunter. This is the incredible instinctual drive that men have to provide for their families – a drive sometimes misunderstood in our modern world because women also hunt deer now too. Indeed, some women are better deer hunters than their male partners because they bring home a bigger pay packet. On some deep level, this can cause some men confusion and a sense of feeling emasculated. This is a good example of how the male map of the world and the female map of the world can be different and, without good communication, reassurance and combining abilities for the betterment of the family, some men struggle enormously. Fortunately, many boys today are being raised with mothers who are quite competent deer hunters so this old conditioning is being replaced by a more equitable view that it's OK for women to be deer hunters.

A man's internalised beliefs about being a deer hunter are largely influenced by his father's journey. Unconsciously, many men simply play out their dad's own path without questioning whether it is appropriate for them in a totally different relationship at a totally different time. Society, too, has laid down these stereotypes. One positive aspect of these changing times is the ever-increasing number of at-home dads we are now seeing. These are men who share the deer-hunting duties in their family. We are starting to see relationships as being more about teams than individuals working in specific roles. Does it really matter who is the deer hunter? Hopefully men will learn that contributing more in the traditional female roles of washing, cleaning and caring for children is essential in healthy committed heterosexual relationships, especially when the female is deer hunting. Research is suggesting that women are still doing more of the home duties than their male partners despite working similar hours.

So how does this second drive play out in the lives of our boys and how does it impact our boys on the bridge? Being a deer hunter can mean more than just bringing home food for the family. A deer hunter is also someone who can solve family problems, provide solutions and fix things, especially things that require physical strength. So often in early childhood little girls have a superior ability to organise, structure, negotiate rules and to be the problem-solvers. Generally, they think better and communicate more effectively, so often little boys are sidelined as being ineffective. Sometimes they learn to be quiet and to avoid contributing. Engaging boys before puberty in being helpful around the home and having regular chores is important. We need to create meaningful tasks where they can feel really useful and that they are contributing as deer hunters. Having family meetings where everyone has an opportunity to be heard is also a great preparation for being a healthy deer hunter in adolescence and later in life. Ideally, these habits need to be in place well before the first pubic hair arrives! Please be mindful that for our boys' developing psyche it is really important to keep them contributing in some way in the family, especially during adolescence.

The pursuit of self-worth

Michael Gurian, author of *The Wonder of Boys* (1996) and *The Good Son* (1999), and most recently *Saving Our Sons: A New Path for Raising Healthy and Resilient Boys* (2017), believes that the invisible drive at the biological core of manhood is the pursuit to prove self-worth. No-one can give a man his self-worth; he has to give this to himself. To find this place, boys and men often seek external ways or experiences to demonstrate potency, victory and independence, and this is what helps shape their search for meaning and purpose in life from a very early age. This is the 'inner warrior' unfolding from within. Boys seem to be generally competitive, active and constantly in search of moments to prove their worth and value. All boys seek the same evidence of worth from their experiences, so they can feel that they have done well. We might think of this as being like a 'self-worth barometer'. When boys are happy with what they have achieved, they feel good about themselves. If they have failed to achieve what they set out to do or, even worse, they have upset their parents or their teacher, it really hurts inside. Even from a very young age, boys will attack themselves for not being good enough or for failing.

We need to keep in mind this emotional barometer of self-worth that exists within every little boy and man and learn to treat it with respect and understanding.

Michael Gurian also writes that the amygdala (the primary aggression centre in the brain) is larger in males than females and this could be linked to *creating more aggression in males*. Given the expectations for our early civilisations, that the gender with the strongest muscles would be better at killing mammoths and sabre-tooth tigers, it makes sense that the amygdala would be larger in males. When this is combined with massive surges of testosterone, it may give us a clue as to why boys seem more wired to like risky behaviour and 'warrior' behaviour. The effect of the neurotransmitter vasopressin has also been linked to tendencies of territorialism, competition and persistence and this may explain why teen boys seek status and acceptance in the boy world. The biggest challenge we have in parenting boys is to work with these tendencies so that they can learn how to channel them in healthy and positive ways. Generally, girls have different hormones and tendencies in their brain development (and social conditioning) to boys. But this does not mean that boys are shallow and cannot learn how to contain their impulsive behaviours, especially when they impact others.

It is so important for younger boys to learn ways to regulate this impulsivity because it is really difficult once they have begun the journey over the bridge to adulthood. It is not impossible, just much more difficult.

Of course, we still often hear the phrase 'boys will be boys' when boys are being warrior-like or highly physical. However, these boys still need to be respectful of other people. All boys need to learn about boundaries that are fair and respectful with discipline that respects them. I will explore this in more depth in chapter 10.

The changing man code

Toxic masculinity has destroyed marriages, diminished father-son connectedness, impaired father-daughter relationships, sabotaged men's parenting reputation, fractured men's sense of what it means to be a man, and continued the cycle of raising more boys to be toxic masculine men.

– Thomas Haller, *Dissolving Toxic Masculinity* (2018)

Gender stereotypes still exist strongly in our society. Gender stereotypes are shifting across the spectrum, where men can now be more openly loving and caring, while women can be seen as strong, fit and brave. Having equity in pay, job opportunities and true equity in front of the courts is slowly happening in many countries.

It is worth questioning some of the messages about gender that come from our conditioning: from our childhood, from our life experiences, from popular culture, and social constructivism that we have experienced throughout our life.

Gender stereotypes that have been shaped socially and culturally can be obvious, like boys wear blue and girls pink, and as shown by different toy sections in shops for boys and girls, and messages that pervade culture and fashion. Slowly these are changing. However, there are such messages in the arts and literature which are less obvious to notice.

As a secondary English teacher there were times I had to use the *Lord of the Flies* as a text to study and there is no question that the pervading sense left at the end was that humans were really just a step away from being uncivilised and prone to domination through aggression and violence. Even though William Golding's Nobel Prize winning book was fiction, it was considered a mirror of human ecology, evolutionary biology and philosophy. The main characters were boys and so the perception was shaped that men especially had this wild, nasty streak hidden deep within them. Rutger Bregman in his recent book, *Humankind: A Hopeful History*, has seriously questioned this premise about humankind, especially about boys and men.

Bregman tells a true story about a group of teen boys who were marooned on a deserted Pacific island for a year. Unlike Golding's story of desperation, aggression and death, Bregman found these boys had worked together cooperatively and with concern to ensure the survival of everyone. It is a fascinating story that may bring into question the 'man box' view of not only teen boys and men but whole communities. Underneath horror stories of war, natural disasters and even pandemics the overwhelming majority of human behaviour is focused on the greater good and the survival of all. It just seems that the stories of the opposite that include Joseph Stalin, Adolf Hitler, Idi Amin and Robert Mugabe, just to name a few, get the most exposure in history and the media. Perhaps Bregman has made an excellent contribution to the shifting consciousness about the patriarchy and his overriding premise that humans are actually wired for friendliness and kindness, instead of control and power, may bring some serious hope for all of us parents.

Once we give these messages light, we can then have a chance of changing them. It is starting to happen and ultimately it will help our teen boys eventually traverse the bridge to manhood.

Thankfully our world is finally pulling down many of the unhealthy conditioned stereotypes of the past that were forced onto little boys such as the need to be stoic, to never show emotions and to be fearless and brave at all times. This old-world view of masculinity forced many little boys to suppress their tender emotions and their struggles to hide all moments of vulnerability, which flows through into adolescence and certainly into manhood. It makes sense that at times of failure, disappointment, loss and separation our teen boys are most at risk because it can trigger strong feelings of personal shame.

Once boys have been shamed enough for failing to be fully masculine, once they have been told enough times that they should suppress their vulnerable feelings, once they've actually been physically injured for failing to meet the mark, boys allow the wounds to scar over and cover any remaining soft tissue and act as if everything is all right.

– William Pollack, *Real Boys* (1998)

Given that many boys today are still being given messages, explicitly or implicitly, that they need to shut down their vulnerable feelings, is it any wonder they can struggle to understand empathy as they voyage towards adulthood? In their book, *The Boy Crisis*, Warren Farrell and John Gray explore the notion of 'heroic intelligence'.

Heroic intelligence teaches a man to kill, not to listen; to repress feelings, not express feelings; to take risks more than assess risks; to fake confidence, rather than acknowledge fear; to pretend he knows what he doesn't know, to not ask for help.

Farrell and Gray argue that these messages, which become deeply embedded in our boys, make it easier for them to take unassessed risks and to appear confident when really they are full of fear. In a way, boys can experience a 'compassion void' because they will find it quite difficult, especially in a high school setting, to express authentic feelings without losing status among their peers – or even worse, respect from their peers. Possibly many of our boys are caught in this catch-22 situation in the 21st century, between the old code and the new code.

Boys can learn empathy from both mums and dads during boyhood. In my survey, 56 per cent of men named their mum as their most important person during adolescence, which suggests that often mum was a safer base for them when things became challenging. Interestingly many dads are likely to empathetically protect their son until he steps on the bridge towards manhood. Unconsciously, the father may fear that too much empathy may cause problems for his son because he may be perceived as weak or not tough enough to get the respect and acceptance that he yearns for. Warm, connected mums and female teachers possibly have the best chance of working underneath the mask of masculinity and filling the 'compassion void'.

> What worries me is teen boys acting tough for show and being forced to be tough to avoid being seen as 'weak' by other teen boys. Coming from a small rural town, drinking is commonplace in teen boys. What annoyed me about this was the amount of bragging about how much drinking was taking place and some of the inappropriate comments about others that occurred while the drinking took place e.g. sexual comments/harassment and bullying.

Research shows in early childhood settings that boys are spoken to more harshly than girls. Sadly, this happens right through life. In my book *Mothering Our Boys*, I explore research around male fragility. Even from before birth males have a higher mortality rate and statistically this continues right into adulthood. It is such an interesting irony that the old male code stresses the need for toughness, without any acknowledgement of fragility of any kind.

Our tween and teen boys have the same invisible layers of sensitivity – even before adolescence starts. As parents and teachers get increasingly frustrated with our boys on the bridge, we tend to use more harsh words of criticism and ridicule that we don't tend to use towards girls.

Most boys have a tendency to have favourite clothes and comforters somewhere in their bedroom. Please be mindful not to have a big clean-up in your son's bedroom without checking in with him. I have had to counsel boys whose mums have thrown out a cricket bat from when they were about six – they were now 15! That cricket bat was one of the special things that meant something deep in his heart. You'll notice that there will be days that your tween or teen boy will still be wearing the same T-shirt. Take a deep breath, and let it be. In a way, a boy wears his favourite T-shirt because it helps him feel better about himself. He is choosing something that realistically will allow him to feel calmer and more secure in himself.

3

Important and interesting information on behaviour common to boys

From my years of experience and research into the literature around boys, I have found some general trends in boy behaviour (warning, broad generalisations ahead!). Not all boys, and definitely some girls, display some or all of the behaviour detailed in this chapter.

Temperament: roosters and lambs

I call the temperament spectrum 'the rooster and lamb continuum'. Imagine the cartoon character Linus (from the Peanuts comic strip); he would be a lamb. Lambs are generally quieter children, more accommodating and content with life. They are often more caring, thoughtful and sensitive. However, lambs often cop criticism from adults because they are 'too soft'. They make us look like fantastic parents.

Then imagine Dennis the Menace; he would be a rooster. Roosters are often loud, strong-willed and full of beans. They are brave, fearless risk-takers and often have enormous amounts of energy. Roosters' parents frequently feel like they're doing a terrible job. Alpha men are roosters!

What works best is for rooster children to learn some lamb characteristics, especially empathy and compassion, and for lambs to learn some rooster qualities that allow them to be braver and more confident.

Sadly, traditional patriarchy has only valued the rooster temperament in the past – often the biggest and loudest winners were seen as the best versions of manhood. Hopefully we can now discover that our gentler, sensitive men and boys are equally valid.

Some common behavioural traits of girls

I was a high school teacher for almost 17 years in co-ed schools. What I *frequently* noticed most about girls, compared to boys, in my classrooms was the following:

- Girls could follow instructions better.
- Girls' concentration spans were longer.
- Girls sat on their seats a lot more with less squirming and fidgeting.
- Girls tended to remember details better.
- Girls were easier to engage in activities.
- Girls needed less reminding about assessment dates.
- Girls thrived in group situations better than most boys.
- Girls came to class expecting to work.
- Girls had better organisational skills.
- Girls seldom needed to fart or burp in public.
- Girls spoke more quietly than boys.
- Girls tended to be more punctual to class than boys.
- Girls remembered their manners more often than boys.
- Girls used fewer swear words and profanities in class.

Some common behavioural traits of boys

Some autonomy helped boys perform better. In our classrooms one of the contributors to disengagement is that teachers often demand that a boy complete a set task without any autonomy or choice on how to do the task. There were times in my classrooms where if there was a written assessment to be completed, I invited the boys to choose where they would do it: on the desk, on the floor or standing on their head in the corner. This really did help to get them started on the task. The fact they could choose where they did their work was deceptively important to them and a small sign of respect. Little things matter and operating under complete authority with mandated instructions – which is a very big thing in the traditional ways of raising boys – simply makes most boys defensive and resistant.

We need to keep this in mind as parents and as teachers.
When we want our sons to do something, we increase the
chances of getting it done if they are allowed to have
some autonomy in how to get it done.

Listening can be a challenge for boys. One of the most common sources of conflict between parents and their sons – and especially mums – is that sons never listen or they seem to never hear what we say! Let me give you a possible explanation as to why it may seem like that.

Let's pretend that your son is playing Fortnite in the lounge room maybe only a few metres away from you and when you call him to come to dinner, he doesn't move. You can call out a few times with the same result. And it isn't until you scream at him that he appears to notice you are talking to him. Let me reassure you he's not doing this deliberately or intentionally. You see, in a way he was really busy; his single focus was completely consumed by the game and the burning desire to win and he did not hear you the first two times – no seriously, he didn't! Males tend to be more single-focused while females are capable of multi-focus, which is driven by instinctual behaviours and biology. So often I meet mums who genuinely think their son is deliberately ignoring them. Almost every time you will find they are completely consumed in a single-focus moment and genuinely do not hear you.

Boys generally hear less or maybe understand less. It would seem that boys' capacity to hear, especially to take in long-winded explanations and directions, is significantly different to how girls hear. In my classrooms I would often give a detailed description of what was required with an assessment task but, inevitably, two or three boys would put their hands up and ask what they needed to do. WTH? Even when I included points on the whiteboard so they could check up after I had finished explaining – they still put their hands up. 'What you want me to do, Miss?!' More recent research suggests that rather than boys hearing less, especially when women talk, this trend may have more to do with boys *understanding* less. Either way, this can be really frustrating for mums of sons. Many dads experience this too!

Boys get 'information overload'. Boys tend to struggle with too many requests given at one time or when too many words are spoken. You may often see a glazed look on their faces because they can't remember any of the requests you have just given them. This is often because of an information overload. By adolescence, many boys have been struggling with information overload, especially from the females in their life, for a long time. Many of them have learned how to look like they are listening, when they have completely zoned out and are not listening at all!

The cycle of requesting and nagging and more nagging is a sign that your communication is not working with your son and not a sign that he is deliberately being disobedient, no matter how frustrating it can be. Remember that he really does want to please you. Give your boy a good chance to be a success in communication by following these tips.

> **HOW TO ASK A BOY TO DO SOMETHING**
>
> - Get his attention before you make your request, and you really do give your son a much better chance of succeeding. The best way to get his attention is through connection – either by using a term of endearment or a head ruffle or a punch on the arm. Connect and then request.
> - Try to ask boys to do one thing at a time and then when that's done, ask them to do the next thing.
> - Often single words with clear non-verbal messages like waving hands and arms can get better results. For example, you may say, 'David – shoes' (pause and point to shoes) 'in your bag' (point to bag), 'now, please' (big smile or wink).
> - If you can keep your requests to **around 10 words or fewer**, you also increase the chances of him succeeding.

Boys have shorter attention spans. Boys' attention spans appear to be shorter if they perceive that the *activity they are doing no longer deserves their attention* or they do not think it is worthwhile. Remember the inner self-worth barometer that he is continually gauging himself against? He simply does not want to waste his energy on things that are not going to make him feel better about himself or that are not going to be fun. I believe this may be to do with boys processing dopamine differently from girls – as soon as the dopamine level drops, boys will start moving in order to build the level back up again. Boredom to boys is akin to failing or losing and that is why sometimes a young lad who is watching TV might also be jumping up and down on the couch.

Boys are biologically wired to be physically active for longer periods of time than girls and at a later age than girls. If we continue to ignore this, we do so at the peril of more little boys who struggle in their transition to big school. Movement matters and today's boys are more passive than ever before. There are some serious concerns that this passivity is contributing to the delay in the development of self-regulation. This is why there needs to be a balance between the digital world and the real world.

Boys need greater stimulation. Boys need to be sure that the activity they are about to participate in is worthwhile, interesting and something they want to do. When this tendency is combined with his teen drive for autonomy – it is obvious why conflict can occur!

Boys have memory issues. If there's one issue that drives mothers to need more coffee and chocolate, it is how frustrating it is when our sons forget things. What we do know is that memories are anchored when there are strong emotions present, which is possibly one of the reasons why we remember quite vividly very painful moments of childhood and tend to forget the blander, normal moments. So boys will tend to remember their successes and their failures, and most of the other stuff just seems to 'go through to the keeper'.

Behaviour

Dr Ross W. Greene, a psychologist and author of many excellent books, argues that many of our boys who struggle to behave 'appropriately' in our homes and our schools do so because they are lacking the skills, *not because they are innately naughty or bad*. He also argues that we need to change our focus from reactive punishment to proactive prevention because reactive punishment has a tendency, especially for boys, to quickly fuel a 'schools to prison' pipeline.

As we know, one of the biological drivers of adolescence is the need to belong with peers or friends of a similar age and the equally strong drive for acceptance and validation, not just from others but also from oneself. This inner striving also plays out within the boy world where boys are constantly striving to maintain a level of 'status' within the circle of boys they find themselves in. This is a really powerful force that almost hamstrings boys from making their own choices. Fear of losing status is behind many dumb decisions boys make at school, and when they bring home their sense of disappointment it is often poor mum who will wear their emotional angst in many different ways.

Sadly, many of our boys who have been raised with a deep understanding of a moral conscience have succumbed to this incredible pressure, much to the heartbreak of their parents.

This is why I see the window between 12 and 15 years of age as the most critical window of a boy's life. This is where we either make or break the future trajectory of their life depending on how we guide them.

Much of the homophobic language that is bandied around among tween and teen boys is driven by this need to belong with their boy mates. The hunger to be accepted or, better still, popular and well-liked, which gives a sense of validation and acceptance from outside of themselves, drives many boys to make poor choices. If a boy feels he can't belong with the cool boys, then despite his family values, he may very well choose to join the boys who are messing around in class or even smoking marijuana after class, sharing explicit intimate images or who sing disgusting sexist songs in public.

I once worked with a boy, Oliver (15), who had been struggling with the death of his grandmother, who had lived in the family home. Oliver had been quite a popular football player and said he thought he had some mates in his classroom. During one class, one of the boys called out something derogatory about his grandmother dying, and before Oliver knew it most of the boys had joined in the catcalling. He was so embarrassed that he never returned to high school and his parents could not get him to try a new school. Being so publicly humiliated by boys he thought were his mates cut him so deeply that he struggled to trust males for a very long time. The boys in the classroom probably still have no idea why Oliver suddenly left the school and never returned. They would have no idea of the part that they played in this either.

Boys can struggle with verbal communication and often their behaviour is something they use to compensate for this. Often their behaviour is their language. A boy who starts rocking on his chair in class, or flicking the person sitting in front of him on the school bus, or throwing an apple at someone during lunch is not necessarily showing signs that he is bad or stupid, he is simply struggling with a high level of cortisol, often from boredom, and is trying to make dopamine by having fun. His capacity to think about his actions beforehand is seriously compromised until his brain is fully developed, which might not be until his mid to late twenties!

> While girls communicate verbally, boys express their emotions through actions rather than words, seeking attachment indirectly through activities or play.
>
> – Dr William Pollack, *Real Boys* (1998)

If there is one thing to remember when you need to have the conversation with your son after he has 'mucked up' and made a poor choice (maybe yet again), it's that he never planned to hurt himself. No, seriously – boys are so often surprised when they do hurt themselves!

'What's in it for me?'

When asked to do things, many boys have the tendency to consider 'what's in it for me?', which is strongly linked to their self-worth barometer. A part of him wants to know if fulfilling that request is going to add to his self-worth barometer or is going to diminish his self-worth barometer. This is one of the underlying principles that I'll explore in more depth later in the book. Essentially, if you can create a deal with your son, where you make a commitment and he makes a commitment, and he can see you both win, you will have a much higher chance of getting things done than just by asking him. He genuinely cannot see what benefit having a tidy bedroom gives him. When he makes an agreement, he is putting his own integrity and self-worth on the line and it does increase the chances of success.

Pragmatism

Males have a strong instinctual drive to be problem solvers. This means that there can be a wonderful pragmatism to boys and men that we women can sometimes struggle with. This pragmatism is often misunderstood by mums in particular. If you are a woman in a boy's life, I suggest that you listen to him very carefully if he is doing something differently to the way you'd like him to be doing it.

For example, if you have a son who enjoys toast after school and you have growled at him for not cleaning down the bench after he has made his toast, listen to him. I had a similar discussion with one of my lads once and he said, 'Mum, why would I clean down the bench after I had my first toast when I know I'm going to come back in an hour and cook some more toast? It really is a waste of effort!'

On any given day, how can a son know how many pieces of toast he might need to cook given that boys get hungry very quickly, especially after physical exertion? I needed to see that through my son's eyes and realise that I was creating tension and conflict where I could simply let it go. Given I had four sons (equally hungry), I could see it was a battle that wasn't worth fighting.

Choosing the battles that are worth fighting and letting go of the ones that can wait is very much a part of parenting sons positively.

The same goes for many mammas about the need for a plate to put your toast on. So many boys think that is what your hand is made for and seriously, they have got a good point. The same goes for a napkin – the hand handles that job pretty well too!

I suspect that many boys have the same pragmatism in wearing the same pair of underpants several days in a row. If the pair he's wearing does not have a skiddy on them, then technically they are still clean! And maybe the passion that many boys seem to have for wearing no underpants at all is to do with saving washing!

Why boys make poor decisions
Boys' behaviour is a form of language

Please keep in mind boys' behaviour is a form of language. Many boys connect with those they love through wrestling and rough-and-tumble play and sometimes that goes wrong. Boys have a fundamental need to move their bodies to discharge excess energy or cortisol, which means they move without thinking. So when their movement goes wrong, we need to remember they had no intention to be disrespectful in the moment. It would seem boys don't tend to spend as much time as girls thinking about their feelings, however, they do feel them just as intensely as girls. Feeling like a failure or like they're excluded triggers big, ugly emotions that can often drown a boy, and he may respond by becoming angry and expressing that through aggression. The increasing numbers of boys being suspended and expelled in our high schools is problematic. We need to look at what is really **under the anger** because anger is a symptom rather than the problem. I explore emotions including anger much more deeply in chapter 5.

Boundaries

It can be quite tricky for our tween and teen boys to understand healthy boundaries. They may have been able to respect them before puberty, however, all of those unique changes that increase their need to be autonomous, independent and to step back from their parents can mean that they can forget family rules and guidelines. Manners that were wonderful before they turned 12 can sadly vanish. The increased need to be egocentric means that they feel their needs are often more important than anyone else's. This is developmentally normal but not exactly easy to parent or teach! For our feisty rooster boys who may have already been low in empathy, this can be a really difficult and challenging time.

Many tween and teen boys make some really poor choices around other people's personal space, often with absolutely no intention to be hurtful or disrespectful. It is excellent to see that many of our high schools are now doing education around respectful relationships and exploring consent especially around personal boundaries. Every parent needs to be having these conversations frequently and enthusiastically with their sons, so that our boys can learn how to make better choices that are respectful of the boundaries in their home, in sporting groups, in classrooms, on the school bus and in shopping centres. The conversations with father figures may be different to the conversations with mother figures but the more conversations the better. If we keep in mind that bullies are not born and know that they are made, it may help us realise that we all play a part in building caring, strong boys.

An essential premise in Meg Meeker's excellent book, *Strong Mothers, Strong Sons* is that mothers need to hold strong boundaries and invest enormous amounts of time and energy into building the moral code and emotional competence that our boys need. Helping our boys learn how to be good losers is incredibly important. You might engage in role-play, or endless noughts and crosses games, let them wrestle, or watch videos on YouTube that show men losing well in competitive situations. Do keep in mind that when a rooster boy fails in public, he will be in a highly vulnerable place, so step forward by helping him to move somewhere private as quickly as possible and avoid asking him how he is feeling. Give him a safe space to process the massive feelings that will be swirling around inside him irrationally and painfully. Emotional buoyancy – where we recover to a calmer place after we have been upset or triggered – takes years for all of us to conquer. If we stop shaming and hurting our younger boys when they make poor choices, our tween and teen boys will become emotionally buoyant much more easily. There is much work to be done before this can happen.

Some rooster boys can definitely benefit from some tough love in our homes. I do not mean any physical punishment, humiliation, hitting or shaming. Take for example an older rooster brother (15) who has taken to punching his younger brother much harder than a playful punch. If he fails to stop making this choice, you need to explain to him what negative consequence will occur as a deterrent. It needs to be something that he really loves to do: removing his surfboard for a week if he loves surfing, removing his device or the Xbox for a week if that's what he loves or if he seriously loves dessert, there will be none for the next week. This will be a very difficult week and you may need to repeat it – but this can teach your son that there are boundaries around his behaviour and some behaviours are simply not acceptable within the home.

Part of the conversation around boundaries needs to be around empathy and *helping them to understand how their behaviour impacts other people*. If you do have a boy who seems incredibly hardened and insensitive and lacking in empathy, please consider getting him a pet rat or dog. Caring for such a small pet or a good dog, especially when knowing it won't judge you or hurt you emotionally, can be transformative. Stroking a pet has been shown to lower stress levels by triggering serotonin, and having something living that likes being with you with no expectations can help open a more empathetic pathway in the brain. Therapy dogs and reading dogs often create huge positive shifts in boys who are struggling.

Many teen boys tell me that high school is a bit like a war zone. There are so many different rules, expectations and unpredictable situations that cause them stress even before they enter the classroom. I believe a poor understanding around healthy boundaries in school grounds is another reason that many boys make poor choices, especially in the presence of other boys of the same age and maturity. Many boys misunderstand personal space with other students and teachers and many struggle with appropriate levels of language and noise levels.

Hot cognition

Tween and teen boys have a tendency to test themselves due to the invisible self-worth barometer that I have explained in depth. This partly explains why many but not all boys are so competitive and why they keep striving to do better than last time. This need to prove his worth to himself is what drives much of a boy's risky behaviour. This also is why many boys often feel they have let themselves down and can get irrationally angry at themselves. And it is also why we need to change the dominant way with which we discipline boys by using a punishment of some kind that usually involves pain, both emotional and physical.

'Hot cognition' occurs when we think under conditions of high arousal and emotion and this state can be really risky for adolescents. Studies have been done comparing computer simulation performances of adults and teens in risky driving scenarios, such as running orange lights. Both groups were similar when tested alone. However, when tested in the company of friends, adults showed no change while teens showed a clear increase in risky behaviour. Teens' ability to make good driving decisions when they have friends in the car drops significantly too. Night-time driving is even more dangerous with friends, and the risk of having an accident goes up enormously, which is why many states now have a curfew on young drivers having more than one other adolescent in their car during certain hours, until they have a full licence. Distractions from mobile phones and accidents caused by texting are also a very real thing in today's world.

A decade ago, an ABC TV program screened about adolescents called *Whatever: The Science of Teens*. In it they compared a 17-year-old adolescent boy and an adult male doing a driving test. They each had to drive around a course without hitting any of the traffic cones. The results of the first attempt were quite similar. The second time they did the test three beautiful teenage girls watched them. The adolescent boy went faster and collected several of the traffic cones, while the adult male performed very similarly to his first attempt. The boy said he felt pressured to perform better and to show off with the girls there. It seems this is linked to an inner biological drive of the adolescent male – to find a mate. In order to do that, he must prove that he is worthy by being brave and fearless. We need to keep this concept of 'hot cognition' in the back of our minds when our teen boys make poor choices sometimes. It will also give you the ammunition to explain to them why you have boundaries around them not driving at night with their mates in the car. Statistically, we can show how much riskier that is and that until his brain has matured, you are setting a boundary around that. To be honest, when boys hear logical and rational explanations, especially when they are backed up by statistics, I have found they are more likely to respect parental monitoring. When we are putting boundaries in place because we have irrational fears, they can often sense that too and find it more difficult to respect. I explore this in more depth in chapter 19.

I worry about the lack of a safety net and what if I'm not good enough?

Consequences

One thing that I explored endlessly in my counselling room was the notion that every choice we make will have a consequence of some kind. Some consequences are great and really helpful and positive, while other consequences are likely to be painful, possibly embarrassing and something we may regret later.

It could be helpful for your son to realise that every choice will have a consequence and *that consequence can be a valuable learning opportunity* – no matter how painful! Given that teens tend to be functioning more from their amygdala than their wise prefrontal cortex, we still need to be understanding that they make these poor choices because they are unable to think them through more deeply like the grown-ups around them.

When my sons were teens, there were several tragic car accidents that claimed the lives of young lads, often several at once. One would think that such terrible events, which had killed boys my sons knew, would mean that they would take caution from that point onwards. Sadly, that was not the case. Developmentally, your son is not able to process the risk versus consequence when driving a car or motorbike until he is much older. Learning from experience, albeit through the experiences of friends and mates, does not always happen. The same goes for a parent or a teacher telling them about one of their own experiences in the hope the boy will avoid the same situation. Genuinely, teen boys do not think it will happen to them. 'That stuff only happens to others, Miss.' How often did I hear that sentence in my years of teaching?

This is not to say we don't share stories. Stories are hugely important in modelling, building connection and teaching empathy. I'm just saying don't have the expectation that they'll take your cautionary tales on board.

There is plenty of research that explores how many children learn by doing rather than listening to someone tell them what to do. Boys tend to disengage from situations where grown-ups talk too much, and this includes their parents and teachers. One of the best teachers for our boys is natural consequences, or where a boy learns as a consequence of a real experience. Repeated pain is a wonderful teacher too! Being hurt by a wooden seesaw up to three times is a great way for a boy to realise that he is accountable for his choices. Verbal warnings of possible dangers might simply not be heard in their hunger to 'have a go' and test themselves.

Celebrate natural consequences even though it may look like you are a lousy parent sometimes! There will be times that the choices they make will cause you incredible stress, and you may end up in the emergency department more often than you think possible. My only suggestion is to keep being grateful that your son is alive even if a little injured. I have worked with many mums and dads helping them plan a funeral for their teenage son who had two seconds of insane thinking that cost him his life, and they would do anything to be able to take him home from an emergency department with a plaster cast or some new stitches.

Testing themselves

Because of tween and teen boys' impulsivity and the need to test themselves physically, they often make poor choices that are seen as naughty or bad, as I have already mentioned. Their sense of failing and letting themselves down also adds a layer to why boys struggle with cortisol overload and the need to discharge it with a meltdown, irrational physical aggression or by running away. Sometimes boys' hunger to have fun means they act really silly, which is a way to release cortisol and make dopamine and other positive endorphins or to reduce anxiety. This can occur through farting, burping, mentioning silly words, as well as by removing their clothes. Some boys make positive neurochemicals by playing air guitar with their penis or by making other funny shapes (aka penis puppetry). When boys are trying to be funny, they are trying to connect with others and also trying to reduce feeling stressed.

Payback

Somehow in the historical conditioning of our boys and men, physical retaliation or 'payback' has been seen as acceptable and OK. In a way, this physically aggressive action has been seen as justifiable in boy world. We seriously need to deconstruct this perception and expectation. Maybe due to the difficulty of expressing big, ugly feelings, especially in the heat of the moment, when combined with the sensitive emotional barometer of self-worth, payback may seem justifiable. Regardless of possible reasonings behind this pattern of behaviour, all parents need to do everything they can to help their boys understand that conflict can be resolved and injustice can be made right *without physical violence*. This is why the emotional coaching of little boys, and then bigger boys, is so incredibly important.

– Maggie Dent, *Mothering Our Boys* (2018)

How to encourage respectful, 'good' behaviour using three simple rules

I encourage families to use these three rules that matter as often as possible for all our children, but particularly for our boys.

The three rules

Please try not to hurt:

1. yourself
2. others
3. things in the world around us.

We need to explain endlessly that hurting any of these three things is not OK – whether through words or actions! If we are able to embed these three rules deeply into our boys' psyches from as early as possible, particularly that hurting others is not okay, then, possibly, we may be able to contribute to the much-needed cultural change around the thinking that it's OK for men to molest, rape and murder women. Maybe if all homes used these simple rules as a guideline then even our girls would stop being so mean to other girls as well.

We then need to explain that there is a really big difference between accidentally hurting ourselves, others and things in the world around us and doing it intentionally. Of course, there are some children who have learned that hurting others is acceptable, or who have been seriously wronged in the past, who choose to deliberately hurt others, however, I have found this to be uncommon. Commonly, there is a reason for their behaviour that I often found had a positive intention attached to it. Sometimes, for example, your boy who was caught fighting may have been trying to defend a friend or to stop someone attacking his sense of fairness. Indeed, in my classrooms and in my counselling rooms, I have often found the boys who deliberately hurt others had often experienced significant trauma early in their boyhood and were projecting that hurt outwards towards others.

So, next time you notice a behaviour or event that
displeases you, pause and ask yourself,
'What is he really trying to say?'

RESPECTFUL SOCIETAL CHOICES

While we strive to understand and sympathise with our boys, we can still encourage them to behave with respect towards others. Manners are a good first step.

- First big message for all boys – excuse yourself when you burp, sneeze, blow your nose, or perform some other bodily function outside of your bedroom. Teach your sons to use basic manners –

excuse me, pardon, please, thank you and may I? Ensure you model the same!

- Teach your sons welcoming and farewelling behaviours. When being introduced to adults, offer them a firm handshake (besides when practising social distancing due to global pandemics!), look them in the eye and say 'nice to meet you' or something similar. Please practise with your son so it becomes comfortable.
- Aim to treat the elderly with respect and offer them a seat on public transport.
- Always offer pregnant women and people with physical disabilities help as well as your seat. Do it with a smile.
- Teach your sons that it is never acceptable to verbally abuse or hit women or children. Avoid doing the same to boys and men.
- Teach your sons to thank bus drivers, taxi drivers and rideshare drivers.
- Teach your sons to thank shop assistants, hospitality staff and anyone who offers a service of any kind.
- Have conversations around the more traditional expectations of male to female behaviour such as opening doors, pulling out chairs, and standing when a woman enters the room. Warn him that some younger women may find these gestures unacceptable while older women see it as a sign of respect!
- Teach your son to thank and maybe compliment the person who has made food for him.
- Ask to be excused at the end of the meal after everyone else has finished eating.
- Have your phone out of sight during mealtimes and avoid answering or responding to alerts during mealtime.
- Remind your son about phone etiquette and encourage him to not look at his phone while having a conversation with someone.
- Teach your son to apologise quickly if he may have caused someone some emotional pain – regardless of whether he intended to or not.
- Teach your son to congratulate winners, especially when he is the loser.
- Teach your son to be on the lookout for people who may need some help and to step up quickly and offer.
- Encourage your son to be patient in queues.

4

The teen brain – what's really happening?

In this chapter I will be exploring in depth some of the invisible changes that occur in our teens' brains to help you understand the emotional volatility that can be a part of the teen years.

It is really important as a parent, or someone who works with tweens and teens, to gain a clear understanding of WHY things change so much and often so quickly. I can tell you no tween or teen wakes up one day suddenly deciding to become more sensitive, moody, forgetful or confused. They can often be as surprised as you!

The child brain that worked well as a kid now needs to begin to be modified so it can become more mature to manage the change from being a carefree child to becoming a grown-up. Makes sense, eh?

> ### MEN'S AND WOMEN'S BRAINS
> There is great debate about whether men's brains are different to women's brains. From my reading, the core differences seem to come more from our hormonal differences, and our social, cultural and biological drivers. However, with more and more research into neuroscience,

we can say that there are some significant differences in the way our brains work rather than in the unique structure of them. It seems that our brains appear very similar and it is just that they often function differently partly due to biological or instinctual tendencies. There are also the instinctual behaviours that may be imprinted on our DNA from the time we lived in indigenous kinship communities. Men and women tend to interpret and process information a little differently at times, but I'm not convinced this is a fixed reality, more like a tendency.

Brain pruning

In order for the child's brain to make room for a smarter, faster, more efficient adult brain, there is a massive 'synaptic pruning' – a shearing off of unnecessary neurons and connectors. This occurs in the brain during the early teenage years.

Teens can lose as much as 15–20 per cent of the synaptic connections in some parts of the brain. This may sound like troubling news but in actual fact it's just the opposite – the brain becomes more efficient, discarding some of its inconsequential information. Unfortunately, the pruning process can unintentionally prune off some useful stuff too!

Forgetfulness

The first sign of brain pruning is an increase in forgetfulness, which is added stress for boys who can already have a less efficient memory.

A boy in your life experiencing the pruning process may do the following:

- Jump off the school bus and leave his backpack, complete with his mobile/MacBook Air and school books sitting on the seat
- Forget to attend the orthodontist appointment even though you texted him a reminder at lunchtime

- Forget to put his dirty washing in the laundry basket in the bathroom – something he has been doing for maybe five years
- Forget his lunch
- Forget what homework needs doing
- Turn up to the wrong classroom
- Leave his football boots/basketball boots in the school change room after PE – several times!
- Frequently forget to put milk and yoghurt back into the fridge
- Leave his bike or skateboard on the driveway instead of putting it in the garage
- Turn up for an exam a day early or a day late
- Lose his house keys – often
- Leave the house unlocked, perhaps even the front door wide open as he leaves
- Forget to wear undies
- Seemingly lose his previously reasonable manners
- Forget his chores
- Leave his wet towel on the bed
- Forget to clean his teeth!

When I was running in-school seminars, I loved to watch the teen boys' faces when I explained their forgetfulness. The sense of relief they felt as they realised it wasn't just them and, even better, that there was a reason for it was beautiful!

How do you feel when you forget important stuff? Pretty lousy? Well, our boys have days when they forget so much stuff and it makes them feel really awful, stupid and useless. Often parents think they need to come down hard on these lapses because he should be more responsible or more mature. So, when our boys are feeling really vulnerable and confused, we often give them more grief!

This then fires up their stress levels and they feel,
yet again, misunderstood and, worse, unworthy
of love from the people they love the most!

Please, when this starts happening have a chat to him or show him a video which explores these early brain changes and work together to think of ways to help him remember important stuff without endless nagging, lecturing, yelling or huffing and puffing with disappointment. I like small Post-it notes and of course you can now send a text with a cute emoji or even send a message through WhatsApp or Messenger.

I know many parents think their adolescents are being deliberately difficult just to annoy them, *however, confusion and frustration with things they have no control over* must now be seen as perfectly normal behaviours. The good news is that this forgetfulness gradually dissipates by around 18 years of age.

Disorganisation

Another sign that brain pruning has happened is the decline in organisational skills. Boys can lose organisational skills like basic planning, keeping rooms tidy, doing home chores and generally managing themselves, especially in our distracting digital world. This change also causes many tween and teen boys to feel stupid, useless and incompetent.

Poor communication

The other way this early brain pruning can be detected is when monosyllabic grunts replace articulation in communication with many boys.

I once had a 14-year-old boy do an oral talk in my English class and there were few words that were clear! He also seemed unaware that his spoken words were distorted. Given our new understanding of the emotional fragility around feeling vulnerable, is it any wonder boys in this window can become incredibly defensive and easily angered when people make fun of them for being forgetful or sounding like they are just grunting? I have had some dads express to me how frustrating they find this incapacity to speak clearly – and many of them struggled to do the same thing at the same age. Try to avoid telling your son to speak clearly or to open his mouth so he can be heard more clearly – *the problem is within his brain*. This might explain why so many boys answer questions with single-syllable answers like 'yep', 'not', and 'dunno!' As the brain gradually rebuilds itself, the capacity to speak clearly will return. However, there are occasions where some boys may need some speech therapy to help them vocalise more clearly because their mouths have simply become used to struggling to articulate. You can help your son understand the reasons for the real challenges in speaking clearly, which can really help a teen boy to not be too hard on himself. In his eyes, every time he tries to speak, he is failing and failing, and this will block his capacity to feel self-worth. Some of the brightest boys I ever taught went through this stage and many of them decided that they were dumb or useless, and they refused to take harder subjects in the final years of schooling, even though they were completely capable of doing well.

Understanding communication from others

Recent studies have found that as children reach puberty their ability to interpret and understand social situations and emotions in others can drop by up to 20 per cent. Most girls tend to have a more mature capacity to understand the nuances of social interaction but many boys, especially those who are neuro divergent, really struggle in this window.

What does this mean? This means that in the window of 12–15 years, boys particularly can struggle with misreading facial expressions and misinterpreting body language that perhaps they could read much more competently before. So often they are trying to build connections with others without words and with physical gestures and actions. This may be the reason why many 14-year-old boys go through a stage of endlessly slapping, shoving, nudging and sitting on other boys. This is a phase and it does pass. There is a noticeable shift around the age 15 to 16, and we will breathe a sigh of relief to see things start to improve. This is where we need enormous patience and compassion for our often awkward, stumbling, frequently non-verbal teen boys. Remember, this is not all boys – I have worked with some delightful young lads who were endlessly talking and couldn't help themselves!

How your teen sees the world: through a cracked windscreen

It took me a while to work out that teens, especially in the early window of 12 to 15, no longer saw the world through the same lens they had before puberty started. I like to use the metaphor of 'cracked windscreen' to explain this. Instead of seeing the world through a clean windscreen, adolescence presents a cracked-windscreen view, and young people simply see things very differently to how they saw things before or after adolescence. Your well-meaning gestures of loving kindness, such as when you ask your son as he leaves the house if he has his jacket, are no longer seen as gestures of loving kindness. These gestures are now seen as some form of criticism! Little things can be blown out of proportion really quickly and easily through the cracked windscreen. The tiny zit on the nose is enormous and many boys struggle as they compare themselves to others in negative ways, often quite irrationally.

This cracked windscreen means that most teens will see themselves in a poorer light and it can be a major contributor to the dark moods or grumpiness that we see in all teens, not just our boys.

Given this is a period where being dark, negative and moody at times and viewing the world through a cracked windscreen can be the norm, in today's digital world where teens are desperately seeking acceptance and validation online, it is much harder to manage the big, ugly feelings of not being good enough.

There was once a television advertising campaign that was run in the hope of educating teenagers to avoid drinking alcohol excessively. The Respect Yourself campaign failed miserably – indeed, it may have done the exact opposite. When an immature teen brain witnesses images of other teens being drunk, staggering around parties, vomiting in the street and obviously misusing alcohol, rather than seeing a cautionary tale, for many it was an example of how to get completely wasted by using alcohol.

There are many similar well-meaning campaigns that fail due to the ignorance that only a mature adult brain will witness such material in the cautionary way it is intended.

The cracked windscreen will also explain why so many of your well-intended lectures and explanations will go unheeded – you are expecting them to appreciate and understand them, as though they have a complete prefrontal lobe. They may look like a grown-up adult, however, their capacity to think and process information is still developing and hence lots of arguments will occur. Developmentally, these arguments are also showing that your teen is gradually developing their own sense of independence and autonomy, which is technically a good thing.

Decision-making through a cracked windscreen

Good decisions involve rationally assessing the risks, benefits and alternative actions that are relevant in any particular case. While adolescents are beginning to think more like adults than children, they often still need help from their parents or other safe grown-ups to make decisions that have serious or long-term consequences. This is because adolescents:

- are likely to be more impulsive
- lack rational thinking strategies
- are looking for novelty experiences
- are less concerned about risk
- are not thinking about the future
- are more susceptible to peer and friendship influence
- are more concerned about physical appearance
- are hungry to be accepted and to belong.

In his wonderful book *Brainstorm*, Dr Daniel Siegel argues that the teen brain's increased drive for reward in adolescence manifests in teens' lives and is one of the reasons for increased impulsiveness (where choices and behaviours occur without thoughtful reflection or any pause). This is why we need to be mindful when we ask a teen boy the question, 'What were you thinking?' after he has made a poor, irrational choice.

Siegel writes about 'increased hyperrationality' – when teens think in small, concrete terms that lack a full appreciation of the bigger picture. This is another reality as a consequence of these brain changes. Teens can often see the positives and negatives around a choice; they just exaggerate the positives and downplay the negatives! Teen boys are so hungry to experience what I call the 'buzz rush' or the dopamine flood that the negatives are often ignored. When a group of teen boys are together this can be exaggerated. Sadly, sometimes for teen boys the pack mentality can override their value systems, especially in the heat of the moment.

ANT attacks

Aside from the cracked windscreen, teens also often suffer with automatic negative thoughts (ANT) attacks, as mentioned earlier. The ego mind creates most of the endless chatter that we hear in our head and this tends to be the layer that becomes the inner critic. This is the layer that creates the ANT attacks, the automatic negative thoughts that can trigger big, ugly feelings that can make all of us, but especially our teens, feel terrible.

> *I'm useless, no-one likes me, I'm not enough, I'm a loser, I'm ugly and stupid, I'm gonna look dumb and fail when I do the English oral, what's the point in studying? I'm too dumb to do well at school, that teacher hates me, my nose is too big, I am so fat, I just don't get it, it's my fault we lost the game, no-one understands me, I can't do that, I hate me, I disgust myself . . .*

This partly explains why teens struggle with self-loathing, low self-esteem and low confidence. It happens to all teens and I myself still have strong memories of this awful place full of self-hatred. Boys who have negative mindsets from childhood, or who have experienced trauma or abuse, or who have other challenges struggle the most.

Overproduction of dendrites and synaptic connections

Some basic neuroscience might be helpful here before explaining this next part of the teen brain development stage. Neurons have specialised projections called dendrites and axons. Dendrites bring information to the cell body and axons take information away from the cell body. Information from one neuron flows to another neuron across a synapse. The synapse contains a small gap separating neurons. By the time adolescence ends, the brain will contain billions of new synaptic connections. Basically, dendrites are found at the end of the axon, which is like the transmission cable of a neuron, which is formed when we learn something new.

Adolescents are acquiring learning and knowledge at an exciting, unprecedented rate due to this massive explosion in dendrites. Now that may seem hard to believe given what I have just explored about brain pruning, but it is true. This is a vitally important window in the journey of human development – it is a *wonderful window of potential*. Learning, especially when it's based on real experiences, happens faster during this time than any other stage in life other than the first five years. The massive increase in dendrites will allow a teen to master new skills like playing a guitar, taking up a new sport, learning a new language, doing a triple flip on a skateboard or even learning to cook *much faster than normal*. Focused practice in an area of interest for a teen such as sport, dance, music, coding or anything creative will see a *significant improvement in terms of their competence and mastery*.

So, during this time of massive dendrite growth the boys who love gaming will become more competent at and more committed to gaming than before or after this window of rapid growth. Potentially this is the window in which they can become addicted much faster too. In ancient times, this is the stage of development where boys would be spending full days beside men learning skills and knowledge about how to be a brave warrior, hunter or protector. They would have been learning how to make tools, how to find water for survival, and how to work together to overcome the unique challenges that they met.

This is where the role of mentors, teachers and guides was such a critically important part of a young boy's growth through to manhood. He would also listen to stories around campfires at night that would be building his moral code and his understanding of how people lived and worked together in harmony. He would learn about how challenging and unforgiving nature can be at times – both when it was freezing cold, and stinking hot. All these practical life skills took years to master gradually in the real world with real people.

Nowadays many boys learn life skills from YouTube and Google. What they are missing out on is the experience of relationships with significant others, and for this we need to be concerned. They will always still be a human biologically wired to live in relationships with other humans, and the capacities to form and maintain meaningful relationships will not be found on YouTube or Google.

Addiction

There is one incredible downside to the massive overproduction of dendrites in this window of potential for our teens. Just as our boys can learn to do positive things really quickly – faster than ever if they focus on them – they are also at risk of becoming addicted to all the unhealthiest things imaginable, such as alcohol, illicit drugs, smoking, vaping, watching pornography, gaming, fighting and becoming lazy and sloth-like.

Sadly, the addictions that are formed in this window are harder to change or overcome than at any other time of your life. This is one of the reasons why we need to be their guardians and protectors so that we can ensure that any of the risk-taking behaviour, or behaviour they class as 'fun', is contained within boundaries.

In his book *Teen Brain*, David Gillespie shares research that explains in more depth the reasons why the teen brain can struggle with potential addiction issues. And it has to do with GABA, which stands for gamma amino butyric acid. So, what is GABA? It is a naturally occurring amino acid that works as a neurotransmitter in your brain, which means it's a kind of chemical messenger. GABA is considered an inhibitory neurotransmitter because it blocks, or inhibits, certain brain signals and decreases activity in your nervous system.

Essentially, GABA in children and adults works as an inhibitor in our reward centre – and it silently helps us not eat the family block of chocolate on our own or drink too much alcohol at one time.

Well, this hidden protector turns off during adolescence, so that when a teen boy is experiencing spikes of dopamine in the reward centre, he just wants more and more!

Gillespie argues that this is why teenagers have always been susceptible to risky behaviours such as drugs, alcohol and sex – and the overarching danger is that addiction can open up pathways to depression, anxiety and other mental health issues.

Studies in humans have been able to directly measure the relationship between GABA levels in our brains and our levels of impulsivity, self-control and reaction time. The lower the GABA level, the more impulsive we are. We also think less about our actions, and as a result our responses are significantly faster. On low GABA, as all humans experiencing puberty are, we act on impulse, make poor decisions and over-react. Sound like any teenagers you know?

– David Gillespie, *Teen Brain* (2019)

It is really important for the grown-ups in our teen boys' lives to understand the science behind much of their less-than-positive behaviours. *They are driven by changes that are beyond their control.* However, when they are given this information and reminded often, with compassion and enormous amounts of patience, we can help them to see that it's not always their fault. So many boys I have worked with were convinced that they were bad or stupid, or both when they were simply going through normal and natural neurological changes associated with adolescence.

Dopamine

Dopamine is the reward brain chemical that gives us pleasure. It increases our motivation, focus and interest. Everyone feels better with healthy neurotransmitters flooding their brain. Dopamine is really *the feel-good neurochemical* that boys are hunting. And given the link between external experiences and events and how a boy perceives his self-worth, you may appreciate why they often test themselves in potentially risky ways.

In their book *The Boy Crisis*, Warren Farrell and John Gray explore what they call the 'new neural crisis' that is happening for boys. They argue that many modern lifestyle factors including air and water pollution, some toxic farming practices, nutritional deficiencies, overuse of antibiotics and over-the-counter and prescription drugs, and significant overstimulation from the screen world are all contributing to unhealthier brain functions that can inhibit development and optimal growth. They argue that the consequences of these changes have contributed to inhibited dopamine function in the brain.

It seems that for those of us who have healthy dopamine function, we can find relaxing and fulfilling experiences such as reading, learning, talking with close friends or family, going for a walk or socialising enjoyable. In other words, it triggers our dopamine to flood us with those beautiful feel-good sensations. Unfortunately for those with an inhibited dopamine function, these activities very quickly become boring, tiring, empty or completely unsatisfying. Welcome to a large number of our teen boys who need a higher than normal stimulation to experience those normal levels of pleasure. The digital world is definitely a major contributor to the hunger for more/faster/brighter/louder stimuli.

All of those other factors, when combined with the highly stimulating digital environment, are making it harder and harder for some to find contentment, relaxation and happiness.

> Overexposure to high dopamine stimulation over time will cause inhibited dopamine function in the brain. Simply put too much high stimulation inhibits normal brain function.
> – Warren Farrell and John Gray, *The Boy Crisis* (2019)

The overstimulated world can be problematic in our teen boys, especially when it triggers boredom and disengagement and apathy in life in general. Boys who struggle with this are also less likely to follow their parents' wishes and guidance, and they have a higher chance of making more impulsive, poor choices. There are four characteristics of healthy dopamine function: focus, motivation, interest and pleasure. Adolescent stress and confusion, when added to low dopamine, make a powerful combination that can make life difficult for our boys. Trying to reduce the stress hormone cortisol drives so much tween and teen boy behaviour!

Hopefully this explanation will help you understand why your son loves gaming, or watching funny videos on YouTube, or watching people gaming.

The buzz that comes from the good dopamine hit that our boys get from conquering a physical challenge, an artistic one or a mechanical one feels really good. Video games with either first-person military or sport simulations and other action games that emphasise physical reaction time and role-playing are so popular with tween, teen and

18 plus boys because they give them heaps of dopamine spurts from the comfort of their own home.

For more information about this check out chapter 18.

Myelination and the development of the prefrontal lobe

This is the final stage of brain development for our teens and beyond, and involves the thickening of the 'white matter' or myelin on the axons. This is the process of insulating the neurons and synaptic connections, which allows more connections and more efficient usage. One of the things to understand is that poor decision-making for teens is often *as a consequence of having an underdeveloped prefrontal lobe.* What this means is that their quality of thinking doesn't improve until the prefrontal development takes place, which – as I mentioned earlier – may not be until around 25 for most boys. Once that executive functioning of the brain kicks in, they will be mature enough to ensure that improved decision-making can take place. This is when parents can start to breathe a sigh of relief, as they have less emotional unpredictability, more impulse control and better organisational skills. There were times when I was teaching when I noticed the same boy sitting outside the principal's office several times a week. Teen boys can repeat the same poor choices over and over again because the prefrontal lobe is slow to develop enough myelin to improve their thinking and the choices they make. This is one of the reasons why so many tween and teen boys injure themselves accidentally. Their impulsivity and their hunger to conquer experiences that make them feel really alive and successful means they do make poor choices.

Making the assumption that they are deliberately making poor choices and that given the same situation again they are capable of making a better one is erroneous.

I will explore in more depth later how we help our boys when they muck up – and how we can gradually encourage them to pause and make better decisions.

WHAT WAS HE THINKING?

Over the last 40 years as a teacher, counsellor, parent, aunty and friend I have heard some fascinating stories of things that boys have done without thinking.

One story was about Oliver (14) who struggled with ADHD. Oliver decided to graffiti the deputy principal's car because he was really annoyed at the disrespectful way he had been spoken to. He wrote his own name on the car! *What was he thinking?*

There was also another Oliver (17) who thought it was a great idea to skate down a very steep road in the middle of the night while he was drunk. After breaking both wrists and removing enormous amounts of skin, he confessed it was a dumb thing to do and said he wouldn't do it again. Sadly, he forgot and he tried the same stunt a couple of months later and re-broke one wrist. *What was he thinking – both times?*

During the 2018 winter Olympics, there was a classic example of teen boy behaviour from 17-year-old Red Gerard, who almost missed his event because he overslept after a Netflix binge, then couldn't find his jacket and yet rushed to his event and still bagged an Olympic gold medal. *What was he thinking?*

The impacts of gaming and technology on the teen brain

So, what else is delaying the growth of that prefrontal cortex, which can give our teen boys a better chance of making good decisions and moving from boy psychology to man psychology? I'll cover this more in chapter 18 but for now here are some issues to consider.

Distractibility in this digital landscape is causing some serious concerns for teachers and neuroscientists. Teachers have been telling me for a number of years that they have noticed a drop in the attention span of today's children in their classrooms. Given that most curriculums have expanded, this needs to be something concerning us all.

This is a concern not just for our boys of course, but for everyone. Constantly having our mind focusing on several things, multitasking, switch-tasking and struggling to stay focused on one thing is a reality. Boys already have a tendency to be impulsive, are quick to act without thinking, and are averse to activities that don't make them feel better. They're hunting that dopamine fix.

Dr Kristy Goodwin, author of *Raising Your Child in a Digital World,* shares my concern for today's children and teens:

'If you cannot direct and control your attention, you are going to get lost in this digital world,' she told delegates at the 2019 Generation Next conference in Sydney.

The overriding messages around families and technology at the moment are very much about parents monitoring our teens' usage, and that is essential but only up to a point. If our teens do not have opportunities to self-monitor or to develop healthy autonomous choices around boundaries and screens, we run the risk of them not developing these at all.

In her book *i-Minds*, neuroscientist and researcher Dr Mari Swingle has more concerns around the impacts excessive use of technology is having on the developing brains of our children, particularly our teens, given the massive brain changes that occur during puberty.

Swingle argues that technology is conditioning us to need higher and higher arousal states to function. Sadly, this will come at a cost that impacts our capacity to focus attention, and so can increase anxiety. In a way, it creates a kind of brain strain or techno brain burnout. It also makes it harder to fall asleep, and lack of sleep stimulates more cortisol and stress, which floods the teen emotional barometer, meaning meltdowns will happen quicker.

Swingle has another concern other than poor attention:

As early as 2005 to 2008 we were aware that higher arousal and the dual or divided attention required for multitasking on multiple devices in multiple modes – doing homework while messaging and listening to music – was stressful and could reduce efficiency. But it also slows the development of the frontal cortex.

I am deeply concerned about any further delays in the growth of the prefrontal cortex or the maturation to an adult brain, given full brain development is not complete until the mid-twenties now for most boys!

We need to prioritise helping our teen boys to be massively engaged in pursuits that involve human interaction that are good for their mind and the body. It will give those rapidly changing brains an opportunity to be focused and concentrated in the real world, which moves a lot slower than the digital world. Having significant times away from the endlessly stimulating technology world and screens will benefit your son in so many unmeasurable ways. I will explore this in more depth in chapter 13.

I'm hoping that this information about the teen brain can help you reframe how you see your son's forgetfulness, his messy bedroom, the milk he leaves out of the fridge and his endless requests to locate his socks! Seriously, he's not enjoying this either. His brain is under construction. Hopefully armed with information, you will both be able to understand where he is at with his brain development.

5

What's with all
these emotions?

There is a mistaken perception that boys and men don't feel emotions
as much as girls and women – they do. They just process them and
often communicate them very differently.

– Maggie Dent, *Mothering Our Boys* (2018)

The sensitive nature of boys

Male vulnerability in terms of health and wellbeing has been well
researched. This research continues to bring forward evidence that
from conception little girls develop faster and more thoroughly than
little boys. Boys are not inherently tough, even though they have a
larger amount of muscle than girls. Physical strength is one thing but
mental and emotional strength that can impact cognitive abilities and
linguistic capacities is something else.

Emotional vulnerability

When boys are struggling with emotional vulnerability, they will do one of three things. Either they will come out fighting, or they'll act out their emotions through angry outbursts or with irrational behaviour towards other children and their parents. Or they will simply withdraw and seek isolation. One of the key things to always remember with boys is that:

Any time there is a significant change in a boy's behaviour, he is usually struggling with something in his world that is overloading his nervous system and troubling his mind.

It is important to keep this in mind as your son starts walking the bridge.

While he is struggling, he may not be sure what it is that's causing the sense of being overwhelmed and distressed. I have worked with boys who became very aggressive suddenly and the apparent trigger was a disaster that happened in another part of the world, which they saw on TV. I repeat my previous plea to all parents of boys and especially to mums of boys to avoid seeing your son as 'bad' or 'naughty'. Know that, in some way, he is struggling to cope with our world and he needs our help. This reframing around boys' sometimes-irrational behaviour is imperative if we are to stop all boys from being confused by strong emotions.

Social conditioning around boys and feelings: the new man code

We must keep in mind the social conditioning around telling boys that they need to be tough and not show any emotions at all. The consequences this has later in life when things get tough can be devastating and yes, sometimes fatal. Being told not to cry, and that to be accepted they need to 'man up', is still happening in the lives of many little boys. The narrative we need to be teaching our boys is that the most courageous thing you can do is to own up to your vulnerability and to open up and admit when you are struggling the most.

Thankfully, slowly we are changing the social constructs of the old male code, however, for many of our tween and teen boys they have been marinated in these old messages throughout their boyhood.

> Feeling like there was an expectation that I had to be tough, that I had to be a man. I felt as though I couldn't ask for help when I was struggling because men are supposed to be tough.

I have found boys' behaviour that is particularly aggressive and irrational is often linked to the more vulnerable emotions like fear, sadness, embarrassment and feeling dumb or inadequate. The same behaviour can keep happening in manhood and that is why we need to spend considerable time and energy in the first five years of a boy's life to help him navigate the confusing world of emotions, feelings and moods.

I clearly remember a 15-year-old boy who came into my English class after a maths class. Not long into our lesson, he just stood up, kicked his chair backwards and walked over to the closest wall, which was brick, and punched it really hard. He then walked out. I followed him to find him sitting on a bench with his head in his hands. Eventually he explained that he lost it because he had failed his maths test. He had actually broken three knuckles. This was the first time I had witnessed the incredible intensity of adolescent emotional angst as a teacher and it was sobering.

Teens and the emotional part of the brain

> I can sometimes have big mood swings and get very annoyed and angry if I do something even the slightest bit wrong, e.g. putting a pan in the cupboard and it doesn't stay in place.

The limbic brain, often known as the emotional brain, does some serious growing in adolescence. Again we need to remember that no teen – girl or boy – would choose to become more emotionally volatile!

Indeed the intensity of emotions is significantly higher in the tween and teen years than before or after early adolescence.

The dominance of the amygdala is also partly why so many tweens and teens can be obsessive about clothes, music, personal image, peer pressure and infatuations with others. They also experience big highs and lows that occur rapidly. This can be very confusing and confronting for adolescents and very stressful – however, very normal!

So much of teens' responses to their world and experiences are coming from the least developed part of the brain. The slowly developing prefrontal lobe affects the ability of young adolescents to manage emotional states such as anger, frustration, fear, boredom, shame and feelings of worthlessness. Their way of thinking – if they are thinking at all – can often allow them to catastrophise rather than accurately assess the current situation. Self-talk, especially the inner critic, also becomes louder once puberty has begun, as I have already explained.

It takes the development of the prefrontal lobe of an individual's brain for them to have the capacity to make a different, more mature choice, although their *automatic impulsive* response will be the most likely first choice. When confronted by a threatening situation – and often this can be a perceived threat not a real threat – the primitive brain tends to respond automatically in one of three ways:

1. Flight – wanting to run away
2. Freeze – suppressing emotions
3. Fight – physical or verbal conflict

So many boys who have had adverse childhood experiences or who feel disconnected from safe adults struggle more in the teen years as their reactive responses are linked to the primitive fear of survival. When high schools struggle to help these boys and possibly add to their angst by not exploring what is driving the behaviour, many disengage or leave.

Given the poor access to the prefrontal cortex, many things that trigger a teen's amygdala are often not life-threatening at all, however, in the heat of the moment they are perceived that way. Their emotional response can seem unrealistic, excessive, irrational and over-the-top and we need to keep in mind that often there is very little they can do about it while they are in meltdown. It is very much like toddler meltdowns – the cortisol needs to be discharged, and while they are in this state, they have no access to the prefrontal cortex and so they actually can't hear you at all.

Emotions can also continue to exist within our nervous system long after an event that has triggered them. Anyone who has lost a loved one will know that grief and sadness, and sometimes anger, can last a very long time. Many boys are carrying deep shame from their early childhood that just keeps festering in their nervous system. Blocked, stuck or repressed emotions can stay buried in our nervous system and sometimes this can be problematic for individuals in adolescence and adulthood.

I have worked with a number of boys who have come very close to physically hurting their mums in a heated conflict situation. The boys are already flooded with stress hormones and completely unable to withstand any more distress. Their mums have kept on venting their big emotional feelings and this can trigger a completely irrational response from a teen boy, such as shoving or hitting. He will need to do everything he can to get away. These are the tricky moments when all our teens need us to model our emotional maturity by containing our own big, ugly feelings and being the safe base that our kids need. I am not remotely suggesting that this is easy – there were many times I had to bite my tongue, and quietly step outside away from the battlefront and do some serious breathing.

Managing emotional volatility

Emotional volatility needs to be seen as a normal part of the journey of adolescence, no matter how difficult and confronting it can be.

Parents and educators need to have a serious understanding of the emotional barometer, the tipping point and how we can use these as teachable moments for our boys. Of course prevention is always better than trying to fix something – but between 12 and 25 we have some years where we can help our young lads come to understand that we are all emotional and social beings. Some emotions make us feel really good and others can make us feel really lousy. All emotions are equally valid. We can help our boys to be mindful of how emotions are felt in the body and can help them be aware that they can influence what they do with them.

One of the most important distinctions to make for our teen boys is that no-one can make you feel anything – you can only choose your response. With practice, our boys can get better at defusing their own emotional angst. We will later explore other ways that boys can fill their own emotional cup in positive ways so that they have a much longer fuse before they reach their tipping point. I am a huge fan of mindfulness programs in our high schools because I often find the boys benefit the most.

WHAT ANNOYS YOU MOST ABOUT BEING A TEEN BOY TODAY?

- Being pressured to talk about our feelings [by] teachers and family.
- Having to deal with so many things at once. You have to cope with school stress, particularly the pressures I put on myself to achieve high results. Then there's social issues, trying to figure out girls (that's almost impossible!) and whether they like you and even if you like them. [And] dealing with other people's overprotective parents.
- Other teenage boys who make fun of boys who cry and have mental health issues.

- Having helicopter parents.
- Being stereotyped as a typical lazy, up-to-no good person.
- Can't show my feelings without being judged by others who expect me to act like a man.
- Hearing and reading about problems happening around the world, knowing if something happens it will be in my future that problems will arise.
- Being too young for some things and too old for others!
- You always seem to be blamed! Great.

All emotions are normal – it's what we do with them that matters

Even with our executive functioning brain, we can all struggle with big, ugly feelings at times, however, our adult brains allow us to soothe ourselves by first identifying that we are in fight-flight-freeze mode and then helping us make choices to change how we feel.

We might notice that we are feeling stressed or even anxious or irritable, so we choose to help ourselves feel better by, for example, making a cup of tea, sitting outside for a while, eating a piece of chocolate, taking three deep breaths, doing a downward dog or going for a walk and a stretch. Many of you have heard me speak about occasionally locking myself in the toilet or wardrobe (with some chocolate) for some peace and quiet – whatever works!

Our brain actually doesn't always discern the difference between real and imagined events; the thoughts associated with either will create emotions and feelings. The limbic part of the brain is where these thoughts become emotional tension and this can then flow through our bodies. Sometimes, with intense emotions, we can feel like we're caught in a maelstrom of emotions and confusion, and this creates even more unpleasant feelings. Without a mature prefrontal cortex, our teens struggle to make sense of what's happening and calm down.

There is a lot of anger in adolescence, especially for those boys who have been conditioned to think that anger is OK – and that feeling sad or frightened is not.

How men and women process emotion differently

Michael Gurian writes about how males and females tend to process emotion differently in the brain. Females tend to quickly shift emotions from the brain's limbic system to the word centres of the brain which means they're able to verbalise very quickly when they are upset. It is quite different for our boys and indeed many men. Gurian writes that males tend to move emotions very quickly from their brains into their bodies. This explains why the boy I mentioned before punched the wall when his disappointment with his maths mark became too hard to contain. So often when boys of any age are really upset they will kick, hit, shove or run away. They often need to physically discharge the excess cortisol and this needs to be respected and understood.

A teen boy's mum's default mechanism might be to verbally express her unhappy feelings quite quickly. In her volatility, she may express these feelings in ways she may later regret. Most boys and men feel blindsided by these outbursts and may have no idea what triggered them. I usually suggest to men and boys to avoid taking these outbursts personally. Most adult men learn to avoid defending, or buying in to the volatile emotions, however, our boys and adolescent boys can find it frightening and scary. They genuinely hate to upset their mum, especially if they are frightened that she may become emotionally explosive. They hunger for her acceptance and love. Being typically pragmatic boys, they often feel they are responsible for their mother's anger or unhappiness.

The emotional barometer

We all have a nervous system within our bodies and unexpressed emotions can lay dormant for years. However, a significantly distressing conflict, disappointment or major stressor can trigger our nervous system to want to discharge tension and, given the emotional volatility of adolescence, this can happen often. Intentional self-harm is a way that some teens release excessive emotional tension in their body. Every teen needs safe grown-ups who can accept that this is a time of emotional volatility and who can allow our teen boys to express big, ugly feelings without judgement or shame. We need to avoid trying to fix our boys' emotional angst because much of it is quite irrational and they are unable to articulate what is driving those heated emotional states. Again, this is why they need a safe tribe of family and significant others who can be the safe space they need when things get really tough and who can show they can still love their boys even after emotional meltdowns.

When I was working with groups of teens, I began using the metaphor of the emotional barometer to help teens understand that there is only so much that they can manage and handle before they can be tipped into an irrationally frightening place.

I explained to them that the barometer rises gradually as one thing after another contributes to them feeling emotionally volatile. It might start with their brother breaking something of theirs, then the realisation they've forgotten a homework sheet, and then their mum getting annoyed because they didn't put the bin out. Sometimes it is something small like this that can tip a teen over the edge. Helping them to understand this metaphor and showing them ways that they can lower the intensity of their emotional barometer, are things we need to teach our tweens – well before the most significant challenging moments of adolescence.

WHAT WAS YOUR MOST CHALLENGING EXPERIENCE AS A TEEN BOY?

- Pimples and boils – I had a blood disorder which caused severe skin stuff.
- Being underweight.
- Got sick at 15 for nine months – lost 18 kg in the first two months – missed a lot.
- Tearing my cruciate ligament when I was 18.
- Having acne and being teased because of it.
- I had a smelly penis because I wasn't washing properly and wasn't masturbating and hadn't talked to anyone about either issue and this led to a lot of bullying at school.
- Being physically smaller and reaching puberty later than my friends.
- Dealing with intense burning anger. For what at the time seemed like no reason.
- Being six foot five and a skinny beanpole.
- Getting random erections.
- Going through puberty later than everyone else was tough. I was always comparing myself and then when I went through puberty it got at me really bad! It took any and all of my confidence away.
- Being slightly bullied about having a below average penis size.

I have worked with teens who have run away from home because their mum nagged them about a wet towel on their bed when their system was in overload. A mother shared how a break-up with his girlfriend (they had broken up and reconnected many times) was the tipping point for her son to attempt to take his own life. This incredible vulnerability can be triggered by a rolled eye from one of the cool kids, being chastised in front of your class and even falling over in front of your peers. It can be tiny . . . like the flutter of a butterfly's wing.

Of course, these stressful moments can also be triggered by something quite big. I once had a 15-year-old boy who came into my classroom and suddenly just picked up his desk and threw it, kicked his chair and raced out of the room, slamming the door. The class had been doing some silent reading! Later the boy was found at home, fortunately safe. That morning he had heard that his special, much-loved Pop had died suddenly.

Michael Gurian's excellent book *The Wonder of Boys* explores how a boy's brain may develop through his teen years. Gurian believes many boys become less able to connect feelings with verbal communication, which is why trying to talk to your son about his feelings can seem like an impossible feat.

In our nervous system we store emotional tension – even from our early childhood – and those who come from dysfunctional and especially abusive homes have lots of tension stored.

> Almost in the same way that we care for toddlers who also experience the same levels of confusion and frustration, the most important thing to do is to **validate what they are feeling**. Accept that it is developmentally normal and that this phase will pass.

There are a few big emotional states that I feel need to be explored in a little more detail in terms of our tween and teen boys.

Anger

Anger is a symptom, not the problem.

Many parents want their teen son to stop being angry because they see the anger as the problem. The parent does not understand that anger can be a response to feeling rejected, disappointed, confused, scared, unloved, misunderstood, disconnected, grief, sadness, ugly, embarrassed, ashamed, useless, powerless or out of control. We need to keep in mind that most boys have been conditioned that anger is an acceptable warrior emotion – it is a manly emotion! So keep in mind the metaphor of an iceberg and know that under the anger you may be witnessing so many other emotions, plus anxiety.

It is important to remember that no matter how nonsensical and frustrating our teens' feelings may seem to us, **they are real and valid** to our teen and discharging emotions safely, especially anger, can be helpful to our teen boys. Shutting it down and making it wrong can simply make it worse later!

Steven Stosny, author of the excellent book *Treating Attachment Abuse*, suggests:

> ... [by] the act of getting angry, by producing chemical changes in the brain that serve as a psychological analgesic (i.e. pain-killer/self-soothing agent), it is possible that, just as we can become addicted to other pain-killing drugs (such as morphine), *some of us may become addicted to anger as a means of coping with unbearable mental anguish.*

Managing anger

It can be helpful to have a conversation with a boy *when he is not angry or upset* as to what can work for him in managing his anger. Never try to talk to him when he is dysregulated! Heck, most adults can struggle with well-meaning people wanting to talk when they are wound up or really upset. The physical discharge of this enormous emotional distress is something we need to talk to our tween and teen boys about. To be honest, any significant physical activity of teen boys, especially if it gets their heart rate up quite high, will help them stay calmer throughout the day.

Here are a few ideas and activities for your son to manage anger and process excess cortisol:

- a boxing bag at home
- running
- a walk in nature
- spending time with the family dog
- spending alone time in his bedroom without being interrupted.

NB: Just escaping into an online game when he is angry will distract him BUT the energy is likely to escalate and he will reach his tipping point even quicker very soon after, often over something tiny.

Pride

Pride can be tricky for many of our tween and teen boys. If you remember the tendency for boys to need an external experience with which to evaluate their own sense of self-worth, you will see that a healthy sense of pride in something they have done well can be really important. Especially for our strong, feisty 'rooster' boys, keeping a healthy sense of pride and feeling proud of oneself without becoming arrogant can be a little tricky with that aforementioned underdeveloped prefrontal cortex. Healthy pride means that they can feel proud of something they have done that is a socially valued outcome, such as passing a test or even being able to fix a motorbike. For some of our teen boys being able to steal things or do graffiti can make them feel good about themselves, and yet we know these are not socially valued outcomes.

Often in my counselling room, I would have a boy expressing deep feelings of shame and disappointment because the only time his parents were proud of him was when he scored high marks on a test. Even a teen boy can recognise that this means that he is loved conditionally, and that really hurts. Of course, we want to feel proud of our kids when they achieve things that they have strived for, however, it can be helpful to reframe pride in just a tiny way.

Rather than feeling proud of your son for his achievement,
how about feeling proud for him? This allows your son
to fill his self-worth cup through his own efforts and
achievements rather than filling them through yours.

Our boys have been conditioned to believe that winning is incredibly important to feeling proud of oneself, especially under the old male code. Heck, I was a girl and I also loved to win! We need to make sure that boys can feel worthy and proud of themselves for participating, for training hard, for giving it a go, not just for winning. I worked with a boy who struggled with enormous rage because the coach of the soccer team did not put him on for the final minutes of a grand final and the boy felt he was the best player who had the best chance of kicking a goal in the dying minutes of the game! I have worked with a boy who had hurt his knee quite badly and convinced his coach that he could win the football match by returning onto the ground. By playing those last 10 minutes – where sadly he did not win the game – he caused serious damage to his knee and needed a full knee reconstruction. His immature pride simply got the better of him.

We need to have conversations about male pride – and how it can quite easily become unhealthy and even border on narcissism.

Embarrassment

Given that boys are often seeking that external validation that they have 'done good' or they are worthwhile, it's important to understand why sometimes they can become incredibly embarrassed in public situations. Embarrassment is the feeling of discomfort we experience when some aspect of ourselves undermines (or could potentially undermine) the image we hope others have of us.

'Looking stupid' is a particular fear of teen boys! Classrooms are a common place where our boys suddenly become consumed by embarrassment. Maybe one of their mates has called out that they have an erection, or called them a really disgusting name. Maybe they have accidentally done a loud, unplanned fart. Often when they feel embarrassed, they retaliate with aggression, quite spontaneously and very quickly. What I have found is that the safer the classroom and the stronger the relationship that the boys in the class have with the teacher, the less chance that boys become embarrassed when things like this happen.

Given that boys can be quite fond of teasing and banter as a way to connect with their mates and friends, it can be easy to see how embarrassment can be triggered. The intention behind the teasing, banter and name-calling is really the key to understanding what happens when instead of increasing connectedness, there is massive embarrassment. Often this is a misreading of the intention, and that incredibly sensitive part of our boys, which is often covered up by fake bravado, can be triggered very powerfully.

One of the things to keep in mind to avoid triggering this reaction in our boys is to remember how sensitive our boys are to feeling stupid, bad, useless or excluded in some way. Much of this stems from the way they have been treated as little boys where we may have still been thinking that hitting, hurting and shaming them was the way you teach them to be a good boy. But in fact, it does the opposite in the long-term. Always avoid admonishing a boy publicly or harshly. Quietly taking a boy aside and speaking really softly to him, or asking to chat to him away from others – even siblings – is incredibly helpful to avoid triggering the embarrassment monster!

Shame

Shame is the name we give to the overwhelming feeling that we need to crawl under a rock because we see ourselves as unworthy, unpleasant, dislikeable or reprehensible, and because of this we expect to be judged or rejected accordingly. We feel so deeply flawed or just wrong and unlovable.

Shaming starts very early, especially for our boys, and often is created through quite innocent, seemingly innocuous comments from grown-ups and even loving parents. The impossible pressures being placed on today's parents are contributing significantly to more shaming in our children.

Simplistically, shame is where we make people feel they are wrong and due to the incorrect perception that boys are tough, shame has been used a lot in previous generations. American shame researcher Dr Brené Brown says there is an important distinction between shame and guilt, which she feels is essential for parents to understand. The way we talk to ourselves is paramount. Brown defines shame self-talk as thinking, *I am bad*, whereas guilt self-talk says, *I did something bad*.

Shame has been linked to a range of issues including anxiety, depression, obsessive compulsive disorder, personality disorders, addiction, eating disorders and even phobias.

Examples of shaming behaviour

- Deliberately ignoring a boy
- Being sarcastic
- *Tsk-tsking*
- Walking away as though he does not exist
- Rolling your eyes
- Glaring at the boy with disgust
- Shouting, yelling and swearing at a child
- Freezing a boy out.

Shaming language

Shaming language implies that a young person is bad, naughty or in some way flawed – rather than describing them as a child or adolescent who is simply learning how to manage and interpret this crazy world.

Examples of shaming language:

- You ought to be ashamed of yourself.
- You naughty boy!
- Grow up!
- Stop acting like a baby.
- Don't be a sissy.
- You're hopeless.
- You're not even trying.
- Why can't you be more like your brother?
- What are people going to think?
- Is your name stupid?
- Stop being so stupid.
- Stop being a sook.

- Get out of my face.
- Be a man.
- What is wrong with you?

Please do everything you can to avoid shaming language and shaming gestures to our tween and teen boys.

Deep shame is distressing for our psyches and can happen so early in life. Shaming makes it difficult for children and adults to come to a healthy place of self-love and acceptance, and instead leaves a person feeling deeply unlovable and unworthy of happiness.

In my counselling experience with boys suffering despair, depression or even ideas of suicide, I found these lads often feel overwhelmed by their emotions triggered by shaming. Emotions were unidentified and unresolved, lying buried inside them. Many of these boys felt deeply flawed and like a failure; they believed that those closest to them did not love them. This deep sense of alienation and feeling separate came up so often when listening to these troubled lads. They were starving for deep, meaningful connection, not only with their parents but also with other significant adults in their life. They often felt completely misunderstood. Many schools still use shaming, sarcasm and strong criticism when dealing with poor behaviour, and many boys carry these scars right through life. We must remove the old boy code that existed in the 20th century because it is no longer valid; in fact, it wasn't valid back then.

When boys are punished harshly and unfairly, especially for long periods of time, it can set them up to struggle with themselves, relationships, work and poor mental health later in their life.

Being aware of the influences of unhealthy pride, embarrassment and shame are huge factors in really understanding and supporting our tween and teen boys. It's incredibly important we help them to make sense of these huge emotional states and give them some tools to manage them.

Navigating the tipping point

When a boy's barometer reaches its limit, this tipping point can see our emotionally fragile teen boys act irrationally and totally out of character and often they want to attack someone – if not themselves, then others or even just the world around them. It is a classic primitive brain response to an enormous threat, even though there may only be a tiny threat present. When they have seen what they have done, it can cause another irrationally frightening response as a consequence of the shame they feel. Things can rapidly escalate in a very short space of time. We must keep in mind this is not a bad teen boy; it's a teen boy in flight-fight mode struggling to survive. Many teen boys have expressed their deep sense of remorse and shame afterwards, especially for hurting their mum, either verbally or physically.

So please beware of the emotional vulnerability of our teen boys and the risk of the tipping point being triggered. They live in a much harsher world than their parents, and the cracked windscreen is even more cracked than before the digital world appeared. Boys who had low attachment or poor attachment with their significant caregivers in the early years of life will struggle more in this window. While they desperately hunger for deep connectedness and love, they often behave in ways that make it difficult for significant safe adults to give them what they really need. In our school settings, inappropriate behaviour tends to be punished, rather than seen as a sign that a boy is hurting and needs help. More punishment usually means more anger, which will push the boy's emotional barometer into his tipping point. This cycle can go around and around.

WHAT DO YOU WISH YOUR PARENTS HAD DONE DIFFERENTLY WHEN YOU WERE A TEENAGER?

- I wish they'd been open and supportive of my feelings instead of repressive, and that they'd listened to psychologists instead of calling them quacks.

- Supported me, loved me in the ways I needed them to. Opted not to use guilt as their primary parenting strategy.
- I wish they'd been more supportive and listened more.
- I wish my parents had provided support and encouragement, and less criticism.
- I would have just liked to have spent more time listening and learning from them.
- My parents always said that they were there for me – so it was great. The problem was I either didn't want to or didn't know how to initiate that conversation.
- I wished my parents initiated an emotional conversation with me rather than leaving it up to me. They had no idea that I would have been likely diagnosed with mental-health issues, but I would have told them if they had asked.
- I wish they'd been more approachable. Always felt I couldn't really talk to them for fear of getting into trouble or being thought less of.
- I wish my parents had showed and talked about their emotions.
- I wish they'd talked to me. Asked me questions. Listened to me. Observed how I was behaving, paid more attention to what I was doing and who I was mixing with. Not imposed their own views and beliefs onto me.

Some suggestions that can help with all these big emotions!

So, what can you do for your son when he reaches his tipping point?

- Be the grown-up who has a fully functioning prefrontal cortex and care for your own son and his friends with gestures of kindness, compassion, messages of encouragement and moments of lightness. Smile often, be lighthearted, offer refreshments and check in on them.

- Accept that emotional turmoil and confusion is a completely normal part of this major life transition.
- Know that discharging big, ugly feelings that have been triggered is healthier than suppressing and stopping them.
- Model kindness and fairness above all else while adolescents are walking the bridge to adulthood. They cannot be what they haven't seen or experienced. Remember to ask your teen often, 'What can I do to support you now?' Better still, write that message on a Post-it note and pop it on his pillow.
- Choose to bring hope and light into our teens' lives. The world is often a big nasty place and we need to reassure them that things do get better. I have found that teens are very easily influenced either positively or negatively. Please choose to influence them positively.
- Remind him that he is loved unconditionally.
- Check in with him. Again. And again.

What can I suggest my teen boy do to help him manage his tipping point and discharge his big, ugly feelings?

- Help your son work out how to fill his own self-worth cup – what activities make him feel good, happy, strong, connected, brave, or content?
- Suggest he defuse energy through physical activity: punching bag, practising a martial art, swimming, surfing, bike riding, skating
- Play music
- Spend time at a special place in nature
- Practise relaxation and mindfulness
- Tapping on acupressure points (particularly beside the nail on the middle finger)
- Deep breathing
- Yoga.

Some 'wounds' boys struggle to understand

So often when working with teen boys who were experiencing difficulties at home and school, I found they were struggling to understand exactly 'what' was making them so angry or frustrated. Once they identified what the problem was underneath their emotional angst, they were often able to make sense of what was happening and could then make better choices around it.

These are some of the areas that boys commonly found confusing and which may come up in your conversations with your sons.

Feeling excluded and that you don't belong

Every human being has a primary need to feel that we belong. With teen boys, this need is amplified for all the reasons I explained in the earlier chapters. When a friend or mate says something hurtful or even hits too hard in a play fight, it can cause some serious inner angst. Not being invited to something, even to walk home from school, can cut deeply.

Frustration is different from anger

Help boys to understand that it's normal to feel frustrated or upset because you just can't seem to do what you want to do, or get what you want to get, or maybe you don't even know why you can't get what you want. Often boys feel frustrated when they feel misunderstood, or the task they have set themselves seems harder than they originally thought, or they have not been given an opportunity to do something their own way, i.e. lack of autonomy and independence. Frustration can quickly become anger and we need to help boys work out how to manage these big, ugly emotions without hurting themselves, others or the world around them.

Feeling intimidated and threatened

Sometimes when boys are in new situations or are placed in social situations with unfamiliar boys, they can suddenly feel threatened and full of uncertainty. We must remember a boy gives himself his self-worth and if he is placed in a situation where he suddenly feels that he will be unable to succeed, to belong or to do well, he can feel intimidated by the situation, and often will want to remove himself from the threat he perceives. It is almost like asking him to play a game without him knowing what the rules are.

Boundaries and consent

Boys often seek to connect with one another through rough physical play (what Michael Gurian calls 'aggression nurturance'). This rough play is not violence but rather normal, developmentally appropriate physical bonding. Sometimes this rough play can go too far. Boys also can be quite naturally impulsive and often make mistakes around boundaries and other people's personal space. A simple check of consent can be a thumbs-up sign – and teaching our boys to say no when they feel uncomfortable with other people's behaviour will take some time. A good place to start is with siblings in your own home, if you have more than one child.

Understanding arousal states

Managing our energy levels is technically about self-regulation. Dr Stuart Shanker writes about arousal states and in many ways this can help us to understand what is happening with the energy levels in our children, especially our boys. Using the metaphor of a cup to explore energy can make it easier to understand. Invisible changes cause confusion in our tween and teen boys, which triggers stress that needs to be discharged. We grown-ups, who have mature, executive-functioning brains, can really help our boys know when their arousal states have become *too volatile or too sluggish*. Sometimes boys can simply become overwhelmed, energetically swamped or absolutely drained and then be completely confused as to how to feel better quickly. Given the random rushes of testosterone that happen, especially during the teen years, surging energy, especially unexpectedly, can be common and really confusing unless we help them understand it better. Sometimes what is seen as misbehaviour is more a *stress behaviour* or a sign your son is not coping with their world. So often in high schools, I have seen boys who have been struggling with high-energy arousal states do some really silly things like jump off the top balcony, or slide down the banister on a steep stairwell and then get punished for being stupid! I will explore how to help boys when they muck-up in more depth in chapter 10.

Dr Shanker suggests there are different states of arousal. For a statistically significant number of boys, they are often in a hyper alert or flooded state. They seldom have opportunities to move their bodies as often as they need to discharge the excess energy that has accumulated from being too passive.

A classic example is a boy who has been engaged with a device for more than 30 minutes to an hour. He is most likely going to become a little bit unpleasant once he stops his very stimulating, highly visual, largely passive, sitting activity. Techno tantrums are a real thing for boys of any age, but particularly for our tween and early teen boys as they are dopamine hunters (the feel-good neurochemical). When our boys run out of energy, it can feel unpleasant and they can become whiny, whingy and difficult to communicate with. Teaching our boys to recognise how their body feels as it loses energy as well as how it feels when there is an energy build-up can be really helpful for them before they do something irrational, often silly, often aggressive, often really risky and often without any consideration for anyone else in the vicinity. Essentially, they are taking action to move cortisol, the stress hormone which has begun to flood their brain and their body.

Sometimes taking a good-quality snack in to a boy before he comes off his Fortnite gaming or giving him a wonderful warm back massage will help to trigger enough positive neurochemicals that it means he does not need to go into the hyper alert or the flooded arousal state as he transitions off his device.

Also, be mindful of timing. If he's in the middle of a gaming campaign and you force him off, he'll naturally be annoyed. Check in with him, rub his back or maybe drop a fart and get him to agree to come off when he next reaches a point where he can save or pause or when he next 'dies'.

Connect before you redirect is a fabulous mantra to remember!

Maybe now you can appreciate why food, being physically active or busy, having fun and farting are so helpful around boys of any age to help them manage their arousal states.

Time out

A boy can struggle to understand when others need time out from them or when they might need some down time. The concept of needing time out is one that every boy needs to understand, especially our volatile teen boys. There are times when the often endless play fighting, teasing, toilet humour and seemingly ridiculous antics can become too much, especially for parents and some siblings. We must help our boys to understand that they *are not being rejected or excluded or in any way disrespected* when we may choose to have some time out. That may look like going for a walk, sitting outside or, for me, I often needed to escape and have a long, calm bath – with the door locked. I have worked with boys who find this concept potentially confusing and so it is really important to help them learn that sometimes others need space and that sometimes they are going to need to give themselves some space in certain social situations. I may have repeated the line 'please take it outside' approximately a million times when I had four sons at home. Indeed, from an early age, I found that life was easier to manage while the boys were outside the house rather than inside the house.

I hope you now have a much better understanding of the normal volatility of the emotional world of our tween/teen boys.

6

When the going gets really tough mentally

Simplistically, resilience is about managing the ups and downs of life. I explore this in depth in my book *Real Kids in an Unreal World: How to build resilience and self-esteem in today's children.* Today's kids of all ages are less resilient than previous generations and that applies to both boys and girls. They are struggling to cope with many of life's challenges.

Some of our teen boys can develop phobias and strong anxiety patterns around things that they have misinterpreted, misunderstood or simply have no idea about. I worked with one 14-year-old boy who had developed a strong anxiety about using public toilets. This had originated from another teen boy joking about the size of his penis. This irrational thought pattern took some time to reprogram and he found it difficult to resolve.

Another boy who had been bullied for being fat began an extreme exercise and eating program that saw him often running in the middle of the night with a torch. Eating food became a really traumatic thing for him and he did need some serious psychological support to be able to unravel this body-dysmorphia experience. He was so desperate to have a six-pack that it became all encompassing.

By now you will appreciate that much of adolescent angst and behaviour is driven by things that teens have little awareness about and their capacity to more often make sound choices is impaired due to an immature brain, at a time of enormous confusion and stress. You cannot build resilience on your own – you need the rails on the bridge to help you do that. Statistically, all teens are struggling more in an uncertain, often harsh world and far too many of our emerging men are ending their lives.

In October 2018 during Mental Health Week, the Australian Men's Health Forum shared some interesting realities about men's mental health:

1. Most male suicide is not linked to depression.
2. Boys have more mental-health issues than girls.
3. Men aren't as bad at getting help as we think.

4. Men have lots of coping strategies that don't involve talking.
5. Men have less depression and anxiety but more drink and drug disorders.
6. Mental health is having a big impact on men's physical health.
7. Gambling is linked to mental-health issues.
8. Men get eating disorders too.
9. Dads experience postnatal depression too.
10. Gender blind mental health services may struggle to help men (and women).

'Fighting' depression versus managing it

Gradually we are seeing glimpses of this metaphor in our world. More and more well-known figures are owning their own struggles with mental illness, which is a positive thing, and owning the fact that life can cause times of struggle and vulnerability. Often 'warrior' terms come out when we're talking about mental illness as we mention beating it, shaking it off, fighting it and ending the battle of mental illness. Sometimes it cannot be overcome completely. I have some concerns that many forms of mental illness need to be managed often for a long time, even a lifetime, and that we need to learn how to live with mental illness, because often it's complex and ongoing.

If we keep portraying that depression is a battle that needs to be won, maybe we are adding to the problem when a man is unable to completely overcome his depression without ongoing support, possibly medication and other wellbeing strategies. He may feel he has failed yet again.

Danny 'Spud' Frawley was an AFL legend in Australia who was widely loved and respected. Sadly in 2019 he ended his own life tragically in a car crash despite being a strong advocate for being more open around mental illness – something he had experienced during his life. This was part of the message that his family, including his wife Anita and their three daughters Chelsea, Danielle and Keeley, released in a statement:

> Danny was to all who knew him a caring, loyal, selfless, loving person who would always put others first before himself and aside from his work in football and media he worked hard to use his profile to remove the stigma associated with depression and encouraged acceptance and support for those who suffered with mental health issues.

Please have conversations with your teen and tween boys about mental illness, especially depression, because so many boys and men hide the debilitating impact that depression has on their lives and their relationships. Ask them to keep an eye on their friends and to let you know if they are ever worried about them.

When the going gets really tough

Statistically, our boys are struggling mentally. According to the 2017 study *Child and Adolescent Mental Health and Educational Outcomes – An analysis of educational outcomes from Young Minds Matter: the second Australian Child and Adolescent Survey of Mental Health and Wellbeing*, completed at The University of Western Australia, the following statistics show boys struggling at a higher rate than girls.

Who is most susceptible to having a mental disorder?
Males 4 to 11 years old: 17 per cent
Male adolescents: 15.7 per cent
Girls 4 to 11 years old: 11 per cent
Girl adolescents: 12.1 per cent

The higher rates for boys, according to the report, are attributed to males having higher rates of ADHD, which was 'twice as common in males than females at ages 4–11 years (11.3 per cent vs. 5.7 per cent), and four times as common in males compared to females at ages 12–17 years (9.9 per cent vs. 2.5 per cent)'.

I have often found that naivety and an inability to identify there is a problem or being too trusting of manipulative adults are all problematic contributors to teen boys developing mental health issues or, worse still, a serious mental health disorder.

When a client of mine, Gary, shared his story with me he was 40 years of age and he said he had never shared the full story with anyone before in his life. Gary had been raised in the tough days of the '50s and '60s when physical punishment was considered the norm, especially for boys. He can remember being hit and beaten first by his mum, and then later when his dad came home he would also inflict pain. The only person whom he felt close to was his elderly grandmother, who lived in the family home. When she died, things went from bad to worse. He struggled academically at school and remembers being hit by the nuns for not being able to spell well. About a month after his grandmother died, when he was almost 15 years of age, somebody in the classroom teased him for being such 'a miserable prick'. One of the other boys in the classroom said he was glad his grandmother was dead, and he reached his tipping point. He threw a desk or two, yelled abuse at the boys responsible and took off from the classroom. Over the next few weeks, he never returned to the classroom but left home every day dressed for school. He was spending his days at a local arcade that had lots of games.

At some point, a middle-aged man befriended him and started chatting with him and buying him food and cool drinks. Gary shared the story of the death of his grandmother with him, and the man was the first person who showed he cared. Vulnerable boys are easy targets for sexual predators, as was heard often in the Royal Commission into Institutional Responses to Child Sexual Abuse – especially in the Catholic Church. One afternoon the man suggested that Gary leave Sydney and come with him and get a job in Perth.

All Gary remembers thinking was that nobody would care if he wasn't there and finally he had found somebody who really cared about him. So he left without telling anyone where he was going. Once the man had Gary in a hotel in Perth, he began molesting him. At first Gary was horrified, but he had been groomed well and the man had convinced him that he really loved him. About a month after they had relocated, the man brought Gary along to a party and gave him alcohol and he became very drunk. It was at this point that his male abuser told him that he wanted him to have sex with his newfound Perth mates as well. Fortunately for Gary he was able to escape but found himself on the street, now homeless in a city he did not know, crushed and wounded yet again. Fortunately for Gary he had found a job the week before and he was able to find somewhere safe to live as well. Gary could not believe how naïve he had been at 15 to believe a stranger. He kept this deep dark painful secret for over 20 years. He hopes his story may be a lesson to the young lads who are struggling to feel accepted, valued or loved.

The Royal Commission discovered the disturbing reality of sexual abuse of tens of thousands of children – both girls and boys – within churches and institutions. Tween and teen boys can become victims who remain silent for all the reasons around shame and feeling powerless. It has been suggested that boys who have suffered abuse often remain silent for at least 20 years – if not forever. Sexual abuse is a major contributor to mental illness, addiction and violence. Teaching our boys about healthy boundaries, consent and respectful behaviours can keep them safe from potential predators as well as help them make better choices themselves.

WHAT WAS YOUR MOST CHALLENGING EXPERIENCE AS A TEEN BOY?

- Coping with undiagnosed depression and lack of self-worth
- Poor mental health

- Learning difficulties – which caused me to feel a lot of shame, embarrassment and vulnerability
- OCD: it happened when I was 14. An unreasonable need to wash my hands and other weird behaviours. Could not pass the front door [if] I saw a car. It passed around 15.
- My struggles with depression, anxiety and anorexia
- Struggling with self-worth driven by my confused sexuality
- Being constantly bullied about my body image.

Suicide

The saddest and most worrying statistic that we need to be concerned about are the numbers of our young lads who feel they need to end their lives by suicide. Rates of death by suicide among our teens and almost men (up to 24) are seriously troubling. Suicide is the leading cause of death among this age group.

Listed below are comparative numbers for suicide deaths for 15–24-year-old males per 100,000, from World Health Organization and other sources:

	Australia	Canada	NZ*	UK	US
2000	20.3	20.17	30.38	10.51	17.05
2001	20.7	18.36	32.29	9.88	16.64
2002	17.92	17.51	23.53	8.59	16.48
2003	17.41	18.5	23.53	8.20	15.96
2004	14.43	16.99	27.99	7.97	16.77
2005	N/A	16.80	27.97	7.34	16.16
2006	15.9	14.47	31.12	7.50	16.15
2007	15.44	15.48	22.58	7.37	15.81
2008	14.60	14.69	26.39	7.66	16.05
2009	13.08	14.82	29.35	7.88	16.09
2010	13.71	15.73	23.56	8.14	16.79
2011	16.41	15.45	29.01	8.16	17.5
2012	13.73	16.14	32.32	8.66	17.25
2013	16.77	12.7	23.49	7.92	17.17
2014	16.88	N/A	N/A	7.96	18.01

	Australia	Canada	NZ*	UK	US
2015	17.46	14 (15–19yo)	N/A	9.00	19.27
2016	13.4 (15–19yo)	N/A	N/A	7.9 (10–24yo)	13.15
2017	13.9 (15–19yo) 22.2 (20–24yo)	N/A	20.49 (15–19yo) 29.5 (20–25yo)	7.2 (10–24yo) 7.6 (15–19yo) 12.9 (20–24yo)	14.46 (15–24yo) 17 (20–24yo) 12 (15–19yo)
2018	N/A	N/A	36.37 (20–24yo) 29.69 (15–19yo) (July 2018– June 2019)	9.0 (10–24yo) 9.0 (15–19yo) 16.9 (20–24yo)	N/A

A news bulletin issued by the World Health Organization in September 2019 reported that across WHO countries the second leading cause of death among people aged 15–29 years, after road injury, was suicide. In the age bracket of 15–19 years for girls, suicide was second only to maternal conditions, and third for boys in the same age group, after road injury and interpersonal violence.

In Australia in 2017, suicide remained the leading cause of death for both Aboriginal and Torres Strait Islander and non-Indigenous children and young people (5–17), accounting for 40 per cent of all Indigenous child deaths. Tragically, deaths among those aged 15–17 contributed to 94.4 per cent of all suicide deaths in young Indigenous people. When we take gender differences into account, 91.6 per cent of Indigenous male youth suicides were aged 15–17.

The New Zealand numbers are deeply worrying and similar to Australian numbers for Aboriginal and Torres Strait Islander boys. Maori lads represent almost 24 per 100,000 of the almost 30 per 100,000 who suicided in 2017–2018.

These tragic numbers are a clear sign that we are failing our tween and teen boys – in particular our Indigenous boys who often struggle with intergenerational trauma – badly as a society.

The old-fashioned way of raising boys involved denying vulner-ability, and overvalued the powerful controlling systems of the patriarchy. In trying to dismantle these old man-code rules, we hope we can help our confused boys find a way to manhood that allows them to have a strong backbone and a strong heart. But we must do more if we are to stop these awful statistics. We cannot continue to expect that our mental-health services can meet the growing demands of our disconnected, wounded and often lost boys. In a way, for many boys today the bridge to manhood does not have any guard-rails – and many are falling off the edge. We need to put those railings back up in a respectful and compassionate way and we need to do it now before we lose any more of our precious, confused lads.

I have shared in this book several stories of teen boys who have had serious suicidal ideation or who have attempted to end their lives. One thing I think needs consideration is that boys and men by nature tend to be problem solvers, as I explored in the early chapters on biologi-cal drivers from our ancestry. So when they see a problem, especially one that requires a practical solution, they will be driven to fix it, and when it's fixed they feel capable and worthwhile. When 'the problem' involves deeper challenges, especially relationships with parents, friends or intimate partners, or a perceived lack of status, or a loss or failure of *something significant to the boy*, their problem-solving is much more difficult. When a teen boy feels the world is letting him down, or he has ruined his whole life and/or there is no-one he can turn to, his risk of ending his life is very real. He wants to end the pain of feeling so worthless and so hopeless and he lacks the executive brain to help him explore what is challenging him and work out how to resolve it. When this heavy load just feels too heavy, the last straw can be quite small. There is a possibility that maybe he also considers, irrationally, that he's saving his family from his struggles and failings? This may be one of the reasons why some teen boys and young men who have very loving families end their lives suddenly and with no obvious reason.

*

We need to teach our younger boys that life can be tough at times and help-seeking behaviour is not a sign of weakness.

Having a brain under construction is only one of the many things that can make it hard for boys to transition into becoming mature, responsible men. Suicide is complex and different for every young person. We cannot just rely on our mental-health services because they are sadly inadequate and often confronting for boys to approach. We need to begin to address the failings of our early childhood system and our schooling system, which are allowing so many of our boys to get lost in the cracks or to grow up struggling in the system that is failing many of them badly. What all our teens need is a nest or a safe base to catch them when things get tough. They need deep, strong, unconditionally supportive relationships so that they have somewhere to turn when the world just seems too much to handle – if not at home, then somewhere in the community. Boys are as emotionally fragile as girls during adolescence – regardless of the mask they may be wearing, the words they may be saying or the actions they are displaying.

We need to keep in mind that suicide is still statistically uncommon even though it's incredibly tragic. Mental Health First Aid is a program run in communities and schools in response to the increasing levels of mental illness among our children and our teenagers. If you get the chance, please take the time to complete the course. This will help you recognise that there are some significant myths about suicide that need to be corrected.

Those who work as psychiatrists in youth mental health come across young lads who end their lives with *absolutely no warning that they are struggling.* Professor Matthew Large from the University of New South Wales has written that clinicians should not assume that patients experiencing mental distress without reporting suicidal ideas were not at elevated risk of suicide. Asking about suicidal thoughts was a central skill for health professionals, he said, but clinicians should be not be persuaded into false confidence generated by a lack of ideation.

One way to consider reducing the risk of suicide, particularly in our young, is to learn from traditional communities in the past and build more human connectedness in our families, our homes and our communities. The transition from being a boy to becoming a man was very carefully facilitated and mentored within these communities. The need for a sense of purpose and direction is paramount in helping all our teens. Boys in these communities had a strong sense of camaraderie; they were all in it together, which gave them a sense of predictability. Those relationships existed in real time not virtual reality. They had opportunities to stretch themselves and test themselves and learn self-discipline. At some point, there would be a silent quest that would challenge them deeply. Again, to become an authentic warrior, respected by others, one must first learn to respect oneself. So many of today's boys are seeking their own rites of passage without the rails on the bridge – or the guidance of good men.

The need for connectedness

Many teen boys have expressed to me that they feel alone on this teen-boy journey. Rachael Kessler was a wise teacher, researcher and author from Boulder, Colorado who explored the various ways we humans can be connected. I feel her work can be a part of a call to action to improve the outcomes for all today's young people. She described six different ways that we can build connectedness. When I was working with a troubled teen who had contemplated suicide, I often found they felt disconnected from all six of these. Please have this conversation with whoever you are co-parenting your son with, as I believe it will give you some sense of direction on how to support your son when he is at his most difficult!

Six ways of deep connectedness

Deep connection to self

Deep connection to another (family, friends)

Deep connection to community (school, sport, faith, local, cadets)

Deep connection to lineage (ancestry, cultural)

Deep connection to Nature and the environment

Deep Connection to a Higher Power (the mysterious, the spiritual, the non-logical)

– Rachael Kessler, The Soul of Education (2000)

Building resilience takes time and often real-life experience is the best teacher for our tween and teen boys.

This is a blog I wrote that shows how significant time in nature plus the guiding influence of older men plus the gift of natural consequence can teach important life lessons. Similar experiences can happen in other natural settings like farms, stations, mountains and sailing.

Why I'm glad my sons took up surfing

When I grew up in the '50s and '60s in a conservative rural farming area, surfing was still in its infancy. To be perfectly honest, surfers were considered to be dope-smoking, unemployed bums. So when my eldest son expressed an interest in taking up surfing I have to confess a part of me was deeply concerned that this would create a serious moral decline of some kind.

Thankfully I was able to overcome the unhealthy stereotypical perception of surfing and, one after the other, all four Dent boys have become lifelong surfers.

Obviously growing up so close to the coast – Albany in Western Australia – made surfing a doable pastime.

Another thing that made surfing doable was that all my boys were competent swimmers before they ventured out into the surf. Over the years I have learned that being a strong swimmer can definitely be helpful, but if you are being pummelled by a massive wave you also need a lot of luck to be able to survive.

Being such a risky sport, you may wonder why I'm secretly glad my boys became surfers. Those scrawny young lads have grown into physically strong, healthy, resilient men and the ocean and surfing are still very much a part of their lives.

Surfing has given my sons lessons in life that I'm really grateful for and which I'm not sure we loving parents alone could have delivered.

Six lessons my sons learned from surfing

1. Reconnection

Surfing takes place in nature, and a powerful and strong connection to nature helps build a sense of belonging in the world. No matter how confusing and stressful the adolescent journey was for my boys, the ocean could hold them with a sense of familiarity and reassure them that all was well in the world.

Surfers will go out in all different weather conditions including freezing cold. In the early days before any of the Dent lads had a licence, I would be the surfing taxi. Sometimes this meant we drove from beach to beach for ages until we found a good spot. Once they chose the surf break for the day, I would often wait hours until they returned.

Was this how I wanted to spend my Sunday mornings? Did I not have better things to do at home? Of course.

However, when I saw the faces of the lads who returned to the car, I knew something special was happening that I could not comprehend.

The teen mask was gone and it was the happiest I ever saw my sons and their mates.

In a way, surfing reconnected them to what really mattered in life – not school grades, fragile male egos, moments of failure and disappointment, or the need to wear cool clothes and look 'sick'.

They were cleansed and reconnected to one of life's gifts – a positive human experience shared with other humans. Humans are social beings and the fundamental need to be connected to others must be met to ensure a healthy mind-body-heart and soul connection.

Most boys today are connected in the digital world however, and they are missing vital social and emotional learning because they are not sharing real-life experiences.

Boys' friendships in particular are enhanced by sharing common interests. Many of my boys' best mates from their teenage years are still their best mates and surfing has been a glue that has kept them connected over many years.

2. Responsibility

To be a surfer you need to be responsible, especially around taking care of your board, your wetsuit and protecting yourself from the sun. Through experience, all surfers learn that if you really want to enjoy your surfing, you have to put some effort in before you get in the water.

Surfboards are expensive. If a Dent lad broke or badly damaged his surfboard even by accident, he would have to surf on a really daggy, old, solid board until either his next birthday or Christmas. He would also need to earn money to help pay for the new board. This may sound tough but it has given my sons a good appreciation of the value of things and they still take very good care of their boards. Responsibility can be taught through surfing.

While out on the waves, there are unwritten rules (actually, sometimes these days they are written on signs at beaches for those who haven't realised yet that there are rules). These rules are a form of boundary to help ensure safety out on the waves.

There are times when surfers get hurt. One of those unwritten rules is that any other surfer who is nearby to an injured surfer goes to help. There have been many occasions where my boys and their mates have stepped up to help out someone who has been injured.

Many will do this despite the risk to their own safety. Stories abound of heroic acts by surfers who helped rescue those who were hurt, even in the presence of sharks. This unwritten code is definitely one that comes with the territory and is representative of true hero behaviour. Another good lesson learned while out in the waves.

3. Resilience and robustness

There are days when surfers need to walk long distances and traverse over steep sand hills to get to catch a wave.

They sometimes have to scramble over rocks and paddle long distances to actually reach the surf break!

This effort takes a robustness that needs to be acknowledged and celebrated. This is another example of the growth of a boy to a man, one who can delay instant gratification, who can persist when his body is hurting and who can conquer a metaphorical mountain in order to challenge himself to reach the 'holy grail' of a ride in the blue tube or the green room.

This helps build resilience as well as building physical and mental strength.

Getting really cold and really scared can actually be really good for teenage boys. To become a resilient human being, you need to learn about fear, failure and how to overcome life's challenges quickly and efficiently.

Surfing can be a great leveller – you can have a fabulous surf followed by one where you scarcely get a wave and this is also a good lesson when building character.

You will not become too confident and arrogant, and quite frankly you will just be grateful when you have a 'good enough' surf. Surfing helps you to learn how to be able to work in all sorts of conditions – stinking hot or freezing cold and raining.

This is something that concerns me about our bedroom gamers who seldom step outside into the real world. Will this softening be a benefit later in life?

I have to be honest, there were times I shook my head in disbelief as boys who were shivering loudly from the cold then put on their wetsuits to go and spend two hours in a really freezing ocean! And yet this was another way of becoming stronger and braver without needing to hurt anybody else.

Disappointment happens often in the life of surfers. Surf can look fabulous from the car park and yet by the time you get to that magical spot conditions change and things can go crappy.

The wind can change and ruin a surf break or someone can drop in on you and steal the best wave of the day. Your leg rope can snap or your board can get 'dinged' or worse still, snapped.

These times of disappointment are character-building moments that will help you learn to suck it up and keep going. Yet another great lesson in life that can be learned on those big green waves.

4. Risk

One of the best teachers for boys about making poor choices is natural consequences.

Surfing does this beautifully and often painfully. My lads have all experienced physical wounds while surfing. These wounds have also made them realise they are not invincible warriors – that taking risks can come with a price.

In his book *The New Manhood*, Steve Biddulph writes of the need to nurture the wild man within. Surfing does this really well. Risk-taking behaviour is normal in adolescence and beyond that life is a long journey of taking risks, both big and small.

Surfing will give you these opportunities every single time you venture out into the waves. The footage of Mick Fanning fighting off a shark has been seen so many times and it will always remind us mere mortals that surfing is dangerous.

Statistically it's not as dangerous as driving a car, or being a passenger in a car, however it can be a pastime that can end in tragedy and every surfer knows this each time they head out for a surf.

5. Respect and gratitude

I am deeply grateful for the many good men who helped guide my sons on the journey to become lifelong surfers. Many a day, especially when they were in their early teen years, the boys would be collected by one of these good men and taken out surfing for the day.

Good men who step forward to do this are incredibly important in the journey of life. Not only is it helpful for parents, especially mothers of sons, it is a way for boys to develop respect for older men by witnessing good actions.

To the good men around Albany who took the Dent lads and their mates out into the surf – I thank you.

Respect can be a tricky thing to understand, especially when you are a confused, hungry teen boy. Having regular good men take an interest in you certainly helps to learn what respect feels like.

The ocean, in its fierce unforgiving way, also taught respect to the lads who dived eagerly into those waters – hoping for joy and success, never knowing what may eventuate.

Mother Nature deserves to be respected and often surfing helped my growing boys learn about valuing the physical world. Take your rubbish with you, remove any floating plastic you find and every time you leave the water alive – you quietly whisper, 'Thank you.'

6. Rush of success

For many boys and men, they need an external experience or event to help them feel worthwhile and capable. This explains why there is a natural competitiveness in our boys – even though our girls can be just as competitive!

When a boy has completed a task to a standard that he had envisaged would make him feel worthwhile, he almost punches the air because it feels so good.

Surfing can give boys and men this natural high in its undiluted exquisite delight. There is an unbelievable rush of endorphins that occurs with a successful wave – one that I can only imagine.

It is also an individual pursuit of success and there is only one person who is responsible for achieving it – so self-worth has to improve following such a success.

A successful ride is a brilliant feel-good moment that can last for ages, regardless of what else is happening in life.

In a Western world full of boy disengagement at school, this rush of success that can happen out on the waves can have a flow-on effect of building confidence in the boy in our classrooms. Success breeds more success.

It takes time to build mental and physical competence and resilience and there are many ways to build it other than surfing. We simply need to make sure it happens.

Hopefully as you read this book you will have a new appreciation of the unique challenges for our boys as they go through this incredibly enormous time of transformation. The understanding of the vulnerabilities that confront our tween and teen boys is paramount to us providing a healthy environment around them that will allow them to not just survive, but to thrive.

Building connectedness can start as simply as making the time and effort to connect with people we haven't seen in a while. Make plans for beach trips, hiking expeditions or BBQs and picnics or even better, a holiday somewhere.

When sh#% happens to those in our family or community, we need to model to our boys that we need to step up and be there, for as long as it takes, and hope they return the favour if adversity comes a knocking on our door. Modelling help-seeking behaviour and help-providing behaviour right through a boy's childhood can help him to accept that when things get tough, there are people he can turn to. Healthy relationships really are the key to this happening.

Then in our communities, let's reach out and meet our neighbours and make time to volunteer in our schools and clubs to ensure we lift the sense of belonging that *builds linkages and social capital*. Everybody matters, no matter what.

We can prioritise being a part of the positive change needed to ensure that during these tumultuous years our boys and our girls have the right configuration of support and connectedness. We should ensure we follow up with small acts of kindness and compassion.

I believe we can all help heal this profound wound of human disconnectedness. We are all in this together. We can do this and we can start today.

A message from a well-respected adolescent psychiatrist to all parents – please trust your gut instincts around your son. If something feels off or not right, please act on those instincts. Check out the chapter on communication (chapter 12), choose the right time and check in with your son, with the biggest heart full of love you can find and possibly a large block of his favourite chocolate. The Mental Health First Aid guidelines suggest that if you have serious concerns about the wellbeing of a loved one, or a young person whom you care about you should ask them directly one of the following questions:

Are you having thoughts of suicide?
Are you thinking about killing yourself?

You cannot put the idea of suicide into another person's head, and asking these questions will not increase the risk that they will act on these suggestions. The research is very strong about this. For more information about the Mental Health First Aid program go to www.mhfa.com.au.

Watch for the red flags

Help your teen to identify when they may be experiencing unhealthy levels of stress or anxiety (i.e. having three of the main symptoms below for a prolonged time). Do everything you can to get your teen to your family doctor for a mental-health assessment – for your peace of mind and for theirs.

- Headaches, other aches and pains
- Upset stomach, indigestion, diarrhoea
- Changes around eating habits – either excessive or no appetite

- Anger, irritability, entrenched moods
- Lethargy, low energy
- Grades dropping
- School reluctance
- Crying a lot
- Social withdrawal, especially from friends and favourite activities
- Excessive disobedience or aggression
- Racing heart/palpitations and/or hyperventilation
- Tension in muscles and/or excessive perspiration
- Problems with a dry mouth
- Often feeling restless, apprehensive or on edge
- Panic attacks
- Feeling hopeless, helpless and worthless
- Difficulty concentrating or feeling scattered
- Difficulty getting to sleep, disturbed sleep
- Feeling frightened for no obvious reason
- Morbid thoughts regarding people close to them
- Constant worry/apprehension about the future.

Reasons a boy might not want to get help

Adolescents, especially teen boys, have a strong resistance to getting professional help, especially within the school system. Some told me that they thought that until they actually spoke to a professional, they could pretend that they were OK even when they were not.

There are many reasons why adolescents (and probably many adults!) may be reluctant to reach out. Australian researchers who investigated the barriers to seeking help with over 600 Year 8 to Year 12 students found that the most common reasons given for not asking for help were:

- Thinking they could solve problems on their own
- Being embarrassed to speak with a counsellor

- Fearing that they may find out they are 'crazy' if they see a therapist
- Having a sense that their problems wouldn't be understood by an adult
- Lacking time to go to counselling
- Being concerned about privacy/secrets being disclosed
- Feeling that nothing will change
- Not being able to afford to see a psychologist/counsellor
- Fearing that a therapist may want them to do something they don't want to
- Worrying about their family finding out they were seeing a counsellor.

Support services for mental health

Headspace, a national Australian organisation set up to support adolescents specifically, does some really excellent work in communities for teens. However, they have had some challenges. Some parents have reported that teenagers complain they often have to see a different counsellor each time they visit. This is actually really unhelpful as it can diminish the teen's capacity to feel valued and safe, because trust takes time to develop through relationship, especially for boys. Other boys have told me they dislike talking about painful stuff, and if a counsellor or psychologist is unable to build rapport or a sense of understanding of how a boy processes the world, they walk and never come back! Many have told me that they have just given up because of this reason. I believe Headspace is also very heavily utilised so getting an appointment when you need one can be challenging. Mental-health resources are stretched. It is a model that can be improved. They do have some excellent online resources for adolescents and parents.

Reachout is a leading Australian online mental-health organisation for young people and their parents. It has real information about relationships and more.

Fortunately, many services do offer online counselling now, which some teens will be more likely to use than going to see a counsellor in person. Boys tell me they prefer email and messaging to actual talking and that makes sense. There are also several apps that help with mental-health support so these can be very helpful to support teens, or just enable them to find more information so they can get help.

On my website, I keep an up-to-date list of support services for teens and I encourage you to check that out and share it with the adolescents in your life. You can find it at www.maggiedent.com/support-services-teen.

Struggling with your mental health is SO common, especially anxiety and depression. Many of your friends and family, possibly even your parents, have likely struggled with it themselves. It may not be talked about as often as it should, but it's improving and more people than ever are realising that being open and honest (with yourself as well as the people who care about you) about what's happening in your mind is super important to keeping yourself happy. Think about it, talk about it, find some help and support!

Other possible support services

As I have already written, I have found that teen boys can struggle with 'talking therapy' unless they find someone who has an exceptional ability to connect with them easily. When a boy is struggling, he will have a heightened level of emotional intensity that may make him quite defensive and even physically agitated. Sometimes he will project this emotional tension onto others through aggression, verbal abuse or by imploding and shutting down.

Talking about big, ugly feelings can be helpful, but for many boys it can actually overwhelm them even more. There are some more alternative therapies that many psychologists are also weaving into their practice, which seem to have more success with our non-communicative boys.

I have used **SET (Simple Energy Techniques)** or **EFT (Emotional Freedom Techniques)**, now called **tapping**, with huge success with deeply troubled and often grieving teens and adults over the years. The tapping of key acupressure points can relieve some of the intensity of the grief and the more they do it, the better. (See www.eftdownunder. com.au for some guidance on how to use these techniques.)

Another relatively new therapy is called **Neurofeedback Therapy**, also known as **EEG Biofeedback**, which is a brain-based treatment that uses a sophisticated brain–computer interface to 'strengthen' or 'rewire' the brain, by training brainwaves, the tiny electrical signals produced by the brain. Neuroscience has been able to show that neurofeedback therapy can help the brain change to improve emotional self-regulation, cognitive flexibility, impulse control and working memory while also reducing tension in the nervous system. I have met some families whose sons have benefited enormously from this treatment.

Kinesiology is another form of therapy that uses less 'talking therapy'. It has been shown to help reduce the emotional tension within the nervous system, reframe and set new goals for individuals, and in some weird way it can process unexpressed emotions from prior experiences that are problematic. I have known many boys who have experienced this form of therapy and have noticed how immediately they feel better within themselves. Indeed, often they ask their parents for another appointment when they start feeling 'under the weather'.

The effectiveness of these less dialogue-focused therapies is directly linked to the relationship that can be formed with the therapist, rather than just the therapy that is used.

Lastly, encouraging your teen boy to use **mindfulness, guided visualisations,** and do regular **yoga** or **tai chi** all help our boys to access their wise inner compass. I recently met a man at one of my seminars who has been using one of my audio tracks for 15 years. He told me that it had really helped his anxiety when he was in high school, and as he grew older, he used it again as he continued his studies at university. And now as a father he sometimes uses the same audio, Beach Bliss, with his eight-year-old son and they both really enjoy it.

The best thing about being a teen boy today is that there's so many people supporting you and willing to help with any problems, whether it be parents, teachers, friends, girlfriends, psychologists etc.

PART 2

WHAT CAN WE DO TO GUIDE OUR BOYS TO MANHOOD?

7

For confused mammas . . . and mother figures

> Mum loved us unconditionally! Dad was too focused on wealth creation to enjoy his family. He missed out. I wish he made more time for his family for his sake.

Let's start the chapter with the good news from the survey from men. When asked the question, 'Looking back, who helped you most as a teen?', just over 56 per cent responded that the person who helped them the most was their mum. I was reassured to see this figure as, in my experience over the past 40 years around tween and teen boys, I found that having a supportive mum was a strong contributing factor to boys' wellbeing and life success. This does not mean that there are not times that tween and teen boys can still make appalling choices, be incredibly forgetful, sometimes rude, and disrespectful and moody. It simply means that they know that despite all this, they have a safety net underneath them all the way through these tricky years and they know that they are loved.

Who helped you the most when you were a teen?

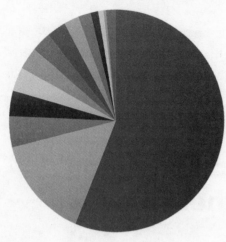

- mum 56.25%
- dad 14.94%
- friend's parent/s 4.54%
- none 3.71%
- grandparent 3.47%
- friend/s 3.29%
- sibling/s 2.93%
- teacher 2.93%
- aunt/uncle 2.27%
- coach 1.9%
- parents (both) 1.14%
- church 0.78%
- military/scouts/cadets 0.35%
- other 1.5%

If you are a mother of a son and you find him really confusing, you may already have read my previous book, *Mothering Our Boys*. In this book I explore in depth (but not specifically from the tween/teen perspective) some of the key confusing aspects for a woman parenting a boy. Through reading the book, so many mothers of sons have discovered a new understanding of their son, and have seen an improved relationship with not only her son, but also her male partner. If you didn't grow up with a brother and/or if your relationship with your father was distant or toxic, you may struggle to be the loving presence that every boy needs.

Respect yourself and others, especially your mum.

Mother wound

A 'mother wound' occurs when a negative relationship between a child and mother causes the child significant emotional and psychological damage. No woman wants to create a mother wound that will impact her son negatively as he leaves childhood behind and becomes a man.

When we carry a father or mother wound, it goes far deeper into our adult psyche and soul, and it often unconsciously impacts our relationships negatively. In my counselling work, I found that many boys and men tended to stay very loyal to their mother despite having experienced major painful moments that caused them enormous heartache. Boys and men who carry a mother wound will tend to struggle significantly in connecting closely and emotionally with women.

The two extremes of mothering – being cold, distant and highly critical or being the smother mother who is constantly invading her son's personal space – tend to create significant mother wounds later in life that can make an intimate relationship with a woman more challenging.

Smother mothering

Every human has a need for individuation and separation and being held too tight can feel suffocating. When a son finally leaves his boyhood behind, hopefully some time in his twenties or even later when his prefrontal lobe finally grows, it is advisable that he walks out of his mother's home with both his testicles intact – metaphorically speaking. I have worked with many men who feel their mother has one testicle and their wife has the other and that he can never please either. The art of letting go of your sons is coming up soon in this book. Smother mothers restrict boys' freedom and often over-invade their boundaries. They tend to check up on them too often, ask endless questions about everything and need to have input into as many choices as possible from subjects chosen at school to what friends a boy should have or avoid.

Cold and distant mothering

So how does the cold and distant mother–son relationship impact our boys later in life? Sometimes it creates an incredible yearning for love and tenderness, and yet they can find that terrifying as well. A boy who has had a cold, distant mother has a seriously armoured heart and can struggle to open it as an adult because he can struggle with deep feelings. Not only can he find them uncomfortable, he can find it hard to share his deepest loving feelings with the woman he loves because he is wary of getting too close to his partner in case it becomes too much. This mirrors how he felt around his mother and he may not want to risk getting hurt again like he was with his own mother.

There is another possibility for men who have had the emotionally unavailable mother and that is that they will attract a woman who will abandon them just like their mother did. Falling in love can happen even if you have had a frigid mother because our primary instincts, when combined with our hormones, can make the phenomes of being attracted too strong to resist. We know that falling in love is the easy bit – staying in a committed relationship is quite different. What can happen for men who had a cold, distant mother relationship is that when the honeymoon period wanes or when his partner gets to be less loving and attentive – for example due to the arrival of a new baby or new work commitments – this can trigger terrifying, irrational fears within the man that he is about to be abandoned again. This can come out as rage or escapism where a man can use his addictions to compensate for the pain in his heart, generated by the thought of being abandoned again. Either of these reactions will make the relationship difficult to sustain.

HERE ARE SOME OF THE REGRETS THAT CAME FROM THE MEN IN THE SURVEY ABOUT THEIR MUM.

- I wish my mother had shown some form of love or an interest in what was going on with me. I don't remember ever getting a hug. I also wish she had been straight up instead of all the fabrications.

- Not having a mother figure nearby.
- Living alone with my mother in an isolated house whilst she went through the menopause.
- When my mum left for another man.
- Seeing my mum experience alcohol and prescription drug addiction and the rehab for that addiction.
- I wish Mum wasn't an alcoholic who left Dad and hated him and I wish Dad wasn't abusive to myself, my brother and his partners.
- Mom was great. She was really 'cool' but I saw with my brother and sister she avoided conflict somewhat too much. Her non-confrontational style became a problem when my brother started to dabble in drugs and alcohol. None of that was her fault of course, but I can see how it didn't help.
- My mother's put-downs, screaming and baiting of my father and my father's explosions and alcohol use.

Behaviours for you to avoid with your son
Overly harsh punishment can do a lot of harm to your relationship with your son

I once coached a friendly, enthusiastic boy in one of my basketball teams. He was a delight to have in the team. He came to me one afternoon before basketball training with a very heavy heart to tell me that he would not be able to play basketball again for the whole season. When I questioned him about why, he said his mother was not happy with his grades and he needed to spend more time studying. There were tears in his eyes and my heart ached for him. His mum had broken a part of his heart with her harsh punishment. Many years later when I met this boy who was now a man, he told me that he was completely estranged from his mother.

When we discipline with unreasonable force or too lengthy a sanction, we don't teach, we hurt deeply – we punish. We also create lots of resentment and anger towards the person who created the unreasonable punishment. Trust me, a withdrawal of privileges does not need to be exceptionally long – it just has to be one they would prefer never to repeat.

Harsh, overtly negative and shaming reactions

Shouting, harsh criticism or displaying your obvious disappointment at your son cuts him very deeply, even if that is not what you are seeing on his face. Indeed, many boys tell me that they believe their mum has simply stopped loving them when she does things like this. So be mindful of reconnecting and reassuring your son after you have had one of your less-than-perfect parenting moments. One of the best things about boys is they forgive quickly and easily when we apologise.

Freezing out

This is a predominantly female technique that we tend to use to express our displeasure at something. I once worked with a 14-year-old boy who had planned to end his life because his mother had frozen him out for a week because she was unhappy with his school report. As he sobbed into my arms in my office he said, 'I thought she had stopped loving me forever. I didn't want to live without my mum's love.'

Mum did a great job with the right amount of discipline and sport involvement to keep us out of trouble. I think I'm well grounded because of her.

Good communication: the art of gentle reminding

Given that the brain pruning in early adolescence makes your son even more forgetful than he was before, gentle reminding needs to become an art form. Endless nagging is a waste of your breath and is rarely successful. I found the power of the Post-it note very handy during adolescence. Sometimes I used a sticky note on their bag to remind them to put their lunch box back in it, or I left a reminder note inside their lunch box, especially if I needed them home straight after school. I have even been known to put a sticky note in the toilet on the wall facing them! Today you could send them an SMS or a quick message via WhatsApp or Snapchat. We just need to accept that boys, and often our good men, can benefit from our exceptional memories. And we need to do this with compassion.

We can reframe tween and teen-boy forgetfulness as not having a deliberate intention and recognise that we can help our men succeed to be better men, partners and fathers by practising the art of gentle reminding. It can be helpful to have a conversation with your son about how you can help him remember important stuff. *Seriously, give him a clear message that we can work together to make sure he remembers important things and about things he needs to have done.*

Boys are known to be a lot less organised than girls and this is another area where you can help your boy manage his life a bit better. Draw up lists, timetables and rosters for chores so that he can go and check them when he can't remember. This means he doesn't feel quite so silly and it saves him asking you.

> Your tween, teen and twenty-something sons will often forget your birthday and Mother's Day and they will forget to call if you have something important on or you're unwell because they get easily distracted. I suggest you learn not to take that personally. Even though they forget, they still absolutely love you!

Farts

I have been known to say on national television that I think mums need to learn to fart more if they have sons. A well-timed fart can lighten the mood, defuse a conflict and be a wonderful bonding connection with a son.

In adolescence, we mums do have to step back a little and I found a little fart every now and then kept me connected.

Tips for positive mothering

1. Be **warm, fair, firm** and sometimes **fun** in your relationship with your son.

2. **Space** and **privacy** – As mothers of sons we do have to step back and give them more space as they head over the bridge towards manhood. This means we need to allow them to have their secrets from us, their times of aloneness, their privacy (online and offline!), and their opportunities for autonomy and freedom – especially in an adventuresome way. Above all, we need to do this with a lightness. Even though our hunger to know everything that happens in their day is real and comes from a place of love, *we must stop interrogating them.* Elsewhere in the book I have explored the power of expectations and labels that can unintentionally force our boys to struggle too. Your tween and teen sons do need you to give them more space – sometimes that's physical, sometimes it's emotional and it's definitely some verbal space. Some of the angriest boys I worked with were trying to tell their mums – whom they loved dearly – 'please give me some more space!'

3. **Practise positive noticing** – You will notice that by acknowledging our sons or *practising positive noticing with them,* you are very much focused on strengthening their attachment and bondedness to us in a loving, supportive way. This is incredibly important. So many boys tell me that they are always getting into trouble and that in some way they feel they are bad. We must flip that switch and we can do that by noticing the things they do well. It will fill our son's self-worth barometer and it will remind him that many of his actions are positive and even helpful.

4. **Mums, aunties and other mother figures** really matter in nurturing a boy's awareness around **gender equity**. Have many meaningful

chats about some of the different ways that most girls and boys may unconsciously behave, communicate, manage conflict and get 'hangry'. This will mean decoding many of the phrases your boys will hear like 'run like a girl', 'don't be a sissy', 'toughen up' and 'don't be gay'. Rather than just telling them not to use these phrases themselves, it is important that you decode them and deconstruct them so they can understand why they are unhelpful.

5. **Talk about how women experience the world differently** due to sexism and violence against women. A helpful conversation is one about the things girls do to keep themselves safe. There was an article published on Huffington Post Australia in 2015 called '34 Things Women Do To Stay Safe Show The Burden Of "Being Careful"'. In it, Amanda Duberman explored the differences in experience between boys and girls when they go out. For example, women might stay in well-lit areas, walk with their keys held tightly between their fingers in case they need to be used as a weapon, not leave drinks unattended, cross the road if we see a man who looks drunk or a group of men, or text a friend before going out on our own or meeting a stranger. The list goes on. It is a powerfully insightful piece because in the discussion following the article, it was revealed that many boys and men had no idea about these steps that men simply don't do, nor do they worry about.

6. **Teach about temperament differences** – Remind your son that there are gentle, sensitive boys as well as strong, fearless boys, and everything in between and they are all equally valid and accept-able. Teach them that words like 'gay', 'faggot' or 'wuss' are not funny and can be hurtful! Teach your boys to look for the strengths in each individual whom they meet rather than just focusing on their flaws or things they struggle with. And it is helpful to help them identify their own unique blend of strengths and challenges.

7. **Keep teaching your son valuable life skills** and ensure that Dad or whomever else you are co-parenting with is doing the same. Basic housekeeping, cooking, maintaining gardens, managing money,

and being responsible with their digital devices all take practice. On my website (maggiedent.com) I have a list of adolescent life skills that is very comprehensive that will give you a plan. Consider putting it on the side of your fridge so that your son can keep crossing off life skills as he masters them. It's equally good for girls as well, of course.

8. **Keep finding inspirational stories of boys and men doing great things** so that your son can see that the way the media portrays men is often skewed, inaccurate and unhelpful. Keep reminding him the world is full of decent, good men and that one day he will become one too.

9. **Develop mastery** – Find something your son can do really well. If he is not academic or doesn't enjoy sports, find something else. Cooking, gardening, being an environmental warrior, arts or even Pokémon. He must have something he is really good at doing because that will build his sense of confidence and self-worth, which can flow into the other areas of his life where he lacks competence.

10. **Prioritise telling and showing your son how much you love him** – especially when he mucks up, fails, loses or makes a really poor choice. Reassure him that your love is unconditional and everlasting.

Raising our sons to be respectful of themselves, others and the world around them takes patience and endurance from the tribe that circles your son. Every interaction, every conversation, every experience, every meal, every car chat, every success and every failure is a teachable moment in your son's life. Our greatest task is allowing our boys to cross the bridge to manhood with an open heart – rather than a defended heart full of emotional pain and suffering that he has been unable to share with anyone else. Mothers have a huge role to play in helping boys to understand the emotional world that really confuses them.

There's a story I shared in *Mothering Our Boys* that shows how these small moments can have a big impact in our lads' lives.

In 2016 I reconnected with a young man who had been a part of one of the basketball teams that I had coached. He saw me across the room at a function and made his way over with a big grin on his face. I recognised him instantly and remembered that he had been the only child of a solo mum who had some significant mental-health issues. After we made the usual rapport-building chat, he dropped his voice and said he had hoped he would run into me one day because he wanted to thank me for two things that I had done. The first one was that he wanted to thank me for a particular basketball move that I taught him how to do down the middle of the keyway because that move had helped him become a valued basketball player over many years. We laughed that he could remember that that had mattered so much. And then he leaned closer to me and told me about something I had forgotten. Apparently, one day at school when students were coming down the stairway towards the canteen, I had put my hand high up on his back and held it there for a few moments. I am prone to positive touch and sometimes it does happen quite randomly and intuitively, so although I did not remember, I did not find it surprising that I had done this. He said he had been having a really bad time of his life as his mum was being really difficult and unpredictable and he had felt very alone. He said that warm touch on his back on that tough day was something that quite simply gave him hope that he wasn't alone. He had tears in his eyes as he thanked me. That was when I realised that mums of sons have a responsibility to watch out for and nurture the sons of other mums who may be unable to nurture and care for their sons as they need. Make your home welcome to your son's male friends and fill their love cups with genuine concern and affection, because you never know when their cup is empty.

When you are worried about your son and he won't talk to you

Maybe it is the extra oxytocin, but I found most women are better at tuning in to how other people are feeling than most men. That does not mean men cannot do this – I have met many who can. So one of the things that you will find really frustrating with your teen son is that you will quite accurately sense that he's not travelling well but he may deny it. More often than not when you enquire as to how he is, you will be stonewalled with things like 'I'm fine' or 'Just leave me alone'. My suggestion to help break through those walls is to do some emotional priming beforehand. If he has a higher level of cortisol – the stress hormone in his brain – it is not safe enough for him to explore his vulnerability.

In chapter 4, I explore the interplay between positive and negative neurochemicals and hormones. So, if you can help your son override his cortisol levels, you will make him feel safer and make it easier for him to communicate. Your best option is usually to start with food, maybe something of the special-occasion variety. Consider a yummy beverage like a cup of Milo, tea, coffee or a smoothie. This small gesture of kindness is a great way to start. Then start the conversation on really safe ground about a hobby, his favourite sport or sporting team, asking about how his last battle on Fortnite went or check on how one of his best mates is doing. About now you might be able to try to lighten him up with some humorous attempts at being ridiculous – this means you are displaying vulnerability in front of him, which gives him a chance to feel less ridiculous if he chooses to expose his vulnerability. If he is still not forthcoming, just remind him that you are always there for him any time he might like to chat. This is one of those moments where a well-timed fart would be appreciated as a gesture of love and connection.

See chapter 12 for tips about timing this conversation and the location – these are really important to your teen son.

Sometimes the toughest thing you can do as a mother is not let him see how much you worry and *to avoid catastrophising.* Surround yourself with a safe sisterhood that allows you to do serious debriefing often. And frequently repeat the mantra, 'This too will pass.'

The mum letter

When your sons are in the midst of adolescence things can get really tricky and they can sometimes find it difficult to really hear you, especially when you are saying something they don't really want to hear.

Sometimes my sons were so defensive when things were a bit rocky that rather than risk a conversation that could make things worse, I resorted to a written conversation instead but only with a big issue.

Mum letters address serious concerns, the concerns that wake you at two o'clock in the morning. And my gut instinct would always let me know when I needed to write something. I'm a firm believer in using effective communication when writing such letters. These letters have always been written with respect and honesty and with my heart wide open. A part of the mum letter is that there is no need for your son to ever mention receiving the letter and there is no need to talk about it. It is merely a letter of concern from a loving mum to a strong, feisty son in the hope he may hear the information and consider it.

Here is an example of a possible mum letter to a 12 plus boy.

Letter for your son when you are worried

Dear . . . .

I love you more than all the stars in the night sky, more than every grain of sand on every beach in the world and all the hairs on all the bears – I really, really do.

Bud, please take a few moments to read this letter. I know you think I am always worrying, and I try too hard or I am a try-hard (?) but I am your mum and that's part of what parents are meant to do.

Just lately something is different about you and, yes, I am worried. You haven't smiled for weeks, and you are struggling to get good sleep. You are spending much more time than usual in your bedroom and your friends haven't been around for ages. You really seem down and I am worried.

I have been online and checked out some youth websites and some of these things are listed as being a sign that you may be struggling. There is just so much pressure on you kids these days, and too much stress can make you sick. Our world can look nasty and unfriendly too. I also know that you won't want to worry me – and that you might think you will be OK soon – and yet my mum radar is ringing loud bells.

Can we have a chat? If not me, my love, can you please have a chat with some other adult?? If you want to chat to Dr . . . ., I am happy and I will let you go without me if that's what you want. Or maybe a school counsellor or maybe someone online anonymously.

I really want you to let someone listen to you and see if there's anything I can do to help you ride out this bumpy bit.

I have printed off some fact sheets and would love it if you could glance through them.

If you really are OK, maybe we could just go for a hot choco-late sundae, bike ride or a swim at the beach. Massage? Hot bath with bubbles? Swim with dolphins? Holiday in Monaco or Italy? OK, maybe not the last one . . .

I am happy if you just write me a note – that will be a great start.

Maybe you need a new teddy bear? You know they never hog the bathroom or pinch the doona or finish your favourite cereal before you at breakfast. They also don't fart.

Remember that adolescence is a time of intense turmoil and confusion and it will one day get better when your brain finishes growing.

I love you with every fibre in my being.

Mum

Showing love in the difficult years

Your tween and teen boy may pull away from you and become very difficult to communicate with, especially during the first stages of adolescence. Filling his emotional cup will require a different approach for each boy. The less that you question him and explain things to him with lots of words, the safer your son will feel. Try to keep your requests – given lovingly with an endearment – to just one at a time. You will become incredibly frustrated at your son during this time and you may not believe me when I say he will come back from this place. It can be a really long couple of years but gradually he will return.

Do you remember what your son enjoyed before he became an adolescent? Whatever those things were, ensure you keep trying to provide those opportunities as you go through this really stressful time of change. Strive to be the most positive and optimistic mother you can possibly be and if you need to, seek some professional help so that your emotional world – which could be being triggered from your own experiences as a teen – can be resolved away from your son. You may also explore the issue with a therapist or a highly qualified kinesiologist. That emotional baggage is not his – it is yours.

Work out the ways you can non-verbally fill your son's cup. Try to do it at least once a week – *even when he least deserves it*. Indeed, that is when it will have the most powerful impact.

There were times near exams and near the end of terms when I was really conscious about cooking, especially their favourite food. The smell of a favourite food cooking triggers positive neurochemicals and endorphins that immediately lifted my sons' moods. Roasts, curries and, in winter, soups were all fabulous mood shifters. We usually had a dessert a few times a week and I would put a little bit more effort into them rather than just a scoop of ice cream and fruit salad. I also sometimes put a small chocolate treat on their pillows – for no other reason than I knew it would make them feel a tiny bit better. Of course, they would love a whole block of chocolate – family size, if possible – but I knew just a small bit of chocolate would still lift the spirits. So ponder, dear boy mamma, in what ways can you fill your son's love cup during these difficult years? What gestures of kindness can you give him because you now know and understand how difficult and confusing this time of their lives really is?

IF YOU HAD YOUR TEEN YEARS OVER AGAIN, WHAT WOULD YOU CHANGE?

- I wouldn't worry as much. I'd enjoy the moment. I'd have been nicer to my mum.
- I'd have started playing guitar . . . and helped out Mum more.
- I've have had more respect for my mum.
- I'd have seen more music shows and told Mum how great she was.
- I would say thank you to my mum more often.
- I would be kinder to my mum.
- How I treated people. Especially my mum.

FAMILY VIOLENCE

Firstly, if you are in a situation of family violence, I would encourage you to seek help to ensure that you and your children are safe, and to get some support. There are countless support services and, in Australia, you can start by calling 1800RESPECT or visiting their website. I know this is a HUGE issue but it's also a darkness in our society that has had a very bright light shone on it in recent years and I think the less we all tolerate living with it, the greater dent we will make in this problem over time. Asking for help is a first step.

Seek out other wise, caring women in your community to support you and your son if you are struggling. Is there a loving teacher, aunty, or next-door neighbour whom your son can reach out to and spend some time with?

I really want to make the point here, particularly for any woman whose son may have a father who is an angry, controlling, perhaps violent man. **Please know that biology does not equal destiny. There is refuge and there is hope, no matter how far away it may seem at times.**

As for your son, yes he may have witnessed or been a victim of violence but that does not automatically mean he will grow up to be a violent man. We now know, thanks to studies into our brain's neuro-plasticity, that we all have the capacity to change the way we think and act – it is NEVER too late. Statistics are not certainty. Time and time again in my counselling work, and even now in my work as a speaker, I have met countless men who have broken the mould. Despite their fathers being violent or hateful or distant, these men have sought help and chosen a different path and worked to become wonderful partners and fathers.

8

For confused dads . . . and father figures

Boys are starving for dads or father figures with open hearts to give them the precious gift of time – often.

- I would have liked my dad to be a bit more open in his love and support, I know he loved me in his own way but he often used teasing/humour instead of being openly loving and supportive.
- I wish my dad had said he loved me, just once. I wish he had encouraged me to do things and told/showed me that he believed in me. I wish I felt that he had had the time to support me and engage in my ideas and dreams. I wish we had had more meaningful conversations.
- I wish my father had been more involved, open and honest and not parented with fear. Been more supportive.
- I wish my dad had been more present. He was there but never really in the moment or situation.
- We really didn't talk about things that were important. My father's mental/physical illness and death left us all a bit shell-shocked, but it was not talked about. Being so stoic had helped them cope with the depression, WW2, etc. I guess.

- My father not facing his own issues/demons openly and getting help that he needed. Him not sorting help for his anger issues. To this day he holds in.
- I wish my father had spent more time discussing the importance of being a good person and respect for women.

Good dads help children to grow into being the best expression of themselves. Fatherless boys are more likely to struggle in school, with addictions, with criminality, with violence and depression. I believe they are also more likely to struggle to grow up to be men with a man's psychology, rather than a boy psychology, as I mentioned earlier.

In their book *The Boy Crisis,* Warren Farrell and John Gray argue that the primary cause of the boy crisis is dad-deprived boys. The deprivation of a dad can come in two ways – the lack of father involvement and secondly, from devaluing what a father contributes when he is an involved father. For far too long dads have been por-trayed in movies and TV shows as bumbling, incompetent and a source of mirth.

It seems that having a warm connection to your father can now be measured scientifically. In the publication *Paediatrics* in 2017, it was reported that:

> At nine years of age, children with father loss have significantly shorter telomeres. Telomeres in our cells are what keep our genes from being deleted as our cells divide. Telomere length in early life predicts lifespan. Boys who have had significant father loss by age 9 have telomeres that are 14 per cent shorter.

Statistically, in the US, boys with some form of 'absent father syndrome' feature more highly in school drop-out figures, gangs, mass shootings and the joining of extremist groups such as ISIS. Not only do these hurt boys hurt others, but they are also more vulnerable to being hurt themselves, particularly to being sexually exploited.

The US culture, especially around the right to bear arms, is obviously very different to most countries due to their liberal gun culture, and so many of the views of this book may not match perfectly with other Western countries.

> My father died when I was 11. Teenage years without Dad were tough. I was fortunate to have other male role models to help and guide me. I am grateful my mum made sure I spent time with these other men.

It is pretty easy to become a father, by donating sperm. However, to become a dad or a loving father figure, especially to a teenage son, takes patience, endless moments of frustration and incredible endurance. My common-sense assertion is that every child benefits from the presence of a good father figure in life, whether biological or non-biological. So, we need to be mindful that the presence of a cold, distant, often-grumpy father figure is not necessarily better than no father figure at all at home.

In all of my seminars with dads only, over the last 10 years I have never met a dad who wants to be a lousy dad. Secretly, they are wanting to be the dad they yearned for when they were a little boy. One thing I have noticed over the years is how much deeper the questions are that the fathers ask at the end of the seminar. The other beautiful thing I've noticed is how often the dads tear up at different times when I share stories in my seminar. There has been a genuine softening of the collective male heart towards children and it is beyond beautiful.

I often say it is a fabulous time to be a father historically, anthropologically and emotionally. The restrictive and limiting social norms around the roles of mothers and fathers have softened, and we are witnessing a wonderful, passionate engagement of fathers with their children.

I can't think of any challenges – I was lucky that I had a great group of friends and a very supportive dad. My friends and I surfed after school and weekends and our parents would take it in turns driving us to the beach. My dad would drive my friends and I down south camping and surfing. My parents separated when I was around five years old and I moved in with my dad when I was 7/8 years old. My dad was bloody good to me and my friends.

Parenting dynamics have become more of a team effort, where both mums and dads or co-parents of either gender work together to create the best outcomes for their own family. This means that the traditional roles of who the main provider is have become much more flexible. Many dads are fathering non-biological children and there are many grandfathers who are also being father figures – they're all dads as far as I'm concerned.

Given these shifting expectations around fathering, many dads tell me they are confused. One of the most wonderful things that's been happening is that groups of dads – often with babies and prams – are meeting in communities around Australia. They're going for walks, having coffees and enjoying time in playgrounds with other dads – just as mums have for years. I have had at least one dad tell me how pissed off he feels when well-meaning people congratulate him for spending time with the kids – or even wishing him well for 'baby-sitting' his own children! These dads are and want to be seen as proud co-parents. Hopefully as time goes by, these unhelpful messages will be challenged and the stereotypes will finally be laid to rest.

I've noticed at my seminars when dads come forward and ask questions about not only their children but their female partner, they have such a deep concern about finding a solution to whatever challenge they are explaining.

In a way this reveals that biological protector deep in their DNA that wants to be able to solve any conflict that is causing tension in their home.

Many display a sense of helplessness, as though they should have the answer and they should be able to fix it. Their failure to do so often makes them feel they are letting their families down, and they should be doing better. Many men find this difficult to express and articulate, and often go quiet or withdraw or they display frustration and anger.

One of the unspoken challenges for many dads today is the paradox between wanting to spend more time with his children, and still needing to work hard, often long hours, to ensure he provides for his children. Men are strongly driven by a sense of purpose – and when two very important purposes collide, it can be difficult for men to find a peaceful solution for their heart and their mind. Fortunately, the softening of gender roles is allowing some serious and honest communication between mums and dads to create a unique parenting plan that works for both parents.

Interestingly, the 'work from home' situation caused by the COVID-19 pandemic has taught many dads that they can work from home more than they thought.

- I wish I'd had more time with Dad. He was a bit stiff, and worked long hours – not so available. He's much looser and more open with his grandkids than he was with his kids.
- I wish they had had more time to spend with us kids and been more emotionally available. It wasn't in their nature, culturally or from the point of their own upbringing. But I still wish it were otherwise.
- I wish Dad had made more opportunities for me to speak to him. I was fearful and ashamed of things and thought he'd be disappointed in me.
- I wish my dad was more present; he was there but never really in the moment or situation.
- I would have loved for my dad to have spent more time with me when he got home from work/on weekends. We never really did much together and I feel quite disconnected from him.

- I wish my dad had carved out quality one-on-one time with me, rather than prioritising his new partner and life. I wish he had been more nurturing and approachable to talk to as I never felt safe to express myself fully around him.

Fathering a teen boy

Fathering a toddler, or a young boy or a primary school aged boy is a very different kettle of fish to fathering a tween or teen boy. Many dads really struggle with the surly looks, incoherent communication, untidiness and generally anything that they don't like. It seems that many men have a form of amnesia around how it felt to be a teen boy and may be mirroring the frustration of their own father at exactly the same things. Dads of previous generations were often expected to be the tough disciplinarian rather than the soft, loving, nurturing parent. Many of today's dads would have been parented with shame-based tactics, especially through the awkward early years of adolescence, and no matter how much they want to be different, those same words that came out of their father's mouth can tend to come flying out of their own.

So be reassured it is absolutely normal to find your son particularly annoying and frustrating during the tween and early teen years. But please do all you can to be patient and to imagine being that dad you wanted when you were a confused lad!

One Sunday morning, I received a phone call from a 19-year-old former student whom I had not seen since he had left high school. I had had this boy in my class in Year 12. He had been a large six-foot-four 'rooster' with a dry wit and a good sense of humour. This Oliver had called, in his words, 'to say goodbye'. Even though his voice sounded cheery enough, my gut feelings were scrambling 'alert'. Thankfully, I knew where he lived and told him that he was not saying goodbye without a hug, and that I would be there soon. I distinctly remember racing out to my car with a tracksuit on and no bra. My car was also flashing low on fuel, but I knew deep in my heart that I had not a moment to waste. When I arrived at the place where he was staying, I found him lying in the foetal position on the lounge room floor with two different means of ending his life beside him. I curled myself around him and simply held him and rocked him as though he was a baby. Soon the racking sobs came and I simply held him until they subsided. Eventually he told me that he felt he couldn't live anymore because he was such a disappointment to his career-driven father. It seemed that everything he did was wrong, and the endless criticism and judgement, and lack of acceptance and love had simply become too much. Fortunately, Oliver and his father were able to do some vital restoration through incredibly honest dialogue. Hiding under this desperately dark experience was the message from the 'man box' that Oliver saw himself as a failure at the same time as the dad was trying to help his son strive harder to be more. I suspect that this form of patriarchal conditioned thinking in our tween and teen boys' (and indeed men's) minds is just one of the contributing factors in some of our male youth suicides.

Dads and father figures don't need to be perfect, however, they need to both be on that long bridge.

The gift of presence

For dads who have created a strong bond with their son in boyhood, the teen years can be much better. Dads who have a common interest with their sons can continue this connection through the teenage years, especially if it involves them being away from the females in the house. Tinkering with cars or a motorbike in the garage with music playing and lots of snacks can be a form of paradise for some teenage boys and their dads. Bushwalking, going to the cinema, building a veggie patch, fishing expeditions or surfing trips can also be incredibly helpful. Some modern dads and sons can have some entertaining battles with games online or with a Wii. There are many ways you can still share time with your son.

I once worked in suicide prevention with a wonderful man from the wheatbelt in Western Australia. He told me he had made a promise to his two sons that he would always try to keep Friday night clear so that he could spend it with his boys. Sometimes it was watching football, other times it was doing some stargazing with a telescope, other times they watched a movie or just went out to eat a pizza together. This is what really matters for our boys – that you prioritise time to spend with them and you don't leave it to chance. Please be careful not to break promises – as this came up a lot for many boys in counselling as a part of the frustration with their dad. Dad dates need to be a reality!

Another dad has told me that whenever he picked up his son from football training or swimming training, they always went by a local takeaway and shared some hot chips together. The same thing at the same place every time. Predictable rituals like this are incredibly powerful.

I once worked with Oliver (19) who had had two serious attempts at taking his life. He shared with me that his dad was a controlling man and an alpha male. He drank, smoked, swore, gambled, was a sport freak and was often quite racist and sexist in how he spoke. Oliver was more of the lamb on the temperament spectrum. He was a nature lover who enjoyed music, reading and cooking. He said he'd spent his entire life being a failure to his father. He had a clear memory from when he was five years of age of his father taking his special blanket and his teddy bear and throwing them in the fire and making him watch them burn until there was nothing left. He told me that his dad had then turned to him and told him to toughen up because he was a sissy. His suicide attempts were desperate plans to escape the reality that his father would never accept him, respect him or love him. Men have told me that these are the three things they really yearn for from their father or most significant father figure in their life. Fortunately, he was able to get the help he needed and he is now a father of three beautiful children, and he is being the dad he had hoped for his whole life.

> Sometimes mothers of sons need to invest time and energy in decoding the old male ethos and we need to work hard to convince our sons that they can indeed be accepted, respected and loved exactly as they are.
>
> – Maggie Dent, *Mothering Our Boys* (2018)

One of the main messages I really want to get across in this book is that there is an often invisible fragility with tween and teen boys, especially those who have a very distant relationship with their father.

Many times when I have been counselling men or just listening to their stories in shearing sheds, around a fire pit, chatting on an aeroplane or in some quiet corner of a social event, I have heard men express their sense of inadequacy about being a father. They despair about the times they forget important things like birthdays or even dates for things like assemblies. Normal parent failures they take deeply personally and this really eats away at their sense of self-worth as a dad. Despite what many people believe, dads do worry about their children and their partners. When they are unable to fix things or take away the pain that their children are feeling, again it makes them feel worthless and inadequate.

So many of our dads today were raised with a culture that was very much about lecturing, shouting, hitting and shaming, which was especially inflicted on awkward and confused teenage boys. I still remember a dad talking to me at swimming club one night about how he had found marijuana in his son's bag. He felt the only thing he could do to ensure that his son did not use marijuana again was to do what his father had done to him when he had done something similar. He took him down to the back shed, took his belt off and whipped him many times. The dad told me that later that night he had ended up in the back corner of his garden silently sobbing because he felt so awful.

In his wonderful book *The New Manhood*, Steve Biddulph explores four kinds of defective fathering habits:

1. The man who would be King.
2. The critical father.
3. The passive father.
4. The absent father.

No man intentionally wants to be any of these types of dad. I encourage any dad who wants to be the dad he really wanted, to dive deeply into this book as it is full of golden nuggets – written by a man, for men.

Below is a part of a post from the Facebook page from the men's non-profit group Island of Men that I believe captures some of the invisible thoughts of some dads today. Many worry they will turn out like their own defective dad.

A boy, so hurt by the absence of his father grows up disconnected from himself, seeking acceptance and love from all the wrong places.

He made mistakes in his life that he struggles to live with. He believes deep down that he is bad, beyond help, undeserving of love.

He has shut everything off until only numbness and rage remains. He fears he will turn out like his dad. He looks in the mirror and swears he won't turn out like that fucker.

He now has a son of his own, a tiny, beautiful, innocent baby and he lives with the fear that his son will turn out just like him.

– Nathan Meola, Island of Men Facebook post,
30 August 2019

Tips for better fathering
The dad plan

One of the things that I have found to be helpful when working with dads who want to be better dads is to commit to paper the things they want to improve – in other words create a plan. And then every few weeks or few months they revisit the plan and remind themselves about it. Then they pick one thing they want to focus on until the next time they do their review. It is like creating a new map to commit to and gradually over time this map will replace the ineffective, automatic one that comes from a man's own childhood. Thoughts come and go rapidly in our minds. Having a written plan is a bit like creating a project that needs to be completed, which is something most men like to do.

The dad message

I have written about the mum letter in the previous chapter, which is incredibly effective for communicating to sons, partly because it is something a boy can read over and over again. It also limits the amount of words that mum may use when wanting to chat about something that is worrying.

Let me tell you about the dad message and why it is incredibly important. The dad message is much shorter and straight to the point.

Many years ago, I spoke to a dad after he had attended one of my seminars. During the seminar, he realised that he was repeating his father's distant relationship with him and he wanted to do better. As he drove home from the seminar, he realised that he needed to tell his son how he felt, but he knew he wouldn't be able to say it verbally. So he wrote this short message on his son's bathroom mirror:

Oliver, I am really proud to be your dad. Love Dad.

About ten minutes later, his son came running into the bedroom with tears in his eyes, saying that he didn't even think his dad liked him let alone was proud of him. They hugged. He continued the chat by telling me that while he did walk his son to school every morning, he usually behaved a bit like a Sergeant Major, lecturing him and making sure his son was organised and on time. The next day when he was walking with his son towards school as he did most days, his son suddenly realised that he had left his finished maths assignment at home. The dad said he leant forward gently and asked his son what he would like him to do. He could either write his son a note or he could drop the assignment off at the office a little later. His son was so surprised by his dad's different response and he said, 'Usually you just shout at me!' By then there were serious tears in this good dad's eyes and he choked as he said to me, 'Thank you – you have changed my life and my son's life. Now in the afternoon after school when I hear the front door bang open – my son calls out loudly, "Where is my dad?" Instead of ignoring or avoiding me, he actually comes looking for me. We then have an afternoon snack together. Seriously I cannot believe how happy I am because I am now the dad I wanted to be.'

So come on Dad, write your teen or tween son a dad message – in his lunch box, on a Post-it note, on a birthday card or on a banana! If your son has not blocked you on his phone, send him a funny text or a weird combination of emojis. Make sure you have a photograph of your son in your wallet and show him that you take it around with you every day (of course if you have other children, make sure you have their photo in your wallet as well).

If you did not have a warm loving father who was able to express his affection for you, it can be difficult for you to say these words out loud. So dad messages are the way to go. Of course, if you are more confident at writing longer letters – go for it.

A BEAUTIFUL LETTER FROM A FATHER TO SON

by Jeddy Azuma, *The Rising Man* podcast

My promise to you, little man, is to give you the best of what I've got.

I promise to lead you, barefoot, through the woods. To fan the flames of your curiosity and adventurous spirit so that you can cultivate your own relationship with your world.

I promise to show you gentleness and assertiveness. To not confuse leadership with authority, or to direct you in a way that is more convenient and comfortable for me.

I promise to love and take care of your mother and your sister – and all the women in your life – so that you see what it means to create safety for women. So you can one day be a guardian for the women in your life, and respect them in a good way.

I promise to admit when I'm wrong. To get over my ego and humble myself when I overstep, lose my temper, or misrepresent my message and find my apology as quickly as my human nature will allow.

I promise to get out of your way when you are truly ready to take this world on, as hard as it may be. To let you succeed and fail on your own merit. I will hold your mother gently as she releases you into the world in her own way so you can become your own man.

And for all the things I cannot foresee, I promise to do my best. For you. For your sister. For our family and all that we hold sacred.

I love you, my son.

Despite what you may believe, *boys do like structure* and they do expect parental guidance around the rules of the home. Sometimes as a dad you can just make a small grunting sound as a reminder that a boundary is about to be breached. Mums find this really confusing because if she makes the same noise, she is usually ignored.

Many teen boys appreciate their dad's ability to simplify things that mum may be stressing about, or to lighten a moment that could be getting a little heated.

So, what else can you do to be the dad that best supports your son as he crosses the bridge to manhood in today's unpredictable world?

1. Be as informed as possible about the unique developmental changes that are happening for your son, especially the brain pruning.
2. Be the strong railings on the bridge.
3. Discipline warmly.
4. Let him see you cry.
5. Surround your son with as many other good men as possible.
6. Support the mother of your son (or whomever you are co-parenting with), especially when the going gets tough.
7. Be comfortable with being silently beside your son at times.
8. Create opportunities for building resilience and agency.
9. Create some unique rituals that you only do with him.
10. Get a fire pit. Use it often. Don't forget the marshmallows.
11. Teach him as many life skills as you can.

12. Help him understand the best humour in the world involves laughing with, not laughing at.
13. Always tell him you will always have his back, no matter what.
14. Always hold high expectations for your son about becoming an honourable, respectable man.
15. Have quiet, tough conversations about sex, drugs, alcohol and porn. Please.

> My biggest challenge was not having a father around full time to guide me on man stuff.

Another challenging area that dads over the years have shared with me is the ability to accept your son's views and opinions when they are quite contrary to yours. It is the same with daughters of course. Encourage your son to explain his reasoning and how he has come to that decision and then allow him to do the same for you. It is absolutely OK to have different views and opinions. It does not make one person wrong or another person right. To be honest, in adolescence I would be worried if there were not some differences of opinions between parents and their teen children. The worst thing you can do as a father is to ridicule or make fun of your son's opinions and views. The same goes for his taste in clothes. Learn the art of silent observation and acknowledgement – quietly nod your head a lot – and remember being a boy the same age!

What to do if your son speaks rudely to his mother

If your tween or teen son speaks rudely or disrespectfully to his mother, you are the best person to manage this. As soon as you notice this happening, quietly invite your son outside, well away from other siblings, and go through the five-step process of when they muck-up (see page 190). Many teen boys have explained to me that they are surprised when they speak poorly to their mother! This suggests that speaking like this is less intentional than we may believe. I have found that it is often driven by frustration in situations where the boy's mother has not stepped back that little bit that he needed. It is an attempt to get more space – not just physically but also emotionally. Often mum asking them to do the dishwasher was just the last thing in a crappy day and it flipped his tipping point!

As the dad, your job is to help him realise that that behaviour is unacceptable in your home. It can be helpful if you can explore another choice he can make when he is feeling really frustrated with his relationship with his mother, rather than speaking to her so disrespectfully, or maybe suggest you might chat to mum for him. Together you may be able to communicate his frustration to his mum in a less confrontational way.

Co-parenting with love and respect

Another thing that can be a wonderful gift to your son is the knowledge that men can love deeply, especially the person they have committed themselves to. To verbally own and explain the deep love that you feel for his mother or co-parent is incredibly valuable. Indeed when I was still counselling, I often found that deep under a man's anger and grumpiness in his primary relationship with the mother of his children was an incredibly strong fear that he would lose the woman he loved.

Normalising that it is OK for men to articulate the love they feel, especially in front of both sons and daughters, will help future generations of couples maintain long-term respectful relationships.

Many years ago, I worked with a mum fighting cancer, her husband and two almost adult sons. I got to know this family quite well, as I was also a bereavement support person in our community hospice. I was given the privilege of conducting the funeral ceremony for this beautiful mum. Following the ceremony as I was leaving, I noticed the dad was leaning against his car in the car park. I sensed he wasn't travelling well and thought I'd check in on him before I left. This good man was at war with himself. I had not realised the inner torment that he had been struggling with until now. In his words,

> I am such a useless prick. You know how many times I sat beside my wife – the woman I have adored from the moment I met her, the mother of my two sons, the woman I have been married to for 25 years – I love her beyond words – and not once over the last three months while she has been dying in the hospice, was I able to say the words – I love you. They always got stuck in my throat. And now it is too fucking late.

This good man leant on my shoulder and sobbed. I reassured him that his wife knew how much she was loved, and maybe this was a lesson he needed to pass on to his sons. This is what happens when we shut down our boys' tender feelings in some hopelessly outdated belief that boys and men need to be tough. All tough men can express tender feelings and still be tough. Indeed, expressing tender feelings to those he loves, often, may be one of the signs of true bravery.

Parenting after separation

These thoughts only apply to those situations where no family abuse has occurred either during the relationship or at separation.

I have walked the path of separation and I know that the first months and years can be really difficult until a new normal is created. All kids want the fighting to stop, they want both parents to not speak badly of each other and secretly want both their parents to keep working as a 'team' regarding parenting. One day they want you both to be a positive part of their big life moments – birthdays, graduations and weddings. So choose wisely how you behave if your intimate relationship finishes. You will always be their biological parent. This applies to mums and dads equally.

If he is still alive, how is your relationship with your father?

This relationship is another influence on how your son will be as a father himself one day. Be mindful of how you speak about your dad, especially when he is not around. Even if your dad was one of those tough, emotionally distant fathers – as might have been normal for the time – he actually did the best he could with what he knew. I seriously recommend again that you read Steve Biddulph's *The New Manhood*, where he explains how valuable it is to let your father off the hook. He suggests you find a good time and place to thank him for the things he did that you appreciated.

Great sex vs lousy sex

Your role today around educating your son to know the difference between great sex and lousy sex is very different from when you were a teen boy. Sadly, badly behaved sporting heroes are creating unhelpful perceptions of how to behave sexually with women. There have been stories in the media of disgusting text messages, inappropriate sharing of intimate images, nightclub toilet sex, sharing of women for sex without clear consent, masturbating in front of your mates, brandishing your penis in public places and the shockingly high rate of rape. Online dating apps have also distorted the authentic hunger that men have for intimacy, especially sexual intimacy. It is feeding into the mammoth hunters' need for conquest. Sadly, this behaviour will never deliver the great sex that healthy adults seek regardless of gender or preference.

You need to have conversations with your son explaining that the most important part about having great sex is not the penis – it is the brain. No, seriously you do! Somehow find a way to validate the incredible sexual urges that will unexpectedly surge through your son's body while he is on the bridge to manhood. Validate that managing sexual urges is a part of life and that having a need to feel worthwhile about yourself only because of the number of sexual conquests you have is not something to be proud of. Masturbation and self-pleasuring are healthy ways of keeping sexual urges in check when done in the privacy of your own bedroom.

Caution your son about watching hardcore pornography that uses violence and coercion, especially at the cost of females and worse, children. Explain that he is in a really impressionable window of his life, and sexual perversion can happen that may distort the healthy development of his sexuality. Remind him you want him to have great sex one day when he is mature enough and responsible enough to be able to take part in a respectful, consensual, incredibly pleasant shared experience.

No, you really do want him to have great sex and not lousy sex – keep reminding him there is a really big difference between the two.

I have a lot more tips in chapter 17 and suggestions of stuff you can read and/or watch yourself or with your son – possibly as a conversation starter. I suggest you start with a short video on SBS from Paul Chai called 'How I'm teaching my sons to not talk about women'.

Sexism/gender roles and stereotypes

Dads and father figures really matter as they have an important role to endlessly build and nurture boys' awareness around gender equity. Modelling respect towards women means calling out disrespect publicly and strongly. You need to have many meaningful chats about how to respect women and treat them as equals. As I said in the chapter for mums, this will mean decoding many of the phrases your boys will hear like 'run like a girl', 'don't be a sissy', 'toughen up', and 'don't be gay'. Rather than just telling them not to use these phrases themselves, it is important that you decode them and deconstruct them so they can understand why they are unhelpful.

My son is gay. Help?

- The most challenging experience of my teenage years was realising I was physically and emotionally attracted to my best (guy) friend in a world that didn't accept gay people and knowing that I was different from everyone else in my world. Wearing a mask and lying to my friends and family about who I truly am was the most difficult part of my teenage years. Constantly wondering if they would truly accept me if I revealed my true self.
- The most challenging experience of my teenage years was being gay and surviving a homophobic culture with some self-esteem.
- The most challenging experience of my teenage years was struggling with self-worth driven by my confused sexuality.
- The most challenging experience of my teenage years was being secretly gay and not wanting to be.

We still have a long way as a society to go in understanding and fully accepting gender fluidity and healthy sexuality, although we have definitely made some shifts in this bold 21st century. The incredible levels of homophobic discrimination, violence and shaming, especially of boys, is still quite deeply, invisibly ingrained in humanity. There is still a perception that you can 'stop' being gay if you want to. Genetics and neuroscience over the last 40 years have come to the strong conclusion that same-gender sexual orientation is natural for approximately 5 to 10 per cent of females and males. This orientation is created before birth. Beyond this, young people today are also more regularly identifying as bisexual, asexual, pansexual and otherwise.

As a father, you would very likely have heard and witnessed the insensitivity towards being gay that often exists in our culture. This of course is linked to the unhealthy perception that being gay means you can't be a man; that you are in some way flawed, damaged or unable to tick the 'man box' perceptions of being a real man.

Fortunately, today's under thirties have a much more respectful acceptance of sexual and gender diversity, as well as every other form of diversity. In one generation there has been a significant shift in the language around being gay. In Australia, the passing of same-sex marriage legislation saw an important and profound shift to accepting that gay couples deserve the same respect around committed relationships. Of course, there are many of the older generation and many in traditional religions who still struggle to accept homosexuality as being anything but sinful.

Let's be honest – most heterosexual men would probably prefer their son not to be gay. It is a difficult journey to walk and most dads would prefer their sons to be a part of the 90 per cent rather than the possible 10 per cent because they might feel they understand that better and they don't want life to be difficult for him. I have worked with teen boys who were so terrified of coming out, mainly to their dad, that they had seriously contemplated ending their life. Supporting this, we know that non-heterosexual young people are more highly represented in suicide statistics across the world. I have also worked with other gay men who denied their true sexual identity and married and had families. Many struggled with addictions and poor mental health until they finally were able to own the truth. The shame around being gay, bisexual or otherwise runs deep in Australian society, and even more so in certain countries around the world.

Recently a dad who I will call Gary shared his story about when his son came out to him. They were driving in a car on the way to the son's high school on a busy morning and, completely out of the blue, his 15-year-old son turned to him and said he had something he needed to tell him. Quite simply he said, 'I am gay.' Gary said he had a spontaneous, fear-based reaction in his head – *oh shit!* Then he thought of all the challenges his son may now face and even had a passing thought that he might not get to be a dad. However, despite that, he said to his son, 'That's OK, bud.' This awesome dad then went on to share his thoughts about the need to look for meaningful relationships, having safe sex with people you have feelings for, aka having intimacy rather than just sex for sex's sake, and he reassured him he loved him just the same. He had tears in his eyes as he recalled the story because it was a powerful moment when he and his son felt deeply connected despite the possible challenges that may come his son's way.

Even in our more accepting society, it is normal to worry about your son living a life as a gay man. Homophobia is still strongly embedded in the minds of many, however, you can help him embrace his authentic self by always celebrating who he is and the life he chooses. So, if you suspect your son is gay, or even if he is not, you can set a respectful example by calling out homophobic language and behaviour. Doing this regardless of your son's sexual orientation would be even better. Allow your son to come out when he is ready, regardless of whether you think you know. It is a huge step and he needs to be prepared for the change and confusion that it will bring.

Casting a boy out of a family because of his sexuality sadly still happens in some families. In a way, this is the ultimate shaming experience for a boy because he is shamed for who he is and how he feels, not for what he does. My challenge to those who know these boys is be the lighthouse figure who can give them acceptance and support. You may very well save a life! I am heartened to see in the younger generation friends gathering around each other regardless of sexuality and supporting each other because they are not as fixed in their mindsets as their parents' generations.

WHAT IS THE BEST THING ABOUT BEING A TEEN BOY TODAY?

- The ability to be who you want to be (e.g. sexuality) without worrying about social pressure to conform to old stereotypes.

- I guess the fact that we're able to be a bit more open about our sexuality than we used to be in past generations.
- The best thing about being a teen boy today is the decreased/decreasing societal pressure regarding how men are supposed to behave.
- Emergence of male awareness and not just telling us that our whole gender is evil.
- The declining stigma regarding men having to be tough and hide their feelings.

Being beside

What every son wants to know is can you really love me when I muck-up – especially when I fail big time?

To know what that may really feel like, please go and look up Derek Redmond and 'never give up' on YouTube. After you have watched it, I want you to sit with your son and watch it with him. At the end, tell him that is the dad you want to be. Remind your son there is nothing he will ever do that you won't help him recover from – absolutely nothing.

I remember once listening to a wise man running a seminar for dads. He believed that every son wants to get to a place in his life where he knows that he has three things from his father – unconditionally. Those three things are acceptance, respect and love. This same wise man said that to be able to give these three amazing gifts to your son, you first have to give them to yourself.

Get help if you need it

So, Dad if you are still struggling with this, still beating yourself up that you are not a good-enough dad, man or partner – start by talking to your wife or partner. Then please seek out some help or be brave and join a men's group that can provide a safe place for you to share your story and choose to value healing the wounds that are preventing you from accepting yourself as good enough. A good place to start is to turn up at your local family doctor and have a thorough health check – whether that be a physical or mental-health check or both. Help is available and, when you take the first step, you might be surprised to see the positive difference it can make in your life. This may be the most brave and courageous thing you can do!

No child – not a son or daughter – wants to lose their loving dad. No loving partner wants to lose their good bloke either. So, stand up, be brave and take responsibility for your own health and wellbeing. You will then be teaching your son to grow up to be a man who will value himself enough to do the same.

> Young males rise to the occasion under the approval of men they respect. As fathers, we hold in our hands the opportunity to inspire our sons to achieve, offering support and modelling what it is to be a man.
>
> – Ian Grant, *Growing Great Boys* (2007)

I wish that my dad had more time to spend with me. I totally understand that it was a different generation, and that my dad needed to work to support our family, but I missed having him around. My mum was amazing, but at times a son needs his dad. I'm trying to be there for my son and put work second.

9

Why lighthouses matter so much

According to an article in the *Sydney Morning Herald* back in 2008: 'A major contributor to the worsening mental health of Zeds (Generation Zed) is less support from families, with fewer functioning adults around and a lessened sense of community.' Yikes, that was 12 years ago and things have seriously got so much worse since then!

The article quotes the executive director of the Brain and Mind Institute at the University of Sydney, Professor Ian Hickie: 'It's not increased pressures, it's lack of support. Kids are more stressed because they're doing it on their own.'

These words were spoken over a decade ago and I would argue that today's world functions at an even more unhealthy speed using technology that further reduces real human interaction and connectedness. This disconnectedness is not just within communities; it is also within the three main support structures for adolescents: families, neighbourhoods and schools.

The vital window of adolescence is where the evolving child adapts to become more mature and adult-like. But it seems the adult world has stepped back and left our adolescents without the guidance and support they need to grow into healthy citizens. It is like the world has removed the railings from the bridge that is taking many of our boys to manhood and they are being left to fend for themselves. You cannot learn about managing human relationships or develop life skills by watching teen dramas on Netflix or searching for them on Google or YouTube.

Father Chris Riley's organisation Youth Off The Streets works daily with adolescents and young adults who are lost. They are not bad, damaged or useless – they are lost. Their bumpy ride to adulthood was a journey without enough loving support and they have been scarred by their choices. Father Riley was once asked, 'How can you help these no-hopers?' He replied, 'It's quite easy to help these young people. They all improve with compassion, kindness, food and a safe place to live.'

This is exactly what traditional kinship communities offered when teens stepped away from their parents in their effort to claim independence and autonomy. There were other adults to keep an eye out, guide and support them. These other supports can be extended family. They can also be people who care enough to be there. I call them 'lighthouses'.

A lighthouse represents something that is strong, reliable and immovable, that shines a light showing safe passage. It does not tell you to do something; it simply shows you a safer way to go. A lighthouse says, if you want to do something really risky and smash on the rocks below where I stand, then be my guest, but I won't rescue you. I will keep the light shining so that next time you remember how painful your last choice was and you might choose to follow the safer way where my light shines.

In his book *Raising Boys in the 21st Century*, Steve Biddulph believes there are three stages to boyhood and the third is from age 14 to adult. In this window it is critical for boys to have more mentors outside of mum and dad. In these years,

Mum and Dad step back a little but they must organise some good mentors in their son's life; if not he will have to rely on an ill-equipped peer group for his sense of self. The aim is for your son to learn skills, responsibility and self-respect by joining more and more with the adult community.

Lighting the flame of potential, while being realistic about teen development, is extremely important. Young people are hard on themselves and adept at self-criticism and self-sabotage, and often get stuck in patterns of limitation. Lighthouses can help them see beyond these limitations. Lighthouses do not rescue, advise or make judgements on an adolescent's behaviour, instead they act as a mirror so the young person can see the world from a different perspective.

The benefits of a lighthouse

Many adolescents learn how to be trustworthy from the lighthouses in their life. These adults are helpful in the role they play by using good communication, helping to build life skills and having the courage to connect deeply. Lighthouses shed light on the pathway to adulthood and beyond. They are respectful, reliable, responsive and reciprocal. They provide an open door and retreat, no matter when, what or why.

I have given this message to endless teens, especially all my sons' mates and my nephews – 'there's always a bed at our place if you need it.' Very few have ever needed it, but many have told me over the years how comforting those words were when things got a bit tough.

Lighthouses can be people who play a large role in an adolescent's life like a coach, teacher, aunty or family friend. Sometimes they appear only for a short time, but in that time manage to plant seeds of potential, give ideas or show through their actions and words something new and helpful.

Every adolescent, especially our teen boys,
needs a lighthouse to help them navigate the
uncertain waters of adolescence.

Lighthouses have to be able to develop a relationship that allows them to influence positively the shaping of a teen boy's sense of identity and to shine a light on the invisible sign that hangs around every adolescent's neck: *make me feel I matter*! They also sow seeds of possibility and potential, just like in the following story.

One year I needed to speak to one of my Year 9 boys, Oliver (14), because his behaviour and his schoolwork had become quite worrisome. So, I chose to have a conversation with him after class when everyone had left. When I said to him that I was really worried about him, firstly with his behaviour, which was quite disruptive, he agreed with me. When I also said he would fail English because he had not handed any work in – he also agreed with me. I wanted to offer him the suggestion that Year 9 was the last year that you could mess around and not apply yourself. The following year he needed to put his head down and focus on his grades so that he could give himself a good chance of a career pathway. Out of the blue he said to me, 'But I am dumb, Miss!' This is something many 14-year-old boys feel due to all those brain changes in forgetfulness and disorganisation – many of them just feel they are dumb! I told Oliver that I disagreed with him and I thought he did have a brain, as he did say some really intelligent things from time to time. He was so surprised to hear that! And he exclaimed, 'Really?'

Sadly for me, Oliver did not improve his behaviour or his grades in the six weeks that remained in Year 9. But 15 years later I received an email from him. In it he wondered if I remembered the short conversation that I had had with him when he was in Year 9. I had left the school at the end of that year and so had not known how Oliver had gone in Year 10. In his email he said he took on board the advice I gave him and he did put his head down and that I was right, he did have a brain. Oliver went on to complete high school, continuing on to university. Not only had he completed a degree, he had gone on to do two PhDs and was now one of the most highly qualified submarine scientists in the Australian Navy. His email was just to say thank you for that conversation because he wasn't sure what path his life may have taken without my encouragement.

Without a seed being sown a new plant cannot grow.

The impact of shining a light

One of the most powerful lighthouse relationships is that between an adolescent and one of their mates' parents – whether they are a mother or father figure.

Research shows that it only takes one adult to make a significant difference to an adolescent's outcomes.

There was a longitudinal study done in the Bronx in America with around 230 children. The researchers believed that these children had little chance of living effective and meaningful lives due to the high level of crime, parental imprisonment, drug abuse, drive-by shootings and alcoholism they were exposed to. They followed these children through until their late twenties and found that over 80 per cent were living positive lives. The researchers wanted to know what contributed to these positive results. Every one of the 80 per cent reported that throughout their childhood, they had had one significant person who never gave up on them – sometimes a parent, sometimes a grandparent and often a teacher.

Adolescents need our compassionate support more than ever and they need it from people other than just their parents to ensure they can navigate this vulnerable time of life.

> I like the amazing people I have around me. Like coaches and amazing parents.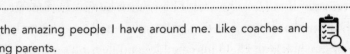

I believe lighthouses have a potential that is still largely untapped to help boys become more resilient and capable, and work through troubled times to a point of recovery. Tween and teen boys in traditional indigenous cultures were surrounded by many men constantly teaching, guiding and supporting them. They were not left alone when they experienced moments of struggle or hardship. Many boys today feel they have no-one watching out for them other than their parents, whom they are biologically trying to separate from.

The men's survey asked almost 1700 men who had helped them the most when they were a teen. If we take out the parent percentage, the remaining 29 per cent shows that the most important 'lighthouse' figures for the men surveyed are as follows:

- 4.5 per cent friend's parent/s
- 3.5 per cent grandparents
- 2.9 per cent teachers.

During times of conflict, lighthouses shine a light of reason, encouragement and acceptance. Adolescents often have poor skills around life management, planning for the future and coping with their chaotic emotional worlds. Lighthouses can be like a personal life coach or a safe sounding board.

When I work with teachers now, I challenge them to take on a special 'project' every year. I encourage them to aim to connect with and shine a light on a student who possibly has a bad reputation or is obviously struggling on the bumpy road to adulthood. Immediately, I see the looks on their faces as they recall a student whom they have helped in the past and they know how good that connection made them feel. In parent seminars, I challenge parents to do the same for a niece or a nephew, a neighbour or any adolescent with whom they connect. Step forward and shine that light. You will be staggered by the potential it can activate in an adolescent who thinks no-one cares.

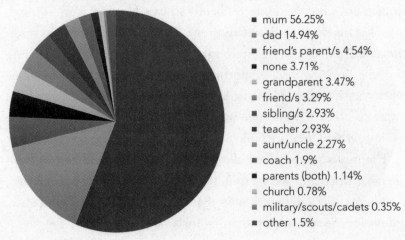

Who helped you the most when you were a teen?

- mum 56.25%
- dad 14.94%
- friend's parent/s 4.54%
- none 3.71%
- grandparent 3.47%
- friend/s 3.29%
- sibling/s 2.93%
- teacher 2.93%
- aunt/uncle 2.27%
- coach 1.9%
- parents (both) 1.14%
- church 0.78%
- military/scouts/cadets 0.35%
- other 1.5%

Now we can compare these results with the boys' survey results. They were asked a different question: 'Who is your "lighthouse" – significant adult ally – not your parents?' Grandparents and teachers continue to play a big role but for this group aunts and uncles were the third most significant allies.

- 26.5 per cent grandparents
- 20.1 per cent teachers
- 13.9 per cent aunt/uncle.

Sadly, 7 per cent of our tween/teen boys said they had no-one outside of their parents they could call on as an adult ally. This is worrying indeed.

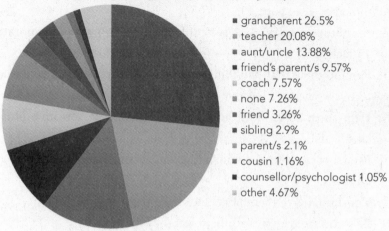

Who is your 'lighthouse' that is not your parents?

- grandparent 26.5%
- teacher 20.08%
- aunt/uncle 13.88%
- friend's parent/s 9.57%
- coach 7.57%
- none 7.26%
- friend 3.26%
- sibling 2.9%
- parent/s 2.1%
- cousin 1.16%
- counsellor/psychologist 1.05%
- other 4.67%

What can lighthouses do?

Essentially, a lighthouse offers the same things that a parent does – they just don't live in the same house. From the outside, we cannot always see the signs that a teen, especially a boy, is reaching their tipping point (i.e. racing heart, dry mouth, suicidal thoughts, feeling frightened, struggling to sleep, to name a handful). They often hide under a mask that says I'm OK. In my experience, I have found troubled teen boys rarely turn to a parent. They are most likely to turn to a lighthouse figure rather than a parent, teacher or school counsellor. (That is, unless the teacher or counsellor is their lighthouse.)

Lighthouses can help tween and teen boys feel noticed, valued, accepted, heard and respected.

They can also help inspire the following:

1. Help them to understand the unique changes that are happening to them, which are causing them to feel stressed, unhappy, confused and moody.
2. Encourage sensible self-care suggestions that include good sleeping, eating and exercise habits.

3. Show them how to survive ANT attacks (automatic negative thoughts – see page 11).
4. Encourage teen boys to see problems and failings as temporary setbacks.
5. Remind them that bad things happen to everyone in life and that recovery needs to be seen as a goal.
6. Help them to explore how to make their own positive brain chemicals.
7. Model meaningful, empowering and caring communication at all times.
8. Constantly give them hope and make them 'feel felt' often.
9. Be someone who makes them feel they matter.
10. Help them find their 'spark'.
11. Help them to work out how to do goal setting and create life plans or maps.

If we can better help our teen boys to understand their capacity for this potential, honour their gifts and talents, and nurture their passions and interests, we can help them find their spark and keep it lit.

When a tween/teen boy has found a lighthouse and a safe place that really offers support in an adolescent-friendly way, it can help in so many ways. It is incredibly important to ensure that issues that arise during this window of sensitivity get the attention and support needed before they become permanent, especially issues around mental and physical health. While thankfully there is a lot of helpful information and support available online now, including online counselling, *this is not a replacement for human connection*. Having a lighthouse figure whom they value and trust can help monitor how a teen boy may really be travelling and if the lighthouse feels the need to seek help, most teens are grateful.

- Find at least one person you can talk to about anything (whether it's a friend, a teacher, an uncle or aunty, a coach or neighbour) and actually talk. What you say has value, has worth and is important!
- Listen to good adult males' advice because they have been in your situation before. Your mates are just like you, making it up as they go along.
- You're at the start of a long journey; many men have been here before, learn from them as much as you can.
- Find a man (uncle, family friend, boss, or even your dad) whom you know deep down is doing the right things and talk to them. Ask them for advice and believe them if they tell you what the right and wrong thing to do is.
- Keep your chin up; you're not alone. It's incredibly important that you develop an enduring face-to-face relationship with a supportive adult who you can feel safe talking to, confiding in. Electronics and social media are not an adequate replacement for the above.

The importance of the man mentor and teacher

There is a strong biological instinctual driver of men to help shape boys into being good men and capable warriors who will take over the key roles of male leadership within the tribe. In traditional cultures, when the boys were removed from the women and taken on their boy-to-manhood journey, they were taught the key life skills required to keep the tribe safe, fed and self-sufficient. While practising these life skills during hunting, fishing, swimming, tree climbing, stargazing and rock climbing, much fun was had by all, even though many of the pursuits were risky.

Our tween and teen boys still really need decent men in their lives to be able to process how to be a man. However, to do this success-fully they need good men, not abusive or toxic men, and men who have grown up to be mature, not adolescents in grown men's bodies. When we can find a male mentor who shares a similar passion to a teen boy and who is prepared to commit some time and energy, this is a seriously wonderful thing. Men tend to mentor differently to female lighthouses, and over the years I have found so many fabulous male mentors in our high schools. When they are able to create that rock-solid relationship that involves genuine connection and respect, tween and teen boys can thrive instead of struggle.

> A fishing club isn't really about fishing or a cricket club about cricket. They are really just ways that men care for each other and take boys into tutelage, give them positive messages and to provide a vehicle for character growth and maturation.
>
> – Steve Biddulph, *The New Manhood* (2019)

Places in our community where your son might find a lighthouse include the following.

- Sports club (football, cricket etc.)
- Surf lifesaving
- Scouts/Sea Scouts
- Church
- Organisations focused on the arts, especially music
- School/teachers
- Uncles, grandfathers, older cousins.

Adults who act as lighthouses need to be mature and conscious of the impact of their relationships with our teen boys, who are potentially fragile and highly impressionable. I have worked with boys who have had unpleasant experiences with significant adults that have made them wary of trusting any other adult.

Given that many of our 12–15-year-old boys can experience strong, irrational, ugly emotional states, they need safe adults to help them move through these without acting from the primitive brain – flight, freeze and fight. With multiple stressors like relationship problems, identity confusion, school failure and disengagement, problematic home lives, school challenges and illness, many teen boys struggle deeply and silently, feeling emotionally overwhelmed. They can become very vulnerable and distressed, and lighthouses need to be as supportive as possible. This is another place where lighthouses can be lifesaving.

I am a firm believer that with the strengthening of neighbourhoods and communities our boys can find the lighthouses they need to help them navigate the journey to manhood. They all need charismatic, caring adults who can act as an anchor, a safe base – especially those who are struggling. This is much like young babies and toddlers, who also need a secure base. Lighthouses are even more critical for immature teen boys because their adult-like, highly aroused bodies are akin to very fast cars being driven by inexperienced and unlicensed drivers. Please step forward and be a lighthouse for a tween or teen boy near you.

WHAT ADVICE DO YOU HAVE FOR TEEN BOYS TODAY?

- Find role models/mentors (men and women) who have characteristics which are positive and that you'd like to have. Spend time with these people and learn as much as you can from them.
- Safely find a mentor outside the family who represents the type of man you'd like to be. Be yourself. Take a chance to challenge yourself, brush your teeth and do what makes you happy.

Sometimes being a lighthouse can be quite simple, especially for men who prefer doing to talking.

A farmer approached me after a seminar one night and thanked me for helping him realise something important. He told me that many years ago a neighbouring father died suddenly by suicide, leaving behind a wife and three children – two girls and a 10-year-old boy.

At times, he would take the boy on long truck trips to Perth where they would listen to whatever sport was on (cricket or football), eat junk food and chocolate, drink soft drink, and fart and burp like young boys. The farmer would also take him to local sporting events, and sometimes just take him for a ride on the quad bikes. He never mentioned the boy's dad or asked how he was coping, and for years had felt he had not done enough. When the boy left the farm and went to university, he would still call occasionally and visit. He would throw a swag on the floor, stay a few days and ride the quad bikes or drive the trucks. Then he would leave again. The farmer finally realised he had been a lighthouse in this boy's life, and the fact the young man came 'home' occasionally just to spend time with someone who had cared meant the world to him. How important was that relationship in that boy's life? I'd say lifesaving! It's often not the big stuff, but the small stuff that can make a difference.

This chapter would not be complete without mentioning New South Wales Rural Fire Service commissioner Shane Fitzsimmons, who modelled exceptional leadership over the time of the horrendous bushfires in NSW in 2019–2020. This is a man who had teachers write comments like 'Shane is capable of so many things if he would just stick with it', or 'Just behave in class', or 'Don't get distracted'. He was unsuccessful securing an apprenticeship – possibly his report cards may have had something to do with it! He joined a local rural fire service as a teen and he found a place with lighthouses who supported him and helped him to grow. He completed a university degree, and gradually worked his way to the top of the RFS and he displayed incredible compassion, strength, honesty and integrity during the months of the crisis. Interestingly, he was reported as saying,

'In the 16-to-25 age group, we have 8500, 9000 members, so don't let anyone tell you young people are not interested in volunteering.'

The power of female lighthouses

Whether she be biological; as in an aunty or grandmother, or non-biological; as in a family friend, neighbour or teacher; the presence of a warm, caring mother figure can be enough to reduce the negative impact of a mother wound (see chapter 7 for confused mammas). In a way, a relationship with a woman whose heart is open to a boy carrying a mother wound can restore the broken heart within him. In many traditional Indigenous communities, the grandmother holds not only the wisdom of the past, but she is the figure of authority for both boys and girls.

Boy mammas, I ask you to be mindful of the boys who look sad and lost, or angry and aggressive. Step forward and be an amazing lighthouse. Show them what female compassion, kindness and love look and feel like and you may change their life positively forever.

Please open your heart to as many boys as possible. If we want boys to grow up to be capable of giving and receiving love from a partner, especially a female partner, they need to have experienced how it feels to have an open, undefended heart.

Female teachers

I have seen massive shifts happen in mid- to late-adolescence when a caring, warm female teacher has shone a beautiful light of positive regard onto a boy who had never known it before. Female teachers who spend a whole year with a tween/teen boy in their class have enormous power to be agents for positive change. This is one of my favourite stories.

During my years of teaching, I realised there was more being learned in my classroom than the English lesson I was giving. I had decided early in my career to make it easy for those who struggled with school, especially those who came to class without their files, paper or pencil cases because their home lives were difficult. Instead of beginning the class with negativity and a punitive focus, I created an easy-to-find space with spare files, paper and a huge pencil case full of biros and pencils (it was in the pre-digital world) that students could use if they came to class unprepared. They didn't need to ask to borrow them, however, most did.

This was such a small thing and I didn't think much about it after I stopped teaching. Then, one day I was stopped in the street by a tough-looking biker covered in tattoos, rings and chains. He had a thick grey beard and wore a black leather jacket. He asked if I remembered him and I replied that he must have grown much bigger and hairier than when I taught him at school! He gave me his name and I was able to instantly recall a small, quiet, unhappy looking boy from a Year 8 English class 20 years earlier.

He explained that he had often slept in a park because of the alcohol and family violence in his home. My classroom was the only one he could attend where he wasn't punished or made fun of because he did not have his files and pens. 'You welcomed me just like every other student and for a time I felt my life was bearable. I learned what kindness was from you.' He went on to tell me that even though he looked tough and mean he always tried to be thoughtful to others.

He volunteered for the local Meals on Wheels and has always been known as a neighbourhood helper in his street. He had stopped me because he had wanted to thank me and to let me know that I had been such a positive influence in his life at a really tough time. When I drove home after this experience, my heart felt really impacted. I realised that I had thought I had missed being a positive influence in this boy's life because I had not felt a meaningful connection or had many conversations with him one on one. *I realised that boys can be really impacted by how others behave and treat them* – the lighthouse effect again.

Please step forward and be a lighthouse for a teen near you.

10

Helping our teen boys with failure and adversity and teaching them how to recover

To err is human, to forgive divine.
– Alexander Pope

I am worried that I'll become a deadbeat and waste my life or I'll chase an unrealistic goal.

When our precious boys step onto the bridge that leads to manhood, they are most vulnerable to being hurt, becoming lost or ending their own lives because the world becomes too full of pain, judgement and confusion. The subtle conditioning of the old male code has so much to answer for. We can start making serious inroads into these challenges by helping our boys learn to lose and fail and recover without shame.

Parents can create a more honest template of expectation around setbacks, moments of disappointment and serious adverse events that encourages boys to see that everyone experiences these tough moments. No-one is a perfect human being who lives a perfect life without moments of challenge and failure. Resilience can be strengthened in all our children to give them the understanding that no matter what happens, there are people who will be with them and help and support them, regardless of the poor choice that may have been made.

Boys and failure

I'm worried about waking up one day and realising that I'm 40, and spent my entire young life wasting away trying to earn money. I don't want to look back on my life and realise that I've wasted 40 years that I can never get back.

Let's be really clear – no-one likes losing or making mistakes or failing. Absolutely no-one! However, for our tween and teen boys these moments can be way more debilitating than for younger boys and older men – and they too can struggle deeply.

From the earlier chapters, you now know that during adolescence your son's brain changes are mainly responsible for an increased intensity of emotions – both good and bad – especially a hunger for risk-taking behaviour, and a tendency to make impulsive decisions that lack thought and consideration.

This means he will make some really poor decisions – sometimes often. A key message to keep giving him is that when this happens it does not mean he is bad, or flawed or dumb. The 'cracked wind-screen' through which he now views himself is very skewed, and he needs your help to correct this faulty perception. If left unbridled, this faulty thinking can create self-shaming, and shame can be potentially lethal. I have heard this phrase so many times from boys and men contemplating ending their lives:

'Everyone would be better off without me around.'

Author and social philosopher Michael Gurian writes about boys' need to achieve some sense of success to feel good about themselves – whether that be climbing a tree, winning a game, hitting a target with a ball, finishing a Lego building or sharing a sporting or artistic achievement. As I've written in earlier chapters, Gurian writes that boys are looking for reasons to give themselves 'self-worth' or a sense of 'I have done good'. When they fail, they are showing they are less than, not good enough, and with an emotional immaturity these moments can impact a boy negatively and powerfully, especially with the looming conditioning of the 'man box'. If they feel like this, they also know they won't get the other thing they seek – respect! *This is the gift that comes with success – something boys and men are secretly hunting every day.*

When boys are faced with confusing expectations that they don't have the ability or understanding to meet, their sense of failure and worthlessness triggers disappointment, frustration and a crushed self-esteem that is then expressed through their behaviour. Then the cycle can begin again when they are punished for lacking the skills and awareness to make better choices in that environment. We need to shift this mindset not just in our schools but also in our homes.

Before the arrival of the digital world, boys spent hours after school doing stuff that was potentially risky, mainly in the company of other boys. Whether it was riding bikes, skateboard riding, playing social basketball or surfing, they tended to be doing these things for hours most days of the week. These experiences also gave boys opportunities for control, connection and competence, which are all aspects that influence motivation later in life. This deeply rich social interaction gave boys endless opportunities to make poor choices around others and to gradually get better at losing. Often, there were injuries and the boys would become quite caring about the injured boy and help get him home safely. This happens less frequently today because our boys are gaming. They're still playing with their mates online, however, without the physical interactions, the physical pain or the losing in the presence of others, they are not getting the same opportunities to learn how to negotiate social interactions and to learn how to lose well.

> A lack of confidence in myself meant I drank a lot of alcohol (as a teen) and avoided trying in some activities. It was better to not try than to try and fail.

Teen boys need to be taught to fully understand that there will be 'bugger moments', those times that life will be difficult and they will struggle to cope. These tough times occur because we are human; they are not a sign that we are in some way weak or undeserving of love. Until we can teach our sons this lesson, we will continue to lose high numbers of men to suicide. Failing and losing cut our boys deeply because of the unhelpful conditioning from the man code plus their inner need to validate their self-worth. The sudden massive release of intense emotions like disappointment, sadness, anger and shame can trigger a boy to act on his pain and/or run away.

Katey McPherson, an American boy advocate, educator and consultant, turned her attention to suicide prevention after a number of teenagers (most of them boys) in Arizona died by suicide. In a podcast episode of *On Boys*, she explained that in the weeks previous to the suicide most of these young people had experienced what she called 'a significant life crisis', such as a break-up, academic or athletic failure or an altercation with the law. For tween and teen boys, given our current culture around raising boys, these are major failure events.

McPherson went on to make this insightful statement:

The reality is some of these children have never failed. And so, when they have a failure, it is epic.

I have noticed some interesting psychological behaviours created by boys I've worked with over the years in order to avoid losing:

- Don't commit 100 per cent (I wasn't trying)
- Keep the game going forever
- Destroy the game
- Cheat
- Keep others from winning
- Be nice and try a bit
- Be the judge/critic – argue a lot
- Be perfect and try ridiculously hard
- Become a problem (mental/physical illness, drug and alcohol addiction)
- Refuse to play or have a go at all
- Quit.

These are all coping techniques that aim to avoid the experience of failing and which happen quite unconsciously.

WHAT WAS YOUR MOST CHALLENGING EXPERIENCE WHEN YOU WERE A TEEN?

- Being bullied as a geek at school with very few friends, and feeling a lack of support from senior school staff who focused on sporting students.
- Getting injured at sport.
- Learning difficulties – which caused me to feel a lot of shame, embarrassment and vulnerability.
- Moving house and changing schools was a bit of a challenge, finding new friends and trying to fit in.
- Overcoming bullying and dealing with suicidal thoughts.
- Dealing with the death of my sister followed by my parents separating.
- Domestic violence, both as a victim and perpetrator.
- Marital difficulties between Mum and Dad. Although they remain married, some of the fallout was not fun to be around. Never physical or anything, but arguing.
- Love and the challenges it brought, heartache, desire, rejection, self-worth. It all felt so crucial and epic at the time.

The old man-code and failure

The old man-code creates an impossibly difficult mindset in many of our tween/teen boys and men, telling them that failure equals weakness, and *that weak men do not deserve to be respected or loved.* In my work in rural areas, I have heard many incredibly sad stories of men who have ended their lives when certain life events had gone bad for them. Sometimes this was following extended drought, the aftermath of bushfires, the unexpected ending of a marriage, or following multiple deaths of people they loved.

For some, the warrior within our men, which is both culturally and biologically influenced, seems to believe that it is actually easier to die than to lose publicly in front of your community and the world. Western culture celebrates the winner and the victor, and if we are to change the disturbing suicide rates of men, we must address the way that failure and losing are experienced by our boys.

The number of our returned servicemen, paramedics, firemen, policemen, rescue and salvage crews and even some of our emergency doctors who are ending their lives is a disgrace in a developed country. These men (and often women) work in areas of high trauma and when they struggle to cope, they often find help can be difficult to find or non-existent. To ask for help is still seen as a negative – indeed in some organisations it means you will be denied future promotion opportunities. These are mature men with fully developed brains who are struggling. It is much harder for our teen boys and young men in their twenties.

I can still vividly remember the moment a 20-year-old Oliver called me to tell me that he had – in his words – 'completely fucked up my whole life'. He was incredibly distressed and it took some time before he shared with me what had happened. He had been studying medical imaging at university and one requirement of his second year was that he had to pass an oral exam as well as a written exam. Due to exam anxiety, during his oral exam he became momentarily distracted and he mixed up the word 'hand' with 'foot'. This meant he failed the oral exam even though he came second top with the written exam, and that he would now have to do an extra year of university. In his eyes, it was a catastrophic failure. Thankfully, he had a strong enough connection with his family that he was able to work out a way through this sudden, unexpected setback.

I have worked with two other male university students who have almost died by suicide when they failed at university. Both of these boys expressed to me how crushing failure was not only for themselves but their perception of how disappointed their parents would be too. *Fear of parental disappointment is one of the reasons your sons will not come to you when they fail.* The old man-code will take time to fully dismantle and so many of today's boys yet to begin the walk over the bridge to manhood will have the same conditioning as their fathers – that being a failure is something to be avoided at all costs.

DISMANTLING THE MAN-CODE AND TEACHING THE POWER OF VULNERABILITY

I was honoured to spend some time in a large shed near the rural community of Esperance almost four months after a serious bushfire had taken the lives of four people and devastated crops and farms in many properties. The gathering was for men only.

As I have a deep passion for men and boys, resilience and loss, I had been invited to speak to over 100 men about the way forward following this natural disaster. One of the key messages I left with the men – which many thanked me for afterwards – was that you are supposed to be feeling lousy, awful and struggling to find joyful moments for months after a traumatic event. This is a normal response to situational distress – that is, distress that is linked to a challenging situation. This is absolutely normal following such a catastrophic event. So many of these men had been raised under the old male-code, which meant that they thought they were being weak if they were struggling emotionally afterwards.

Many also expressed concern that they did not know how to support their wives who were grieving, quite often in different ways. I explored

---

that simply 'being beside someone' and checking in on mates and friends is incredibly powerful. I also gave them permission to cry if they felt they needed to.

One of the local volunteer firefighters shared with me his overwhelming sense of failure even though they had fought a vicious fire for almost five days without any external support. They had fought courageously to the point of exhaustion and instead of feeling like heroes or warriors, they were consumed with feeling inadequate and useless because they had lost lives, especially the life of a much-loved local mate. *We have much work to do to reframe men's thinking and teach that vulnerability is truly courageous and showing it may be the toughest thing you ever do.*

Loss of sporting or other dream

When a teen boy has his heart set on a dream – whether that be a sporting dream or an artistic dream – and that dream is crushed for whatever reason, it can have some seriously worrying consequences.

One young lad (16) I knew was a gifted athlete who was competing at a high level in athletics and was also doing exceptionally well in basketball. He experienced an injury that impacted his lower back. Initially the doctors thought it would only take a couple of months for him to recover. Sadly, the injury was permanent and he was no longer able to compete in either of his much-loved physical pursuits. Over a period of time, he began to withdraw from his friendship circle and because he had missed quite a bit of school, his grades had dropped as well. His family became really worried when he ended his long-term relationship with a lovely young lady, telling her that she 'deserved someone better'. In a way, he was grieving for multiple losses without the tools and strategies with which to understand or process this grief. Fortunately, he agreed to see someone who was able to help him understand it, to plan a new map for his life and he has since recovered his confidence and is doing well academically and socially.

Sadly for the boys who refuse to speak to someone – whether that be a parent, a lighthouse or a professional – this hole of despair can become permanent. It is essentially a combination of a grief experience and an inability to fill their self-worth barometer with anything other than what they feel they are best at.

Significant loss of respect for men can become life-threatening.

> I had numerous hip operations and as a result was very immobile and inactive. I loved sport but couldn't take part and I gained lots of weight. I was lucky to have great friends but as a teenager the hospital and weight gain was a huge hurdle that I didn't overcome until I was near 20.

Reframing failure as normal

Rather than seeing failure as a form of weakness, we must reframe it so that failure is actually a normal part of being human and it can be an opportunity for growth. The more we share our own personal moments of adversity, and how we have grown from them, the better our boys and men will be at managing the tough moments of life. In fact, resilience is all about recovering from failure or overcoming adversity that may make someone feel helpless and powerless for a time.

We must remove the shame that is buried deep inside so many of our boys and men and which is linked to profound disappointment when they are unable to meet their own expectations and the perceived expectations of those most dear to them. The powerlessness that is a part of experiencing setbacks and adversity needs to be spoken about and normalised. The latest research about resilience suggests that the capacity to recover or to manage really difficult life experiences is dependent on the systems within which you live – your families, your communities, your school communities, your sporting communities and your neighbourhood. Within these systems exist the resources that will help you recover and you will sometimes need to ask for help. Unfortunately, among many men help-seeking behaviour is still seen as a form of failure. This must be changed and thankfully there are signs that this is happening with men's groups becoming more mainstream, allowing men to share their stories with the raw truth that men appreciate.

Failing needs to be seen as a consequence of
being human and a normal part of life!

I have written extensively about my concerns about forcing little boys who need more time to shine into our school systems before they are developmentally capable of managing these expectations. Many of these little boys struggle and often create mindsets around feeling dumb, stupid or that they never try hard enough! If we keep in mind the self-worth barometer that drives boys' need to experience moments of success to feel good about themselves, it is obvious that by adolescence many boys have been telling themselves for years that they are simply not good enough.

With lots of coaching and strong emotional support from family and caring teachers, our boys can lose their fear of failure, and they can simply expect failure as a normal part of their life.

Strategies for building resilience in the face of failure

1. Visualising or imagining losing and practising how to respond

One thing that can help tween and teen boys is for a caring adult, either a parent or lighthouse, to take the time to validate how it actually feels in the body when he loses. One example to work with is to have a boy imagine or pretend that he wants to be captain of the basketball team or maybe a school leader. Then have him imagine that he is unsuccessful and that the announcement is made in a public place. Teach him to scrunch his toes up really tight inside his shoes until they hurt. This distracts his amygdala from processing the deep disappointment and instead focuses it on a potential threat in his shoes. It really does work – maybe you could try it sometime as well! This will allow him not to be flooded with these big feelings and it will help him be able to make another choice around how to respond. I recommend you encourage him to practise going over to congratulate the person who did get the position that he wanted. We are teaching him that there are different ways to lose and that yes, it can take a few practices to get it right, and normalising how it feels. Being a sore loser who spontaneously reacts in a way that is disrespectful, rude or embarrassing will simply create even more big, ugly feelings further down the track. Ultimately, this will create more shame for your boy.

2. Sharing failure

To help your son better learn about failure, it's good to have conversations about things you hear in the media where boys and men have experienced failure and how they have recovered.

I think the Jim Stynes story is an excellent one to share with your son. Jim was an AFL footballer who gave away a free kick just before the siren in the 1987 preliminary final. This meant his team lost and did not get into the grand final. He took off to Europe to get away from Australia and the source of his embarrassing wound. One day, thinking he had escaped his shame, on the platform at a train station somewhere in France someone called out to him to remind him that he lost the game. He realised then that running away was not going to bring him the resolution he needed. He came back, threw himself into his football and became extremely well respected. He later set up programs to help struggling youth. He ended up with an Order of Australia and even though he sadly died from cancer in 2012, his work continues today.

More recent is the story of Steve Smith, the former captain of the Australian cricket team, who was involved in a ball-tampering cheating scandal. Technically, he turned a blind eye to it rather than actually participating in it, but he and two other players were found to be guilty of cheating and were banned from cricket. Steve Smith had been an exemplary leader and a very well-respected cricketer until this moment in time. He owned his mistake and then publicly apologised for his poor choice as the team leader and took his punishment without question. He quietly stepped away from the cricket world and took time to rebuild his own sense of self-worth. Smith returned to international cricket, despite crowds expressing their displeasure, and in 2019 he scored 671 runs in three matches, peaking with scores of 211 and 82 at Old Trafford. His batting performance shows that he had clearly used his year away from cricket to work on his skills.

We need our boys to hear stories of the men, especially well-known men, who suffer significant failures and struggles in their lives, who make poor choices, or who fail to make a good choice at an important time, whether it be on our sporting fields, hotels, schools or in our workplaces. They need to see that they can make amends and regain their self-worth and continue to strive to be a better man. Everyone will experience challenge in their life. Everybody will experience failure, and the capacity to overcome these adverse events is called resilience.

Nothing lasts forever. Whatever you're going through, know that there's a whole life of experiences ahead of you. Cherish the memories, good and bad. Every experience you have is preparing you for life in ways you couldn't imagine.

3. Tell your son you will support and love him no matter what

We must teach our sons to know that life is an unpredictable ride and sh#% happens – often unexpectedly. The global impact of the

Coronavirus pandemic is a perfect example! But importantly, let your boy know that when tough stuff happens, he can own it and he can walk through it with the help of others, no matter how painful or sad it is. He does not need to struggle alone. Giving our boys a safe base to fall on and a bucket full of hope will seriously help more boys have a better experience of being a teen. The concept of unconditional love needs to be explored. One of the most important things you can do during this vulnerable window of his life is remind your son that you will continue to love him no matter what. So many of the boys I worked with who were struggling believed that their parents couldn't love them because of some of the dumb things they had done.

So please remind them often that you love them –
with a hug, a loving note, a wrestle, a well-timed fart
or whatever works for them. It does make a difference.

4. Humour

Humour is really important as a protective factor in terms of resilience for both genders and can also help defuse embarrassment and a sense of shame that is so easily triggered in our boys. Having a good sense of humour about yourself and your own failings can model resilient behaviour for your son.

5. It's not all about winning

A really helpful message to give our boys before the tween and teen years is that participating enthusiastically can often be just as important as winning. Also that it takes true courage to turn up and have a go at something that you have very little chance of succeeding at. These messages are drowned out by the endless pressure on boys to be the best and that the winner takes all.

The power of the metaphor – the map and teen boys

A strategy I began to use especially with teen boys and men was the metaphor of their map of the world. The map that we use to navigate the world – especially the journey over the bridge to manhood – is based on our beliefs, prior perceptions, past experiences, genealogy, social conditioning, family values and peer pressure. In a way every teen boy has their own map of the world with which they are navigating their choices. Our job is to help them to create more helpful maps, or to allow them to see the map of the adult world. Remember, our behaviour is the result of choices we make based on our beliefs and past experiences, and we make assumptions and have expectations automatically. For so many teen boys, they often feel when things get difficult that they are the problem, and that they are in some way bad, flawed or useless. Using a map metaphor, they can simply figure out they may just be a bit lost and that by finding a better way to navigate or changing their map they can improve their lives significantly.

Here is an example of a mother–son conflict, which I outlined in my book *Saving Our Adolescents*, that shows how different maps can cause angst.

The son was having difficulty engaging at school and had been wagging occasionally. Mum got a call to say he had not arrived at school and she was pretty angry because she had dropped him off at school before it started.

She frantically phoned his mobile and it was turned off. She went home to check on him and he wasn't there. She then started to get really worried. Then the school called to say he had shown up.

She quickly went to the school and found her son and confronted him in front of other staff and students. After she yelled at him and told him how stupid he had been, he then lost the plot and in front of the same group of people told her to get f#& %$#@!

Mum's map of the world had told her that he had wagged after she had dropped him off and she was worried the school would expel him because he was on a final warning. The son's map of the world was very different.

When he had arrived at school, he had been told there was a seminar for his year group that cost $10. He didn't have the money, plus he didn't want to go so he had gone downtown until the seminar was over. He had left his phone in his bag back at school.

Once they were able to have their different maps decoded, they could understand and appreciate how the conflict had erupted out of misunderstanding – not malicious intent.

Totally different maps and different worlds, and neither side could see the other side. A connected parent, or a supportive lighthouse or an adult ally, can help decode the maps so they can both understand each other's behaviour. The mother had done something very dangerous in adolescent land: publicly shame an adolescent in their territory. Social inclusion and the biological need to belong is profoundly strong, and she had unintentionally made him look wrong and stupid in front of his social group. The son had reached a tipping point and exploded, partly to defend his sense of identity and also to retain his place socially.

Using the map metaphor was my main way of working with teen boys and men in my counselling work. The first visual map I used was the one below because it explained that our ability to be capable and resilient is a balancing act between the things that nurture and protect us and the things that cause us stress and conflict. This balancing act can be helpful to use throughout life, not just during adolescence. A boy would write down a list of things that were causing him problems (stressors) and then he would look at the things that made him feel happy, stronger and capable (protective factors).

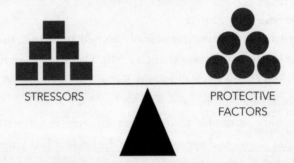

RESILIENCE MODEL

STRESSORS   PROTECTIVE FACTORS

The second part to the mapping was having them give a mark out of 1–10, with 10 being excellent, in the five key areas of their life.

School. Friends. Family. Community. Skills.

Often a boy is unable to see what the problem is that needs fixing and so he can get lost in a cycle of continually making the same poor choices. Then, once he is in that cycle where he cannot see how he can win or do well, he will quit. Once he has clarity, he can then start to become the problem-solver rather than feeling powerless and at the mercy of confusion. As soon as a teen boy is able to see everything visually in front of him, he then begins to notice and understand the areas that may need work and the areas where he is doing OK. This is basic goal setting that opens a boy to a new sense of purpose.

Once a boy was able to see, for example, that the biggest area creating stress and challenge for him was the time he spent at school, then we would help him create another map exploring exactly what it was about his school situation that was causing the problems. The boy would then choose a couple of action steps, both a plan A and a plan B that he needed to do before his next appointment. I have met some of these boys as grown men who still use these mapping strategies when they feel they are struggling in their life!

- I wish my parents had been more outgoing, played with me, had friends around and given me guidance. Shown me they were brave and it's OK to fuck up. That was not there and would have really helped.
- I wish I could have been given more advice, as I made some poor life choices in my late teens.
- I wish they'd listened to me, encouraged me, let me be myself, and given me the freedom I needed to do what I felt I needed to do rather than sheltering me away from the world due to their own mental-health issues.

11

What to do when your son makes a mistake or a poor choice

Inevitably your son will make a mistake; or hurt himself; hurt someone else; or make a very poor, thoughtless, stupid or cruel choice – many times actually! How you react as a parent can significantly impact how he recovers from making this mistake. Your first reactions may be anger, disappointment or the urge to discipline harshly, but there are other ways of reacting that can strengthen your bond with your son and ensure he learns from the experience through growth rather than shame. Your son is going to make poor decisions repeatedly until he has enough myelin in his brain to be more mindful of the choices he makes. That is just a fact of life. As parents, your job is to day-by-day, week-by-week and year-by-year help your son learn a culture of accountability that can be created without a need for severe punishment, shaming or ridicule.

When I asked some of the struggling teen boys in my counselling room why they were unable to tell their parents that they were at a very vulnerable or dangerous place, so many of them responded, 'I just didn't want to disappoint them again and see that look of disappointment in their eyes'. This is so incredibly sad. When boys are repeatedly experiencing moments of emotional rejection, from their mum, their dad or both, a belief that they are unworthy and undeserving of love then feeds straight into their emotional barometer and convinces them that they will be unable to love themselves. This is why we need to look very seriously at how we interact with our boys when they make endless mistakes in early childhood because this is where much of the unconscious programming is laid down in our boys' minds that can make things tricky in those teen years.

In his book *Dissolving Toxic Masculinity*, Thomas Haller writes that having a non-toxic approach to discipline can allow boys to 'experience both the negative and positive outcomes of their choices and behaviours'.

> Implemented consistently, with gentleness and love, outcomes become the cornerstone of your discipline structure and your sons' path to developing responsibility and a healthy masculinity.

There is a story which, again, I told in my *Mothering Our Boys* book which really must be shared in this book since it explores different ways of managing a significant teen muck-up experience.

This story is based on one I heard many years ago in rural Australia.

> Once upon a time there were three 14-year-old mates who had been friends for a number of years. Sometime in the previous year, they had come to like playing golf. On most Saturday mornings, they would meet at the golf club, get their fathers' golf clubs from the buggy room and play at least nine holes of golf before the main competition started late in the morning. This pattern of behaviour had been happening for almost a year before something went horribly wrong.
>
> On this particular Saturday after the boys got back to the club room, they were putting the golf buggy and clubs back into the buggy room when they started a harmless shoving and pushing game

(for want of a better word). One of the boys grabbed one of the golf clubs and pretty soon they were pretending they were fencing. This game then led into a random game of trying to hit each other with the golf clubs. They damaged a few of the walls where the golf clubs cracked the plaster. Then somehow or other the light fittings were smashed and some of the lockers were also hit and damaged in the senseless, mindless 'boys being boys' game-gone-wrong 15 minutes of insanity.

When one of the club members who had arrived early for the competition walked into the room, the boys stopped suddenly. The boys' fathers were called and the boys were made to sit on a bench outside the buggy room facing the car park where many other members were now arriving. The members were obviously very unhappy with the vandalism and damage.

Soon the first father arrived and as he got out of his car, he slammed the car door. As he came up the path towards where his son was sitting, he began shouting abusively calling his son 'a bloody idiot' and asked, 'How could you be so stupid?' When he reached his son, he physically took him by the shoulders and shook him vigorously while continuing to shout in his face. He then shoved his son in the direction of the car and again slammed his car door as he drove off in a furious haste.

The second father arrived and as he got out of his car, he also slammed the door. As he came up the pathway towards his son, his face was black with a silent fury. When he got near his son, he swung and hit him really hard over the head and then he began shouting the same shaming abuse as the first father. As his son began to walk towards the car, his father shoved him so hard from behind the boy sprawled onto the path. He then dragged him to the car. He also slammed his car door and took off in a furious haste.

The third father then arrived and unlike the previous two fathers he did not slam his car door. He walked up the pathway towards his son and held his arms out to his son and gave him a hug. He whispered something to him and then with his arm around his shoulders, he guided him carefully back to the car and they drove off quietly.

An hour later the third father and his son returned to the golf club. They had been to Bunnings and purchased all that was needed to repair the damage that had been done. The father and son worked all afternoon patching the holes and repainting. They repaired the lights and then when they were finished they quietly left.

When I was told this story, it affected me deeply because in my counselling rooms I so often had to hold a boy who had had a similar experience with his father or father figure after he'd made some seriously poor choices, and allow him to sob deeply.

They had been so shamed and wounded by their dad's behaviour and they never forgot that sense of being a huge disappointment to their father. Many still carried that wound far into adulthood.

Were the first two fathers bad men? No. The first two fathers had done what they thought was the right thing so that their sons could learn they had made a mistake. They thought that would teach their sons not to vandalise other people's property. And it is highly likely that their own father would have managed one of their less-than-perfect moments with a similar response. Sadly, rather than feeling they made a bad choice, their sons were left feeling they were wrong, bad or flawed. This is shaming and it has a way of making individuals feel worthless and incapable of being loved. Such punishment as this can often permanently damage the relationship between a father and his son. I have heard so many sad stories from boys and from older men – stories of such profound hurt and pain.

The father that chose to support and love his son and to teach him that when you make a mistake you need to make it right most likely had a loving, warm father when he was a boy the same age. But maybe not.

Josh Shipp lived through the foster-care system in America and grew up to challenge every foster carer he had, including the one who helped him change his life. In his book *The Grown-Up's Guide to Teenage Humans*, Shipp writes extensively about the importance for parents and significant adults to become coaches rather than 'traffic controllers'.

Shipp has a strategy that I would like to share with you for when your teen fails – no matter what it is, no matter how big or small it is, he suggests that you sit down with your teen and ask this question:

'What did we learn from this?'

Shipp explains beautifully that the word 'we' shows that you are both in it together. Why is this important?

> This is disarming because after every failure, teens are afraid of being singled out and punished. There will likely be consequences to their actions, but your first overture must be to send the message that you're in partnership.

This is very similar to the approach of the third father in the story I have just shared about the boys at the golf club. Rather than just shame and punish the boy for his poor choices, he gathered him up and taught him a different way of being accountable and responsible. They did it together.

What to do when your son has made a mistake or a poor choice
Before you dive into the conversation:

- If your son has been physically injured, absolutely attend to his physical injuries with as much love and tenderness as you can find before you explore what happened.
- Allow everyone involved time to calm down, feel safe and process the incident before you begin the resolution process – this may be 24 hours or more after the event.
- Try to see the world through an adolescent boy's eyes and practise responding, not just reacting.

- Be careful to avoid looking disappointed or embarrassed about his behaviour.
- Remember boys are sensitive and not tough so practise warm discipline not shouting, hitting or shaming.
- Do everything you can to contain your emotions *until you get all the facts*. If a boy sees that you are upset and angry or disappointed, he will be less likely to share what has happened in its entirety.
- Remember the tips from the chapter on communication about *your tone and your physiology*.
- Please avoid asking your son 'What were you thinking?' after he has done something that seems really dumb to us parents. This shaming language does not help.

When everyone feels safe and calm, you can begin the conversation

- Start this big conversation about this negative experience *by validating how it might feel for your son*.
- Ask him to tell you what happened and then listen without interrupting. Stay silent after he has explained it – often a boy will contribute more when he thinks you're really listening to him. Often they do not understand why they are in trouble, especially if they did not intend to hurt someone or damage something.
- Gently ask what was his intention when he made that choice: 'What were you trying to do, mate?'
- Remind him about the three rules (see page 54) and ask him which one he broke.
- Help him to make it right. This is such an incredibly important step in your resolution process because your son needs to learn how to be accountable when he has made a poor choice and he has broken one or more of the three rules. He must make it right. Notice, I have suggested that *he* works out how to make things right rather than mum or dad or a teacher making things right

for him. I find this helps boys learn to become more accountable and responsible in the long-term because they are problem-solving their own mistake. This can be quite funny because sometimes they will think up something really awful as a consequence. Our job as a parent is to ensure that this consequence happens. Even if we think he has learned his lesson, please lovingly ensure he does the right thing. Teach him to be accountable for his poor choices – gently and with compassion.

- 'Next time?' Ask him about what he might do next time this situation arises. What choice could he make to avoid breaking the three rules in the same situation again. This is also an incredibly important step. You need to work with your son to work out what would be a better choice if the same thing happens again – he will need some practical suggestions here.

- Forgive him for making a poor choice – quickly. Seriously, there will be a new poor choice coming soon that you will have to deal with. You have to let it go. We are so often tempted to bring up a past misdemeanour or bugger-up moment later but they are best forgotten. I wish this step was easier than it is as I have had to work with many parents to get to this place given the enormity of some muck-ups (especially when it was in a public situation).

- Acknowledge the valuable learning – like Josh Shipp suggests – 'What did we learn from this?' This step can be optional, however, I have often found that it has helped my sons to see that life is a long journey of learning and growing. If you can use the words 'resilience' or 'recovery' it can be helpful for him further down the track. So, again, because our boys tend to learn from natural consequences and experiences that cause them some discomfort, it can be valuable to remind them that life's lessons are not all bad. In a family of four sons, I often found that one son's disastrous muck-up moment could become a valuable life lesson for the other sons.

- **Reassure him you still love him**, non-verbally as well as verbally, by 'showing' rather than 'saying'. I cannot stress how important this is for all teens because they are struggling with their own self-worth every day. Your reassurance of love, your gestures of kindness, your encouragement that things will get better and any other form of non-verbal connection is absolutely noted even if they are unable to respond positively. Even after all this please keep in mind your son could still be beating himself up internally.

> **ALWAYS MAKE SURE YOU GET THE FACTS AND UNDERSTAND HIS INTENTION**
>
> A boy was asked to vacuum the daddy long legs spiders and their webs out of the lounge and hallway but he never did it. When his mum came home, she immediately thought he had forgotten but instead of yelling at him, thankfully, she checked in with him as to why he hadn't done as he was asked. He had remembered but he felt uncomfortable hurting the spiders and felt sorry for them.

Helping our sons make good decisions by listening to intuition

Intuition is a knowingness that stands outside logical, rational thought. Intuition occurs to assist an individual to make choices that are of a positive nature, especially around situations of personal safety.

Over the years I have asked many children and teenagers who have hurt themselves, or made a decision which they later regretted, if they had a thought or a sense that this was something they would later regret. Overwhelmingly, they had all had an intuitive thought or a gut feeling that they chose to ignore.

So, if teenagers do feel this instinct, why don't more tween and teen boys use their intuition? Our fast-paced, overstimulated world is full of visual, auditory and kinaesthetic stimuli. I would suggest this overload of stimuli is a large contributor to a weakening of the capacity of intuition, which is our inner guidance. Children are happy with less unplugged time in the natural world. But fewer children are spending significant amounts of time in nature in today's world. Intuition can become stronger when we become centred and calm down and practise stillness in our lives. Without opportunities for stillness and quiet reflection, it is harder for our tweens and teens to tune into their inner guidance, which is really the best friend they have. Intuition strives to help us become the best person we can be and keeps us safe, healthy and on a positive course in our lives. It is important that all our children are given opportunities to develop their intuition and to hear the silent voice within.

Well-developed intuition is an enormous asset, especially in any teen's life with the high-risk situations that many teenagers find themselves in. Before going into a party or accepting a ride from someone, they can pause and check their intuition – how does their gut feel? Parties can change quickly from being safe and enjoyable into uncontrollable fights and chaos. Teens – both girls and boys – have shared with me how they had intuitively known when to leave a party, BEFORE any conflict started. They found out about the trouble the next day. A real concern is that alcohol and drugs inhibit the power of the intuition. That may be a reason why there are so many accidents among the adolescent population. Weak intuition and inexperience can have deadly consequences.

Many tween and teen boys choose to do risky things because the flood of positive neurochemicals afterwards can give them a rush and a feeling of transcendence, that mind-body state of bliss free of anxiety and worry.

Many boys will struggle with the concept of intuition because it is not logical or provable. The natural pragmatism of males also makes teaching them about the gut feeling or sensation difficult. Often when they have had an experience – either positive or painful – you might be able to tease out some sense of inner knowing that was taking place at the time.

Find a personal space for your mind, whatever that looks like, challenge your thoughts and slow them down, breathe, the waves of emotions and tension will at times seem like the end of your world, breathing slowly and deeply as loopy as it sounds helps.

Encourage your son to do three things before he makes a decision

1. Become quiet, centred and fully present.
2. Breathe deeply and slow the body and the mind.
3. Actively seek the quiet voice within.

You could encourage your son to strengthen his intuition through the following activities:

- Calming audios
- Mindfulness activities
- Guided meditation
- Yoga
- Fishing
- Deliberately disconnecting from overstimulating devices
- Autonomous Sensory Meridian Response (ASMR) videos on YouTube – weird and yet often helpful
- Mindfulness apps like Smiling Mind or Headspace.

Remember, making poor choices and failing is part of being human. Life will throw you a curve ball sometimes – it is what you do next that makes all the difference!

12

Teen boy communication that really works

sucked at that. I needed to piece that together, more or less, on my own and around my mates. I wanted a hands-on set of parents that would trust me (and I them). Yet, my parents struggled to help me – despite being present – at crucial times. I will never make that mistake with my kids.

- Talked to me, not at me. Been less judgemental. Showed more affection.
- I would have liked it if my parents had been more willing to talk about what they were uncomfortable talking about. Their discomfort meant that we didn't talk about what needed to be talked about. There was no communication about anything important unless I had misbehaved in their eyes.
- I know my parents loved me but I wish they'd communicated with me more. I feel that everything I learned about life I had to learn by myself, the hard way.

Communication seems such a simple thing to do, however, poor communication is one of the key factors underlying conflict in our families and our schools.

Just because we are saying words to another person does not necessarily mean we are communicating effectively.

We often misunderstand each other and that is before all the brain changes that create the 'cracked-windscreen view' of the world for our tweens and teens. What you have demonstrated and modelled over his childhood will become your son's template for communicating later. Unfortunately, the unique changes of adolescence can appear to erase all the good work you have done and that is one of the reasons why it sometimes feels like an alien has stolen your son!

In counselling, there were times when very troubled adolescent boys who had attempted suicide – teens who had reached their tipping point – would come to my office so relieved because they had finally found someone who would listen *without judgement*. So many of our boys struggle with past experiences of being unheard, misunderstood, ignored or made to feel there is something wrong with them. This reluctance is understandable and with a good understanding of ways to communicate, especially to our tweens and teen boys, I believe we can improve our communication.

Conflict

Conflict in relationships is normal rather than a sign that something is bad. Boys and men are often really confused when conflict happens, especially with people they love. In his research, John Gottman shows that when parents argue it is the resolution of the argument that is most important for our children to witness – especially our boys. We are all prone to thinking we are right and the other person is wrong because we are human! Early in the book I explained that when the limbic brain becomes fired up in females the next centre to fire up is the word centre – which is why mums are generally quick to have some heated words to say.

Parents need to understand and explain to their sons that the heat of the moment – when everyone is in the emotional 'red room' – is not a good time to talk about the issue you're having. Taking some time out and cooling off is really useful. I did not say this was easy for us women, however, it is not only respectful it can really help our boys, before and after they are teens, to be able to work through a conflict by coming to understand how the other person feels.

Simply say in a calm, gentle voice, *'Bud, let's chat about this tomorrow after we've both had a chance to cool down and think and have a good night's sleep.'* A non-verbal gesture of support would be great. Having a follow-up conversation in the same familiar and non-threatening place every time can be really helpful.

Avoid the following strategies when approaching your teen

- Lecturing
- Nagging

- Arguing
- Unkindness
- Criticism
- Shouting
- Manipulation
- Commanding and demanding
- Guilt games
- Shaming
- Any physical abuse
- Ignoring them or freezing them out
- Comparing them to siblings
- Using 'always', 'never', 'It's easy!', or 'It's going to be hard' as a predictor.

Our brain is wired to zone out things that we hear often and that's one of the reasons why nagging is quite unsuccessful, especially for boys.

Adolescents – both girls and boys – can interpret some parent communication and behaviours to mean very different things than what you intend

Here are some common miscommunications.

Adult communication	Adolescent interpretation
Threaten	I don't matter.
Command	I'm inadequate.
Preach	You don't like me.
Advice	You invalidate me.
Lecture	I can't do anything right.
Shout	I am frightened.
Criticism	I am useless and incapable.

Adult communication	Adolescent interpretation
Shame	I am bad and hopeless.
Smother	I am trapped.
Nag	You disrespect me.
Withhold love	You make my world unsafe.
Disconnect	There's no-one I can trust.
You solve my problems	You crush my search for solutions.
You tell me what I am feeling	You invalidate me and my feelings.
Be unavailable/on your phone	I am invisible and unlovable.

Please do not beat yourself up if you have done any of the above; I am guilty too. It can be difficult for parents to manage the constant shifts and changes in our kids while often struggling with our own levels of over-commitment, work, lack of sleep, home and life. When we are tired and stressed, we will revert back to our critical parent/ reactive parent voice in our head that often came from our own parents – who also did the best they could.

Good communication
Body language
In the early 1990s, I did quite a bit of training in NLP (neuro linguistic programming), which was a fascinating body of information that explored the best communicators at the time. I was able to come to a much better place of understanding about the complexities and nuances of human communication and how we can do it better.

One of the first things that NLP proposes is that communication is less than 10 per cent of the words that are spoken. I'm not sure this is conclusively backed by research, however, it is still a worthwhile thing to consider. The remaining 90 per cent is roughly due to physiology and tonality. Essentially, we are communicating with our bodies and our faces all the time. There are some aspects of physiology that are highly provocative towards teen boys that may surprise you. So often a tween or teen boy will misread the physiology of friends, peers, teachers and certainly parents.

Caring, empowering communication – what is it and how do we do it?

Good communication leads to:	Poor communication leads to:
Warm relationships	Kids who turn away from adults
Cooperation	Conflicts and bickering
Feelings of worth	Feelings of worthlessness

Some tips for effective communication

The less threatening the physical approach and placement of the grown-up and the safer the place where the conversation takes place, the more likely the boy will feel open enough to at least hear the words being spoken.

Eye contact

It is interesting that women often prefer direct eye contact to men and boys, and many boys can find eye contact threatening. Demanding that a boy maintains eye contact with you is more than likely putting him into a position of threat that will trigger his amygdala and mean he will be unable to listen to what you are saying (just in case he needs to run to survive an attack on his life). Don't insist on or expect direct eye contact!

Placement and place

Imagine a person standing in front of you with their hands on their hips about to speak to you. I guarantee it will put you on the defensive immediately. The position of my chair in my counselling room was carefully placed to ensure I was not directly in front of any boy who came to see me. Consider having a conversation in the car, sitting beside them on a couch, or leaning together on the railing of a balcony in order to lower the level of threat in the conversation.

Movement

If you need to have a reasonably serious conversation with any boy but especially any over the age of 10, may I suggest you combine it with some form of movement such as going for a walk, or shooting hoops with a basketball. Choosing a relaxed location can really help him to feel calm and safe to hear you, especially if he feels confident no-one else will hear the conversation.

Tone

I cannot stress the importance of tonality in communication with sensitive teens, particularly our boys, enough. The tone of your voice is enormously important if you choose to communicate meaningfully. So many boys have been conditioned that raised voices, sarcasm, criticism and shaming means that they have done something bad, naughty or upsetting and they are about to be punished. Please remember that they *often misread* your tone just as they do your physiology and this will trigger their amygdala into fight-flight mode.

- Avoid using their full name with a harsh tone.
- Remember the power of using names of endearment, or just less threatening ones like 'mate', 'bud' or even 'dude'.

Timing
Times to avoid important parent conversations with tween/teen boys
- When you are upset, especially angry
- In the heat of the moment!
- Before you know the full facts or the full story
- At breakfast time as they are often still half asleep

- Straight after school
- While they are watching a favourite TV show
- While they are busy on a device, especially when gaming or watching other people gaming on YouTube
- While anyone else is nearby
- When they are hungry
- When they are tired
- While they are eating
- When they are having a growth spurt
- Within hours of the significant misdemeanour
- Within 24 hours of a misdemeanour that happened in public
- Within 24 hours of having returned home from a sleepover or a school camp
- On their birthday/special family day
- Just before visitors arrive.

Top tips for good timing

- Approach them when none of the above is happening.
- Ask them when would be a good time for you to have a chat – most boys are very sensitive to feeling ambushed.
- Remind them gently just before it is chat time, and possibly check if they want a hot drink or a snack.
- Building rapport – a bridge of connection – is incredibly helpful when having conversations with tween and teen boys. A gentle punch in the arm, tussle of the hair or even a wink – these all help boys feel safer before the conversation begins. Oh, and never forget the power of the well-timed fart!

The feedback sandwich

Essentially, we are all wired to protect ourselves from nastiness or criticism by becoming non-listeners. By the time most boys reach adolescence they have had endless experiences of being growled at, criticised, shamed and made fun of so they are particularly likely to become what I call 'selectively deaf' when they hear words of criticism, especially when spoken without warmth.

The feedback sandwich always begins with something positive and life-affirming about the boy to whom we are speaking. Then, we explore the concerning information we need to share – without changing our tone. Finally, we finish the conversation, no matter how long it was, with another love-affirming message about the boy. So it could go something like this:

Oliver, you know how much I love your energy and enthusiasm and passion for life. (Pause and smile!) However, I have been concerned of late that sometimes this enthusiasm has become a little bit of a problem when you are playing with your sisters – and you have become quite bossy when they don't want to do what you want to do. You then seem to become frustrated – and I have noticed you lashing out or shoving them. So I want us to have a little chat about how you might be able to manage that frustration without hurting them because I know it doesn't make you feel good later and it does upset your sisters. (Possible gentle shoulder rub – pause.) Shall we do this now or should we have another chat tomorrow when you've had a chance to think about it a bit more? You do know that you are my most favourite boy on the whole planet, don't you, and that I love you more than every star in the night sky and more than all the bums on all the fishes in the whole wide world?

If you need to have a conversation with your son about a failed assignment, or him overreacting to a missed goal in soccer, or him getting really angry when he was unable to get his own way or when he wasn't allowed another biscuit, the feedback sandwich will always help.

Avoiding arguing with your tween/teen son

Although teens' brain development means they can struggle to present a calm, logical argument, they certainly know how to press our triggers. They also have a lot of energy and their pent-up angst will often be projected onto parents who are a safer base than, for example, teachers at school or a boss at work. Remember the information from the earlier chapters about heightened emotional intensity, inability to see things accurately and a passion for making their own choices and you can understand why having an argument with a teen is an unwise thing to attempt, especially when they're under 16. Please keep in mind if your son is angry at you he is trying to communicate something, not deliberately trying to hurt you.

How to say 'no' to a request from a teen and avoid an argument:

- Often when they ask you for something that they really want, and which they also know may get a negative response – just know they are READY to argue their case!
- Listen to what they are asking. Clarify you have heard the request clearly.
- Pause and think about it and say 'let me give this some thought or chat with dad . . .'
- In a **quiet** voice, let them know you will give them an answer later that night.
- When they are in their room later, around 9 pm knock, pause – **always pause** – enter.
- Say your piece gently – 'sorry bud, the answer to going to the party is no'.
- Turn, leave the room and close the door.
- You can also leave giving the answer until after they have finished eating their breakfast and it is done equally gently.

    Ignore anything that is thrown at you as you leave
    the room as that is none of your business.

Remember, ruling with guilt, endless suspicion, withholding love, irrational fear and making personal attacks are all psychologically damaging to every adolescent regardless of age or gender. This behaviour will inflame the adolescent amygdala and they can reach the 'tipping point' quickly and unexpectedly.

If your tween/teen boy has an explosive moment verbally towards you, and maybe kicks the rubbish bin, slams a door or yells expletives, keep in mind he is struggling with big, ugly feelings and stress, just like a toddler except like one on steroids!

Please try not to take such outbursts personally – rather than firing a teen up any further it's better to hold the safe base that they need you to rest on. Sometimes these challenging times will come in clusters: around the end of term when they are tired, near exams or tests, or when they can't find a thing in their bedroom because their 'floordrobe' has exploded into total chaos. Things can be a bit more inflammatory when they have a growth spurt happening or they are feeling excluded and wounded in some social dynamic happening at school. They will be unable to make the mental link between these extra stressors and their need to explode emotionally at home. However, they will be struggling to manage their emotional barometer and could be close to their tipping point.

Many teen boys won't remember what they said in a day or two, however, we parents, especially mums, can recall them forever. Again, please remember the emotional barometer and that adolescents (boys and girls) need to discharge emotional angst or they may choose to numb the pain by doing far more dangerous things including intentional self-harm. Mothers (and some dads) tend to get a lot of this verbal discharge, so maybe reframe the discharge experience by first reminding yourself, 'My son is not bad, difficult, naughty or cruel. He is struggling to cope right now.' You could try thinking one of the following thoughts:

● Well hopefully he will be less likely to reach his tipping point now he has vented some of his feelings to me.

- I know he feels he can safely discharge his stress verbally at me because he loves me and I am his safe base.
- Imagine any uncomfortable words he's saying to you are just sliding off you like the proverbial water off a duck's back.
- I also used to wash my hands with lots of soap after a teen outburst as a way to symbolically cleanse any of the 'muck' that may have stuck to me. Weird I know, but I found it really helped to not take the discharge personally.
- This is just a phase – I have got this!
- Repeat this mantra often – 'let me be what my son needs right now – a safe base'.

The more you practise the above, the more it becomes automatic – and yes, it can become easier to cope with these really challenging situations. Resist the need to punish this behaviour as it will simply inflame the emotional intensity within him and it can escalate to him becoming even angrier. And often it will make parents even angrier and that is a serious recipe for disaster on all levels and connection is so important to our lads especially when they are struggling.

Often, the temptation will be for us to fight back or to attempt to 'coach' our sons in how to better defuse their anger but, trust me, the heat of the moment is not the time to do that. I am not suggesting either that you be a verbal punching bag for your son's slurs. There is a line between him safely expressing his feelings and him being downright verbally abusive – and you must draw that line. It's about timing again – you can leave the coaching till well after the outburst. Check out chapter 5 on emotions for how you can help him identify what's under that anger.

I intuitively knew that if one of my sons had an outburst like this, at some point they needed to be reassured that I had not stopped loving them. I want you to imagine what could be an olive branch you could offer your son sometime after one of these big emotional outbursts? What worked for me was around 20 minutes after the meltdown, I would gently knock on their door – often to no response – pause, then enter, quietly place a cup of Milo or hot chocolate or orange juice on their desk, with a sweet biscuit of some kind and then shove the dog in and tiptoe out of the bedroom, closing the door quietly. *This silent gesture powerfully spoke that we were all good.* Often later that night there would be either a mumbled 'sorry, Mum' or a silent hug or sometimes their physiology showed me they were sorry.

In his excellent book, *Brain Rules*, John Medina writes of the work of behaviourist John Gottman. According to Gottman, one of the best ways to manage a potential meltdown situation – especially with a young child who has poor executive function – is to acknowledge the child's feelings and empathise. The same goes for our tweens and teens who are also struggling with a poorly functioning prefrontal lobe. As I've said, adolescents, both boys and girls, often misunderstand body language and the words we say. They need to have their feelings validated, be heard and most of all be loved and accepted as they are, not just for *how they could be.*

After acknowledging and empathising, my next top tip is using 'I' statements rather than 'you' statements. 'I feel upset when the bathroom is left in a mess' or 'I am worried that I could run over your skateboard if you keep leaving it on the driveway!'

WHAT TO DO WHEN FAMILY CONFLICT ESCALATES

If you and your son are frequently engaging in very heated fighting and the situation is just getting worse, it might be time to seek some professional therapy to explore what is really driving that conflict. He is often not the problem; he is possibly being a mirror for you. Our own baggage from our adolescence may need some cleaning and airing. Problematic patterns from our families have a tendency to resurface and need to be healed and set free. A professional setting may help you and your son to find common ground and heal the conflict in your family. See your GP or a professional counsellor or coach who specialises in teens.

Being heard

Even though it doesn't look like it, at times our tween and teen boys are hungry for deep connection through meaningful communication and they yearn to be heard just like every other human being. Nothing bonds us together more closely or builds more authentic intimacy in our most important relationships than being heard and understood because this builds the three big things that matter to boys: acceptance, respect and love.

Just because our boys have a tendency to talk less as well as an inability to understand too many words that are spoken at once does not mean they don't have the same fundamental need to be heard.

Here are some phrases you might use to let your son (or another boy in your life) know you are really hearing him:

- 'Let me put this down so I can give you my full attention.'
- 'Wait a second while I turn off the TV/radio/computer, so I can really hear you.'
- 'Tell me more about this.'
- 'Awwww . . . really?'
- 'Wow, that's interesting . . .'
- 'Let me see if I understand you so far . . .'
- 'That must have been _ for you . . .'
- And all sorts of encouraging sounds that are not words – 'oh', 'ah', 'duh'.

To communicate that you are really listening to your son, use your body language: kneel in front of him as he speaks, lean in closer, put your head in your hands or sit really close to him. Remember, physiology speaks before you do!

Your most important words need to be about **acknowledging and then validating his feelings**:

- Failed Maths test – 'oh, that sucks' or 'oh, bummer!'
- Lost his school shoes – 'oh, that sucks' or 'oh, bummer!'

- Forgot his lunch – 'oh, that sucks' or 'oh, bummer!'
- Lost his library book – 'oh, bugger!'
- Forgot he had library – 'oh, bugger!'
- Missed the bus – 'oh, bugger!'

Sometimes if he seems quite upset you might need to say – 'oh, double bugger!' Then pause – no matter how much you want to comment – just pause and see what he wants to say next. By pausing, we are giving him the time and space to consider what has happened and what he can do about what has happened. If we jump in too quickly, firstly to express disappointment, you will shut down the conversation very quickly.

It is similar if a teen/tween boy comes to you with a problem he is trying to solve. *Every fibre of our loving, wise being wants to tell him how to fix it!* Encouraging him to explore and consider possible solutions is a part of developing the thinking skills needed for being an adult, not a child. *If you keep fixing his problems, he will never learn to fix them for himself.* It's also helpful to talk about plan A and plan B – to give him an idea that sometimes it might be the second idea that may ultimately work better than the first idea and that it's always good to have a plan B! This helps our boys to realise that making good decisions is not about making perfect decisions or always the right decision – it is about exploring decision-making and that practice will improve our decision-making capacity and ability.

At times, I offered to give feedback to my sons when it had not been invited, and when they said no, I respected that and said nothing. Saying nothing was so hard to do because I was busting to tell them how flawed their choice appeared to me! The occasional 'I am not sure that is a good idea' did slip out, but the tone with which I said the offending statement had a huge influence on what happened next. When you are able to maintain a calm, caring tone, you can definitely get away with a few small parent cautions without inciting a major reaction. If I said nothing at first as they refused my offer for feedback, often my sons came back a few days later and then asked me for the feedback.

Helpful suggestions at this point may be some of the following

- 'What thoughts do you have about this so far?'
- 'So, do you have an idea or plan to sort this out?'
- 'Do you think that will work well for you?'
- 'Do you need my help right now to sort out what is happening?'
- 'Let me know if I can help in any way.'
- 'I trust you to come up with a positive solution.'

Effective communication in problem-solving

Janet Allison of the Boys Alive! website and the *On Boys* parenting podcast suggests using the idea of apprenticeship when guiding boys. She shares a simple strategy that can work for both lighthouses and parents. Teen boys are often resistant to being told what to do, and using the apprenticeship idea sidesteps that unhelpful parent behaviour. It allows boys to become problem-solvers, with mutually agreed upon solutions, including consequences and rewards.

Janet recommends the following, along with the suggestion to pause often.

1. State the problem as a neutral observer. 'I notice that your lunch was left on the counter.' A good question for boys is, 'What's up with that?' or 'What do you think about that?' (NB not 'how do you feel?' . . . Remember to acknowledge any emotions that come up as being valid.)
2. 'How do you think your lunch could get remembered?' 'What can you do about that?' This is the time where all answers are acceptable – the more creative the better. Write them down if helpful.

3. When you've landed on an idea that you can both agree upon then it's time to declare the consequence and the reward. Again, all needs to be mutually agreed upon.
4. Decide how long you will try the solution – one week is usually good. Then agree that you'll revisit it if it isn't working and try another idea.

I definitely recommend writing this down for when you check in later so your son can remember the plan you decided on.

What if?

Another really powerful communication tool during the teen years instead of lecturing and nagging is to ask 'What if?' So, for example, if your son is really keen to go on a weekend camping trip with three of his mates somewhere out in the bush, rather than say no because it is too dangerous (even if that is going through your mind), give him some scenarios that you are worried about and ask him – what if?

For example, ask him what would they do if one of the boys became really ill in the middle of the night and they had no phone reception? What would they do if one of the boys was bitten by a snake? What would they do if they became lost when they went for a walk?

This gives our teen boys a chance to consider some worst-case scenarios and explore the choices they may make. After they have given their explanations, they are often more open to any other suggestions made by grown-ups. But if the grown-ups tell them what to do from the get-go, they seldom take much notice. This strategy is not only respectful, it is empowering and many teens, both boys and girls, are often quite well-informed about what to do in a crisis.

This same 'what if' questioning technique can also work around choosing subjects and managing organisational skills. For example, what do we do if you forget your lunch – because I'm not bringing it up to the school! I think each of my teen boys forgot their lunch at least once and I was intrigued to find they each had a different strategy to find food at lunchtime. Please try this questioning technique even before your son becomes a tween or teen if possible because it really does help our kids become problem-solvers!

Here are some more questions and suggestions that encourage conversations with boys of all ages.

- 'Does that feel fair to you?'
- 'Tell me what you were hoping to do.'
- 'How can we make this better?'
- 'What do you think needs to happen now?'
- 'Sounds like you/we have a problem.'
- 'Whose problem is this?'
- 'There is a problem here. How can I help you to sort it out?'
- 'Check it out inside. Does it feel right?'
- 'What were you trying to do here?'
- 'What would you like to do now?'
- 'What would a good friend do now?'
- 'I noticed that . . .'
- 'Now that's interesting!'
- 'Having a go is important; we can't all win!'

Post-it note magic

Given that we know boys zone out frequent requests and tend to forget things more easily than girls, there is great power in the Post-it note. Simply put a brief reminder on a note somewhere he'll see it – 'Dishwasher, bud!' 'Sport today!' 'Bin night – your turn!' 'Good luck on Maths test.' I would add a small love heart or smiley face. I have been known to add a note in my sons' lunch boxes to remind them they needed to walk home that day! Not a guarantee that it will work but it really can help with reminders that don't sound like criticism or nagging.

The digital equivalent is an SMS message – heck, how helpful is that for communicating with tween and teen boys? Not only do they look at them, when they respond you can avoid the monosyllabic, hard-to-decipher verbal messages. So essentially this is a digital Post-it note! I must warn you though, too many text messages and he will stop looking at them – don't forget a fun emoji if asking for something they would prefer not to do like an orthodontist appointment or his turn to do the bin!

Learning to apologise
The power of sorry

There is no question that there are no perfect human beings on our planet. Of course, there will be times that we yell, misinterpret our children, misunderstand what they want and generally bugger up. The old male-code told us that men don't apologise, it's a sign of weakness, but one of the most powerful things we can teach our boys is that when we make mistakes, we own up to that mistake and we apologise if need be. This shows them that this is the right thing to do. We need to teach our boys that saying sorry when we really mean it is a sign of courage and strength, not the opposite. It is also about taking responsibility for your actions, which is important for boys to learn. Our boys need to see the men in their lives – particularly their dads – apologise.

Forcing a boy to apologise can be problematic, however, and a genuine apology is very different to a forced apology. A genuine apology has a very real sense of remorse attached to it.

> Words like 'can't, ought, won't, have to and should' often negate growth and optimism. I would often ask my students to upgrade their language by using words and terms like 'I am, I can. I will, I choose' – and often their behaviour and grades would change to follow the language change! The words we use and the beliefs we have influence the way we navigate the world.

Final tips for getting teen boys to listen

- Build rapport first – with a gentle touch or calling them by a name that is a term of endearment
- Check the timing tips
- Match their physiology – what their body is doing . . . but not too much!
- Choose a gentle, low tonality
- Be comfortable with pauses and silences
- Use gestures to help them connect to what-where-when
- Give time warnings/suggestions around transitions
- Don't have an agenda before you start
- Remember, boys are communicating when they are not speaking
- Try whispering
- Give choices and request politely rather than demand or command
- Don't sweat the small stuff.

Finally, Andrew Lines of The Rite Journey has created a conversation-starting card deck called The Man Made Cards, which can really help parents have deeper conversations with their sons. Communication starts with being heard and, even better, being understood and every teen, especially boys, struggles with this. Hopefully, this chapter will help you communicate better with your son. Well, sometimes at least!

13

Raising boys with character who will care about themselves, others and our world

While this book is about teen boys, we obviously have to start thinking about raising boys with good character when they are very young.

When there is a bad news story about teen boys, it gets saturation coverage for days. These sensationalised forms of media reporting can incorrectly influence our perceptions about teen boys and masculinity in general. Not all boys are behaving badly and over the years I have met many who have stepped up to care for siblings, mates, friends and sick parents without a word of complaint.

EQ or emotional intelligence can be nurtured in childhood. Raising boys who care and who show emotional maturity before manhood can happen. In his excellent book *Mindsight*, Daniel Siegel explores a wide concept of the qualities that make up an emotionally mature person, regardless of age. Some of these qualities include attuning to others, being flexible in our responses, soothing fear, being empathetic, having moral awareness and being capable of using intuition.

Siegel argues that due to the plasticity of the human brain, we can build emotional and social awareness and competence at any time in life. This may be true but during adolescence, our tween, teen and early twenties boys really benefit from some emotional coaching in this area. There is no question in my mind that having caring parents, other family members, lighthouses and staff in high schools holds the key to building the emotional intelligence of our confused lads. Boys are watching the grown-ups in their lives and seeing how they interact with each other. Obviously, the relationship of their primary care-givers, their parents, is the major template that they will take forward into their own intimate world later.

Boys who fail to develop these capacities will tend to struggle in relationships and they will struggle to realise their full potential. They will also tend to grapple with poor health outcomes, addictions, mental-health issues and anger and aggression. I explore this in more depth in chapter 17 about relationships.

Modelling kindness, empathy and good character as parents is the first base! Fairness is a huge part of understanding how to care. Dr Matthew Lieberman has done research that shows that when we are treated fairly it ignites the same part of the brain as when we eat chocolate or have a drink of water on a hot day. It makes us feel good and so we get feedback from our brain when we are kind because it is always linked to fairness. So, ask your son when he makes a poor choice – 'Was that fair?' Cultivating an understanding of fairness early in life can be so helpful.

We can raise all our boys, both our roosters and our lambs and everything in between, to be caring when it matters. It is not just one thing that builds the capacity to care in our boys; it is the combination of many things done collectively with an intention to build the character that hides within every one of them.

Helping our boys to feel loved and connected
Healthy attachment

The first five years are an incredibly important timeframe to build the foundations to create a caring man. Healthy attachment is essential in raising boys who will care and it basically means a strong sense of being loved and valued. Of course it is wonderful if a boy has a loving mother and father to do this, however, the research shows it just *needs to be at least one significant, warm, caring grown-up who gives the boy a sense of having a 'safe base' in his life.* Boys are just as sensitive as girls and in some ways can be even more vulnerable to feeling abandoned and unloved. We need to prioritise loving little boys, often by showing rather than telling, and by disciplining with warm discipline rather than harsh punishment. The good news is that healthy attachment can be built during adolescence, especially early adolescence. This is one of the reasons why the roles of lighthouses and parents who never give up are so important.

Model loving touch

Our 'rooster' boys, alpha boys, are often lacking in empathy and can be seen as 'rough' and insensitive to others. Yes, they may have been born feisty with a heightened sense of their own self-importance, but parents need to work out how to put some lamb in that rooster before they get to school and again as they step on the bridge towards adulthood. My best suggestion for both these times is to get a guinea pig or a pet rat. With careful guidance from loving grown-ups, our boisterous rooster boy can learn how to be gentle, although it does take some time. Having him care for that pet by feeding it and cleaning out its cage is also really important to building a sense of responsibility for someone other than themselves. Building pathways to empathy is critically important in raising today's boys to become men with both backbone and heart.

The power of books and films

Prioritising reading stories that have messages about empathy and kindness is another powerful step you can do often in a boy's life. I used a lot of carefully chosen true stories because they definitely touched the hearts of the toughest of boys in my high-school classrooms. Please keep reading or telling boys true stories that open their hearts. You can also share stories together on long car trips, for example, via audio books and podcasts. The podcasting revolution has opened up a whole new medium for listening.

There are so many great classic films and TV series out there which touch on themes that adolescent boys can relate to. Here are a few suggestions to get you started: *The Karate Kid*, *I Am Sam*, *Pete's Dragon*, *The Never Ending Story*, *About a Boy*, *Good Will Hunting*,

Forrest Gump, The Fault in Our Stars, Love Simon, The Perks of Being a Wallflower and *Remember the Titans*.

Check-in moments

Whether your boys are young or adolescent, you can use bedtime as a time to build the habit of 'checking in', which means you ask them if they are doing OK or have any worries, even if they don't acknowledge it! No matter what he says always wish him goodnight before you go to bed, even if it is through a closed, locked door! Occasionally, you can still remind him that you love him more than all the hairs on all the bears and just let that sit with him.

Sometimes you may notice that your son is kind of hanging around in the kitchen or following you out to the laundry or the washing line and that may be out of character. I often saw that as a sign that my son wanted to have a talk about something. They can also have terrible timing and want to talk to you just as you are leaving for an important meeting or are running late for work!

Family values and expectations

As I've mentioned in this book, boys tend to have less efficient memories than girls and often simply forget what your family values may be, especially in the heat of the moment when they're having a lot of fun. Consider creating a very large poster with your family values in full view so that when your son makes a poor choice you can remind him gently what matters most in your family. The toilet is a great place for inspirational posters – no really, it is.

Prioritise kindness

When we are treated with kindness, it allows our nervous system to relax and the pleasant sensations from endorphins, often serotonin and sometimes oxytocin, to flood our body. It makes us feel safe, valued and connected. Avoid causing your son stress and distress because they have significantly negative effects on how children, adolescents and adults interact with the world. Consciously choose kindness often – even if it's counterintuitive. To boys, kindness = love! I cannot stress the importance of this during the tween and teen years for our boys because they get so little kindness and yes, they often deserve it less which is why it matters more!

Validate that big, ugly feelings are OK and indeed normal. Boys often struggle to articulate their big, ugly feelings and this can come out as anger or in some other physical expression like kicking or hitting. Helping boys to identify their emotions – well after they have had a chance to calm down – can really help them better understand themselves. Being empathetic and having the ability to tune into other people's emotional worlds is a really big part of being fair and kind and this can be really confusing for many boys. Remember when your boy is flooded with big, ugly feelings, allow him space and time before trying to help him.

Consider getting a good dog

A good dog can teach empathy and compassion so much better than us humans. Often stroking a much-loved dog can reduce your son's stress, make him feel loved and teach him to be gentle all at the same time. To be honest, the dog will always love your son unconditionally and never let him down, no matter what happens! Having a family cat is also a good idea because sometimes while patting the cat, it may suddenly bite or sink its claws into your son's arm. When he looks up and asks – 'What did I do wrong?' we need to reassure him that he did nothing wrong, that the cat simply changed its mind. I often joke that that experience will help him to live with women later in his life!

Go camping with family and friends

Removing our boys from their familiar environments and allowing them to connect more deeply with other kids and adults who are already a part of their lives can quite often be life-changing. Not only do such trips involve everyone helping each other out, the relaxed nature of the outing can reduce hidden stress levels in our kids. Quite often (especially when there's no wi-fi access!) they'll get out amongst it until they drop from exhaustion and so much learning can happen during those days.

Gather around campfires or fire pits

When people gather around fire, it seems to trigger a very ancient pathway of memory that sadly it seems TV and screens have stolen in our culture. The fire itself has a mesmerising effect, bringing people into a mindfulness state. Listening to people share stories, tell jokes and sing songs brings a strong sense of belonging to all who are present. The sharing of true stories often about challenging experiences is one of the most powerful ways that boys learn how to be good men who care. Seriously consider getting a fire pit at your place through these years.

Marinate boys in stories of men who care

Boys are so easily influenced in the early stages of adolescence that all of us who care about them need to prioritise the witnessing and the sharing of true stories of men who do good things – men who care. Orange Sky Australia, set up by two young men; the Burrumbuttock Hay Runners; and Samuel Johnson's Love Your Sister charity are just three examples.

Become a lighthouse or a mentor for a teen boy

The more people who genuinely care for them the better. See the section in chapter 9 about the importance of lighthouses.

Speak more with your elders, choosing good mentors is really important.

Community involvement

Many of our boys are growing up in their bedrooms in their digital communities. This means many of them are lacking the important growth and development that comes from being a part of a community. Many are struggling with social anxiety as they appear from their bedrooms in their late teens and early twenties because navigating the social nuances of life takes lots of experience. Help your boys be involved in something – anything from organised sport, drama or the arts, environmental volunteering, animal refuges, community or verge gardens, or simply helping their neighbours or their grandparents. Every single interaction makes them feel better about themselves and they will get that caring does matter. Modelling the behaviour we want from our sons is possibly more important than telling them about it!

Prevent access to the harmful and hurtful aspects of the digital world

Do everything you can to educate your son about how to navigate this crazy world with healthy boundaries. See chapter 18 on digital technology.

Rites of passage

Traditional kinship communities would all have a rite of passage for young people as they ventured into adulthood to help boys accept the ending of boyhood. There are many excellent programs now being run in schools thanks to the wonderful work of Dr Arne Rubinstein (Rites of Passage Institute) and Andrew Lines (The Rite Journey). There are many others also being run at a community level like Fathering Adventures, Pathways, The Fatherhood Project, True North Expeditions and others.

Help get high-quality programs into schools for teen boys

Around the ages of 13 to 15 teen boys are highly impressionable and easy to influence. If boys are immersed in positive experiences, they will become very different men to those who are immersed in the opposite. When boys are given an opportunity to be heard and to have some of their unhealthy perceptions deconstructed in a warm, respectful manner, they can be changed for life. It is my dream that every single boy in middle school will have the opportunity to experience the high-quality programs that are offered by organisations in Australia like Enlighten Education's 'Goodfellas' program, Tom Harkin's work and The Man Cave.

We need to speak positively about both genders

Unhelpful messages about either gender are to be avoided at all costs. Indeed, celebrating individuals as people, rather than people defined by gender is what is helpful for both boys and girls, especially during the vulnerable window of adolescence. Tweens and teens all struggle during this time of transformation and we need the foresight to not add to their stress by demonising them, calling them names, shaming them and disrespecting them.

Valuing cooperation and healthy competition

We must help our boys decode the 'man box' message about winning at all costs. Technically, competition is mostly about power, control and the need to be better than others. It encourages a 'me versus you' mentality, and in a way that helps boys to create separation rather than connection. In his excellent book *Dissolving Toxic Masculinity*, Thomas Haller explores the down side to competition among most boys.

The antidote to the toxicity of competition is cooperation. When we teach boys cooperation, they feel a sense of belonging and oneness, they learn to trust others, they demonstrate compassion for the differences of those around them, they communicate openly and honestly and they value building relationships.

14

Please help me with my unmotivated son

> The problem I am having is with my 14-year-old son who does not apply himself to his school work at all. He won't revise, study or plan at all. His grades are weak and failing in some major areas. He just won't apply himself and is lazy. In his own words he can't be bothered. And on top of that he refuses to acknowledge his body odour or wear clean clothes! Help!

This was a message we received via Facebook and it mirrors so many other messages that we receive about tween and teen boys. Remember this is not all boys. Some of them are incredibly motivated, especially around things that make them feel capable and worthwhile. Of course it is an exasperated mum who sends the message because she has tried everything to get him motivated and moving – to absolutely no avail. She feels she is failing him and wants to know what is the secret to getting her son motivated? I often notice a sense of urgency with these requests, as though the mother is running out of time to help her son. In this chapter, I will focus on the lazy, unmotivated boys in our homes and in the next chapter I will explore the issue of disengagement of boys at school.

Hopefully by now you will have a really good understanding of the biological, neurological, physical, hormonal and psychological changes that are impacting your tween/teen son. Remember that your son has an underdeveloped prefrontal cortex, the part of the brain that is responsible for helping with organisational skills, high-level emotional competencies, the capacity to plan for the future including studying for tests and delaying gratification. He does not have an adult brain like you.

Fact 1. No-one else can motivate us but ourselves.

Fact 2. The more you do for your son, including worrying, the less he has to do for himself.

Fact 3. Getting good school grades is really important for you but may not be as important for your son as being accepted by his mates and friends.

Fact 4. Opting out is a strategy often used by boys to cover feelings of inadequacy and a mindset that believes they are dumb.

Fact 5. Given all the pressures that are happening at school and outside of school your son may feel out of control, and by disengaging from the whole process, he is paradoxically gaining a sense of control.

Fact 6. Many boys prioritise things using the 'What's in it for me?' test and under 15 years of age, it is anything that makes them feel good.

Fact 7. You cannot force your son to be motivated.

Fact 8. Procrastination is technically a form of avoidance, not defiance.

Fact 9. You cannot speed up the development of the prefrontal cortex.

Fact 10. Your son might not be mature enough to manage everything that is being thrown his way – yet.

Lack of motivation can be a transient and temporary condition for most boys and is considered quite normal to all of us who have spent years teaching tween and teen boys. While a lack of motivation may be partly developmental, it can become a permanent mindset that stays with a boy right into adulthood. In his book *How to Motivate Your Child for School and Beyond*, Dr Andrew Martin argues that there is a significant statistical difference between boys and girls around a key facet of motivation. Boys are much more inclined than girls to sabotage themselves by putting obstacles in their own path to success. This form of self-sabotage can come in many forms including procrastination, avoidance, wasting time clowning around, or choosing to do fun stuff.

Dr Martin's research has led to the conclusion that there are eight critical factors that underpin boys' motivation.

1. Good relationships
2. Respect
3. Sense of humour
4. Relevance and usefulness
5. Ensuring mastery
6. Experiences of success and reward
7. Control and responsibility
8. Low level of fear.

Obviously, many of these factors impact our girls as well, but Dr Martin argues that they impact boys **more** than girls.

In psychological terms we are hoping to give ourselves the opportunity to develop autonomous motivation rather than controlled motivation – which may involve attempts at coercing, bribing or seducing our sons to behave in a certain way. In a way the turbulent early years of the tweens and teens are an opportunity for us to reset the goalposts of the way we interact with our sons. There are some who argue that today's intensive parenting has created many problems for our children as they launch themselves into the real world. The argument is you have done too much for your children and have left them less capable and resilient than previous generations.

The cost of a lost boyhood

I believe another thing that is contributing to the state of massive inertia that some of our older teen boys are experiencing has to do with some key experiences that they have missed in their boyhoods.

Most boys do still have an instinctual drive to be little warriors and adventurers. This can happen in their superhero play, or when they are building cubbies in the bush with their mates, or when they decide to swim in freezing cold streams in the middle of winter or spend hours climbing trees. They also have a tendency to want to wear shorts and T-shirts when it is freezing. Others enjoy racing mountain bikes, motorbikes or surfing – all real experiences where boys test themselves in so many ways. These real experiences give our boys many opportunities to take risks, fail and recover and develop a greater resilience to the bumps and bruises of life.

These experiences where boys stretch themselves and test themselves without a parent hovering nearby are innately important and healthy for them. Yes, sometimes they will hurt themselves when they make a poor choice but this will give boys the gift of a natural consequence. In other words, a boy will learn through pain that he is not invincible.

So many boys today are not given enough of these opportunities and when they miss these vital learnings, they lose the gift of finding courage within themselves. Please enthuse and encourage these acts of 'stretch and grow' and encourage them to climb high, use a power tool safely and camp overnight with their mates when they ask. Paralysing our boys with fear definitely crushes their innate sense of courage and motivation.

Loving and well-meaning parents can give their sons subconscious messages that they are incapable of managing themselves and that they cannot trust themselves to make choices – especially when they want to stretch themselves. This can lead some boys to create overly cautious mindsets and a distinct fear of failure. The warrior instinct can be weakened, possibly permanently. Ultimately this impacts their capacity to be resilient and confident not only as boys but as emerging men. Competence builds confidence and that builds the innate autonomous motivation that will start to appear as a boy heads towards 16 years of age. Without these opportunities or enough of them, your son could become the 18-year-old stuck on the family couch, feeling powerless to move his life forward.

Dads and other male father figures are seriously needed, maybe more than ever, to take our boys away from worried mammas and allow them to play vigorously, adventurously and to learn to deal with risk to help encourage their innate bravery.

> Also remember again to please make sure you prioritise teaching your boys valuable life skills around the house: how to do washing, how to hang washing out, how to bring it back in (even if it's still got pegs attached) and how to cook and clean. This does give our boys the opportunity to feel confident they can look after themselves. When well-meaning parents allow boys to skip the chores around homes, they can become lazy and even more dependent. Absolutely no-one wants that for their son!

Stickers and extrinsic rewards

There has been an overuse of praise, stickers and extrinsic rewards that have conditioned our children, including our boys, to expect that they need to be given something when they achieve something worthwhile. To be honest, I think the issue goes beyond parenting to the decrease in free neighbourhood play and the changes in our playgrounds when we removed long monkey bars. The way to conquer those long monkey bars was endless effort, lots of striving and failing and being motivated by something within us rather than something waiting at the end other than our own success. Intrinsic motivation is exactly that; it comes from within.

In today's worried world, it seems like many young people get stickers for just about everything short of breathing. This seems to be the downside of the warm, fuzzy self-esteem movement that came out of the US many years ago and it has left our parents and teachers confused. Have you noticed that children don't need to be given a reward for doing things like watching a movie they've been dying to see, or for eating ice cream or chocolate? These are activities that come with a built-in reward and they deliver the immediate reward of positive emotion.

In contrast, teachers and parents often encourage 'less desirable' activities such as learning or helping to clean up with extrinsic rewards that offer the immediate positive emotion lacking in the task. This has become an accepted practice. Children get lollies, chocolate, money and toys for helping out at home. They receive stickers for sitting quietly in class and grade As for handing in well-written reports. However successful this type of extrinsic motivation may appear in the short term, it ultimately inhibits a lifelong love of learning and it certainly does not build motivation in our children.

Such rewards also create competition. I've heard of some parents so focused on stickers, stamps and certificates at assembly they've complained to teachers because their child had only had one certificate while other children had received several. We are so determined not to upset our children that it has led to an irrational quest to make sure our kids 'feel good'. I would refer you back to chapter 10 on the importance of letting our boys fail and lose and recover for more on why it's important that they learn that life sucks sometimes.

One of the world's leading voices against competition and rewards, Dr Alfie Kohn, has explored significant research that shows that extrinsic rewards often end up demotivating our children.

While some extrinsic rewards can have short-term benefit, sadly there is a strong tendency for our children to come to expect them, particularly our boys who in a way reward themselves with a good dose of self-worth when they achieve well. If they get conditioned that they need an external reward from somebody outside of themselves, this could easily be contributing to the demotivation that many parents are finding in today's adolescent boys.

Eventually, our children and teens will need bigger and bigger rewards to do what we would like them to do if they haven't developed an inner locus of control that gives them an intrinsic sense of positive emotion. I believe a 'thank you', a wink, a quick hug, a pat on the head or thumbs up is so much better to validate the effort than a certificate or chocolate bar. These gestures are more an acknowledgement and encouragement than an external reward as such.

Building autonomy

Having high expectations; clear, consistent boundaries; and allowing our teens, especially our boys, some opportunities for autonomy are incredibly important. These things deeply impact the capacity for self-motivation. It's worth noting it gets easier to motivate yourself once your prefrontal cortex is complete, which for a boy may be in his mid to late twenties.

Much of chapter 12 on communication is geared towards giving you the language and communication style to support building the inner motivation of your son to do basic things. Putting rubbish into the bin, putting milk back in the fridge, doing homework as requested by the teacher and being organised enough to not only make their lunch, but to put the same lunch into their backpack are simple tasks that so many of our tween and teen boys seem to fail at often.

Even though I have already explored many reasons why boys can be more forgetful than girls, we do need to help them work out some systems that will help them remember for themselves instead of relying on us to endlessly remind them. Working *with our boys* at how we can help them remember better, maybe by writing lists. There is a big difference between endless nagging and gentle reminding.

For some teen boys, this stage of the brain pruning, when they experience an increase in forgetfulness and disorganisation, can be not only confusing but without an understanding of what's happening, it can be the biggest de-motivator ever.

I have worked with men in their late teens and early twenties, who are convinced that they are dumb as a consequence of this window of the development when they did struggle.

Boys are quite visual, so visual reminders on the side of the fridge of what is coming up in any given week can be helpful – especially if the boy is the one who writes down the events, not the parent. Teach your son how to write lists that are stuck up on the wall somewhere easy for him to see in his bedroom for what to take on PE days, after-school sporting events or music and allow him to wear the consequences of not following through on these things. If he has a phone there are digital reminders set up with some of the online calendars that can be really helpful too – until he loses his phone of course. (Maybe use reverse psychology here and get him to show you how to use the reminders on your phone.)

Positive noticing

Keep in mind that boys are always seeking an external experience with which to give themselves a dose of self-worth. When a boy succeeds in remembering his homework or his lunchbox make sure you acknowledge these events as they do impact how he sees himself. *If you don't notice in a positive and warm way, sometimes that can impact the motivation to keep doing it.*

Use encouraging phrases like, 'I noticed you remembered your PE gear.' Or 'I see you have your backpack and lunchbox ready.'

Again, this is the art of positive noticing – rather than endless questioning or overpraising. It is a subtle shift but in the art of building inner motivation, it is one tiny step at a time. We don't want them to rely on us to check up on them every time or to praise them every time they get it right!

UNMOTIVATED BOYS AND GAMING

Seriously, if you were a teen boy, do you think you would prefer to do your homework or prefer to connect with your best mates in a few battles of Fortnite after school? I am not demonising their love of gaming, however, we need to see how motivated a boy can be through that lens so that we can stay focused on what we need to do to encourage them in the real world. In high school, I think a really simple way to ensure your son does his homework is for you have an agreement that it needs to be completed before he gets to play online with his mates. If you have this expectation for every afternoon, without fail your son will learn to be motivated to get his homework done as quickly as possible. I want to say too that if your son is heavily into gaming (spending more than four hours a day solidly attached to his console, for example), refer to chapter 18 for more information about how to help and support a teen boy who has a problematic gaming habit.

Dr Adam Price has three Cs for motivation: control, competence and connection

Control

Over time we gradually give our sons the ability to control their own choices and consequences as they head off into high school and then beyond. Obviously, you would not throw them off the deep end and expect them to suddenly do everything without your support. I suggest you have a conversation and write a list about the things that you want him to develop capacity to do for himself. Let him prioritise that list and then start the training.

Competence

To develop competence, your son is going to need some practice. Sometimes becoming incredibly competent and having mastery over a task or activity at home can lift their confidence outside of home. Possibly you could train your son to be the best pancake maker, cook the best pizzas or be the best car washer in the family. The activity is not that important; it is that your son finds mastery doing an activity that will give him the self-worth he yearns for, which will lift his confidence in other areas. Giving your son an opportunity to do things, and to do them well, means we may have to step back a little. This will be really difficult for some parents – recognise that and then keep going.

Connection

This simply means that our lads feel attached or feel cared for, connected to, and have a sense of belonging with others. We really do need to look within our homes at how we can improve our relationships with our confused and stressed tween/teen boys. The secret to helping them grow in confidence and competence is buried in our relationships. Keep your warm, fair, fun and firm parenting happening while your son is gradually picking up his ability to take care of himself more. Some days you will see giant leaps forward, other days giant leaps backwards. Keep the goal in mind, and keep checking in with him as to how he is doing as he begins to master taking care of himself more.

When we step in and do it for him, we are lowering our expectations of his potential, and he will behave in accordance to that.

The drive to have a healthy, positive work ethic as an adult is often the end product of having these ingredients as a part of your family life and school life. We want to raise our boys to know the value of hard work, which gives them a sense of mastery or confidence (which will feed their sense of self-worth). We also want them to develop an awareness of working in the relational world of our workplaces both honestly and respectfully.

Sadly, what often happens is a lot of frustration from parents ends up in shouting and shame-based language, which then triggers your son's amygdala. That will make him feel he has to fight for his survival by fighting back, freezing or running away.

> For those of you who have sons who have special needs or who
> are neuro divergent remember this incredibly important message:
> keep telling your son that he is unique and that he will have something
> to offer the world – regardless of his extra challenges. Tell him loudly
> and proudly that he does not have to change to fit the world, that you
> will support him to find his place in our world that will allow him to shine.

Please help me with my lazy, unmotivated 18-year-old son who is stuck on the couch and going nowhere

It has only been in the past few years that I have started to hear from very frustrated parents about boys in their late teens who seem to be stuck or immobilised on their journey to manhood. I have previously written about the potential for teens to struggle in the months post high school, when the excitement of leaving high school and entering the real world can quite suddenly lose its shine, but this phenomenon is quite different.

These boys often come from loving homes and have not experienced any obvious personal trauma or had a problematic journey through school and yet they are stuck. Indeed, often these boys have had incredibly loving parents doing lots of things for them. However, the boys were both stuck and resisting any help!

Tips for helping a 'stuck' son

1. Reassure him that in time he will find a sense of direction and purpose – explain the brain maturity stuff to him.

2. Reassure him that he is here on this planet to make the world a better place in some way.

3. Explain that stuckness = inertia and so movement of some kind, no matter how small, every single day is going to help him. See the deal (page 275) for more.

4. Please don't nag him or force him to get a job. He will have very little confidence and this is too big a leap to start with. It will simply make everything worse.

5. If he is over 18, get him to take a tiny step which may be to choose a small training course like a first-aid course, a Responsible Service of Alcohol (RSA) certificate or barista training. Or consider a small volunteering opportunity.

6. Explore activities or things that he has enjoyed in the past and talk about making feel-good chemicals. If you can make a list of the top five activities that create positive neurochemicals, that can be really helpful.

7. Explore options that may help him build his fitness even if it is just walking the dog – and if you don't have a dog, consider getting one. Physical activity of any kind is incredibly valuable for both physical and mental wellbeing.

8. If you have elderly parents or neighbours, suggest they ask for his help to do something that they can't do.

9. If he's old enough and hasn't passed his driver's licence yet, begin that process – gently and gradually.

10. Some teens have done a one-day cooking course just for fun. Keep an eye out for opportunities like this.

11. Also start teaching your son how to cook favourite dishes. Start with pikelets as they are really hard to mess up.

12. Reach out to family or friends who live on a farm and might be happy to have him come for a short holiday to help out with farmwork.

13. If you know someone who is doing some renovations and might need some help, suggest your son.

14. Go camping with family friends.
15. Invite his friends over for a sleepover – often.
16. If your son is remotely mechanical, one of the age-old processes of boy–man apprenticeship work is restoring or rebuilding an old engine.
17. If you have a Men's Shed nearby, have dad or an uncle take him for a visit and see if he could start a project.
18. Teach him how to mow the lawn and use a few of your power tools.
19. Reassure him this is just a phase and it will pass.
20. Encourage him to consider redecorating his bedroom. Yes, it may end up black, but that's OK for now.
21. Fill his love cup in whatever way works for him so he knows that you are beside him cheering him along.

All of these options are about breaking the inertia of being stuck without putting undue pressure on him that could trigger more stress and anxiety. They are also ways to build those three Cs – control, competence and connection.

The last thing he needs is any more nagging, negativity or criticism because he is already doing that to himself. Gradually building his confidence one small step at a time within the family and within his boy 'tribe' can work. Prioritise compassion, kindness and endless patience – even when you want to scream! And as a last resort, there is always the secret weapon – a well-timed fart to put a smile on his face.

Give at least a month using the suggestions above and if he is still stuck, he may have slipped into depression so please have a mental-health assessment done with the family doctor and seek some professional support if you are worried.

Please remember that inside every teenage boy is a four-year-old boy who is confused about life and desperate to know that you will love him unconditionally, especially when he cannot love himself.

Sometimes boys who seem disinterested, unmotivated and just coasting, especially in middle school, can find a way to be a better version of themselves when their prefrontal finally grows. This Oliver is a great example.

I often share this story about one of my former students that serves as a reminder that school is not the be-all and end-all.

Oliver was a very quiet student in my Year 8 class who was illiterate and academically challenged. He would sit quietly and smile at me when I looked his way, but he didn't learn much due to the huge delay in his learning. I wondered how he was going to create a worthwhile life when he left school with so few skills. I remember lying in bed at night sometimes worrying about Oliver – how would he ever get his licence if he couldn't write or fill in forms? How could he apply for jobs? How could he fill in his Centrelink forms? I felt deeply that our school system had failed him as it fails many boys. We must remember that over 80 per cent of men in prison have low literacy.

Years later, I came across Oliver again. He was working at a service station – this was back in the good ol' days when you were personally served. He came out so enthusiastically when he saw me and filled my car while we chatted away. He wanted to know each of my boys' names and reminded me that I was his favourite teacher ever! He washed my windscreen, my side mirrors and even my back window. If he had had more time, I think he would have washed my whole car while it refuelled. As I drove off, I thought he had treated me special because I was his favourite English teacher.

The next week I went back and to my surprise, I discovered that I hadn't been given any preferential treatment. There was a tradie's ute in front of me and Oliver washed his windscreen, side mirrors and back window just the same as he had done mine the week before. Oliver treated everyone with the same enthusiasm and genuine human concern. When people drove away from him, they felt the world was a better place.

One day I noticed cars lining up on Oliver's side of the service station just so they could be served by him. People preferred to wait so they could experience this man doing what I then saw as unbelievably valuable work.

Later, I almost cried tears of joy when I pulled in to get fuel. There was an elderly person's home just up the street from the service station and I could see two elderly people with their walkers coming through the station. Out Oliver rushed with a cloth and he wiped over their walkers and chatted to them and patted them on the back. Their faces shone with delight as they toddled off. I then saw that Oliver was doing incredibly important, sacred work. On a daily basis, he was making a positive difference in the lives of so many people by being kind and caring.

Oliver may have struggled academically but somehow on his journey through his life, he had found his gifts and was sharing them with our world. How perfect.

15

Navigating middle school and high school

> I wish my parents had put less pressure and expectations on me and offered more support.

Formalised learning has been pushed down into early childhood over the last 5–10 years and many boys have begun their schooling journey with very negative mindsets about learning and education. Even boys who have transitioned well into big school can start struggling with engagement in Years 3 to 5 (and I suspect the massive lure of technology could have something to do with this).

Which school is right for my son?

If your son has not begun middle school yet (age 12 years) and you are making the decision about which school to send your son, may I caution you to think deeply before you commit your son to a particular school environment. Every boy is different and some school systems can be the opposite of what your son needs to nurture him in these incredibly confusing years. I have heard many stories of the reasons why boys have refused to return to school environments in these years, and I need to tell you that when a boy decides a school is not for him, that he hates it, the chances of him returning to that school are almost nil. Academic prowess, sporting competence, artistic talent, and giftedness technologically are all possible considerations when choosing a school for your son. Some schools have special programs to meet these talents while others don't. If your son has learning challenges, this needs to be another consideration when choosing a high school.

If you have the financial means to *choose a school that suits your boy, rather than make your boy suit a school, please do so*. If your son is interested and shows capacity in a certain area, consider going to a school that gives that area priority. Whether it is the arts, technology, soccer or music, giving your son the option of choosing a school around something he loves seriously has some merit. Part of the deal of attending a school of his choice is that he will commit himself to striving to do his best.

Also, seek out what other programs they are running that enhance student wellbeing, especially in middle school. It is often the extra-curricular programs that are run by passionate teachers that can really support your son to grow to be a strong, happy man. The year they turn 14 can be the trickiest year in terms of immature behaviour and the potential to disengage and to make really poor choices, and so having a specific wellbeing program can be life-changing. The Institute of Positive Education at Geelong Grammar School does this really well.

In this fascinating window of potential, your son's brain can make him learn really fast. This is when valuable life skills need to be taught – *through the wonder of real experience*. For example, Scot's College and Belmore Boys High School in Sydney both build in experiential learning. Wesley College in Perth runs a special program for boys of this age where for a whole year, boys are given incredibly practical experiences to help them grow and develop. The Katitjin program embraces the fact that boys go through a number of changes through adolescence that affect their motivation and engagement levels. Katitjin is a Noongar term meaning 'to listen and learn'. This program focuses on teaching life skills such as self-awareness, working in teams, leadership, engagement in the community and more. There are also camps associated with the Katitjin program.

School and the old man-code

Sometimes a school that has a strong patriarchal history can have an underbelly that still supports the old man-code. A good example is St Kevin's College in Toorak in Melbourne. In October 2019, there was an incident on a tram when a group of St Kevin's students were filmed singing a highly inappropriate, sexist song. Apparently, this demeaning song was well known as a part of the school culture.

Soon after, the school found itself at the centre of a new scandal. A former student, Paris Street, made public the sexual-grooming behaviour of former athletics coach, Peter Kehoe, that ended up in a conviction. The ABC *Four Corners* program discovered that in 2015 the headmaster, Stephen Russell, wrote a character reference for the coach after Kehoe was convicted for grooming. The dean of sport at the college, Luke Travers, also gave character evidence for Kehoe at the trial. Once made public, this showed the depth of the unhealthy culture that supported an offender and ignored a vulnerable student. Finally, action was taken and the headmaster resigned and Travers was stood down.

Please do not see this as normal in all boys' schools. I have been incredibly impressed with how many all boys' schools have transformed from the old-world view of an elite boys' school to one that is genuinely accepting of diversity and equity. Sometimes this disrespectful sexist culture was present in some co-ed schools in an all-male department. Thankfully, transparency has improved and things are definitely better for all staff and students.

There were moments when their vulnerability washed over me and I was wondering how we actually manage to get so many of them safely through to adulthood ... Their childlike naivety ... their dependence on their peers to define their behaviour, their desire to live in the moment and their associated unwillingness to plan all combine at a time when male hormones are raging through their bodies and the blood appears to be going down rather than up.

– Celia Lashlie, *He'll Be OK: growing gorgeous boys into good men* (2005)

Why school often fails boys and helps to demotivate them

In our test-driven system of education, the Holy Grail is graduating with high marks at the end of Year 12 as a precursor to heading to university for higher education. This overt carrot is dangled over students' heads right through primary school and so when our boys start to struggle, they also often see themselves as a failure because they are not going to be able to drink from the Holy Grail. We have a tendency to diminish the importance of vocational education and we need to stop doing that because the world is always going to need vocations as well as university-educated professions.

IF YOU HAD YOUR TEEN YEARS OVER AGAIN, WHAT WOULD YOU CHANGE?

I would have done vocational Year 11 and 12 rather than tertiary entrance subjects. I found the practical real world way of learning much more effective for me.

Many boys start to display school boredom around the age of 12. Educators like myself who have taught in high schools share the frustration of many parents around demotivated and disengaged boys, especially around the age of 14. In chapter 14, I have deeply explored the key reasons around why our boys tend to be only motivated while they are on their devices rather than in our classrooms! So, let's be clear – becoming disengaged and bored at school is quite common in the early stage of adolescence for boys particularly. Your son does not choose to do this intentionally, however, when it happens, it has a cumulative effect quite quickly.

Many schooling practices over the years have become feminised so they are more suited to most girls than boys. Continuous assessment, group work, increased desk time and less recess and lunch times, plus having access to phones at school, can all be difficult for boys. This is especially true for those boys who need to find success somewhere external or to use physical movement to build up the neurochemical dopamine that can really help them focus and concentrate.

Boys are also biologically wired to only want to participate in things that they perceive to be of value to them and that they have a good chance of succeeding at. As a former English teacher, I have had many long discussions with teen boys about the value of learning how to write an essay. Many of them believed that to be a waste of their time because they were hoping to be sporting heroes so they wouldn't need to write essays!

Sadly, our test-driven education systems are sending the wrong message to our boys: if you can't pass tests and do well academic-ally, *there is something wrong with you.* I believe this is a serious demotivator as our boys get into high school. We have always had a significant number of boys (and girls) who are not academically inclined but rather inclined to a much more competent use of their hands or their creative talents in positive and helpful ways that benefit our world. Parents and educators need to give our boys lots of messages around finding a fulfilling purpose in life, rather than just promoting an academic pathway to finding a meaningful life. Encourage your son to have dreams when he is little without the need to crush them. Be mindful how you behave when your son is playing sport or competing somewhere, to ensure that you are not giving overly enthusiastic messages about the need to win. Constantly give him messages about the need to have a go, and to participate even if he has no chance of winning. Seriously, this will really help your boy as he progresses through his adolescent journey.

Many 14-year-old boys are just 'cruising' at school, not striving to excel and yet hoping not to fail. Many boys also want to be achieving at a similar level as their best mates and so often it is simply 'not cool' to be achieving academically. While the temptation is to come down hard on your son with punitive measures and punishment, I have found that this often makes things much worse.

One of the reasons that our boys have a tendency to 'cruise' is because they cannot cope with all the things that are happening at once; they prefer to be goal-focused on one thing at a time. Research suggests that boys and men tend to prefer to be single focused rather than multi-focused and with so much happening all at once – body changes, hormonal changes and brain changes – this time is especially confusing for teen boys! Plus, this is the window of the natural awakening of sexual awareness and desire, and as the penis is outside the body, it can make some moments really awkward in the immature boy-soon-to-be-man. Maybe they are just focusing on survival, rather than striving for success. Remember they still do not have access to a prefrontal cortex that would help them to be more focused on striving to achieve.

Also keep in mind that at home these teen boys are struggling to remember things such as putting the milk back in the fridge or where they left their socks, and so they are coming to school already more stressed than they were before puberty began. Then you can add on hormones, poor sleep, hunger, or disorganisation in the moving dynamics of social groupings at school, and is it any wonder many of our boys lack enthusiasm and energy in the school environment?

To cover their stress and sense of inadequacy they create masks. There are many masks: the smart alec, the clown, the jock, the bully, the cool dude, the shy mouse usually with a long fringe hiding their face. They especially need this mask at school, as it is really much like a war zone for boys. There are so many rules, expectations, different teachers, classes and they are often being challenged to do tasks they are not sure they can conquer. Please keep this in mind if you have a parent interview and the teacher is concerned about behaviour that may be coming from your son's protective mask. It is his way of coping and without it, he might not turn up at all. This behaviour may be a sign he needs some guidance, some encouragement, or a check-in to see how things are going from his perspective. Show concern for him – not moral panic!

Mindsets or belief systems are formed by repeated experiences. So, by the time our teen boys get to Year 8 or 9, they have already been significantly bored and disengaged. They would have also been getting growled at, sanctioned and often punished for behaving in unhelpful ways in the classroom. These mindsets that develop (especially with the forgetfulness and the disorganisation) mean many boys start to really believe they are dumb, or stupid or that there is something stopping them from achieving well. Their expectations of themselves have plummeted from where they may have been in middle primary. Mindsets become self-fulfilling prophecies and this is why a lot of boys struggle to transition into upper secondary even if they are capable, because their experiences have convinced them otherwise.

WHAT WAS YOUR MOST CHALLENGING EXPERIENCE WHEN YOU WERE A TEEN?

- School, struggling academically. Not feeling like I had the ability to ask for help.
- High school assessments (solo) – getting started was always the hardest piece of coming up with a concept. Creativity was not my strong suit.
- School due to dyslexia and difficulties with social networking.
- Being at school and learning using methods to learn that didn't suit me.

- Not being able to make sense of school, couldn't see what I might use any of it for.
- Not being able to deal with the stresses of senior levels of school. I had found school easy until Year 11 and was not able to cope when workload and complexity increased. I chose to leave school at 16 instead of learning how to learn.
- I was uninspired with school; it seemed pointless and irrelevant for the most part, to me.
- School – studying wasn't easy as I was always distracted. Felt like I didn't get it. Ended up with ordinary grades. I was youngest in my class and felt other boys had a bit more experience.

Technology, gaming and school

David Gillespie in his book, *Teen Brain*, and Dr Mari K Swingle in her book, *i-Minds*, both explore how teen brains are getting wired differently, especially in those who have been gaming. Teachers today face a challenge verging on the almost impossible in trying to create stimulating and engaging lessons, with an overcrowded, often-irrelevant curriculum, and increased testing regimes for over-stimulated digital natives.

Increased technology in schools has put an extra challenge in our boys' learning. While it meets their need to be in charge of many aspects of a lesson, they are too easily distracted by what else they could be doing while on the screen, especially things that look like more fun.

Many middle-school teachers tell me it's almost impossible to monitor the ways that boys use their phones and screens in the class-room and many boys brag outwardly about accessing pornography and gaming while they are supposed to be doing school work! It is simply far more exciting and engaging for them to choose activities that interest them rather than doing maths or English.

This is a form of escapism from reality. Unfortunately, it is also not helping these teen boys to develop the emotional competences of delaying gratification, impulse control, persistence at a task and doing something less engaging for a goal that may enhance their capacity to improve their educational outcomes. Escapism from some of the more unpleasant, normal aspects of education definitely contributes to the unmotivated son on the couch a few years later.

When this is done over and over – especially from ages 12 to 15 – unhealthy escapism seriously compromises a boy's ability to mature or to develop helpful patterns of behaviour that will help him to set and then strive to achieve many life goals after he leaves school.

One of the good things about technology is that some students, especially boys, can find exceptional teachers who can inspire and engage them. Teacher Eddie Woo has become famous for championing his school's STEAM works (science, technology, engineering, arts and maths) learning space. Woo decided to give his students serious hands-on, powerfully engaging experiences to address real problems – exactly the type of stuff teen boys can get excited about. He bought robotics, 3D printing, virtual reality, drones and more for his program. He put them in the hands of students and gave them real-world problems to solve. Woo tapped into the creativity and problem-solving capacity of his students respectfully, giving them the opportunity to be in the driver's seat. This passionate educator has got thousands of students improving their maths ability, thinking critically, working in teams and communicating by using hands-on, task-focused learning opportunities. Let's hope this is a sign of a better schooling system for adolescent boys in the future.

Classroom behaviour

As I've mentioned in chapter 1, boys in this age group can be beyond frustrating thanks to their poor impulse control and propensity for connecting with their mates in physical ways. I have explored ways to deal with this behaviour in chapter 16. Gentle, repeated guidance is important. Even though this can be really annoying for hard-working teachers, so much of their behaviour is developmentally driven and most boys are not intentionally disruptive in class. This behaviour is about building bonds and connection and is a great way to counter-act the high levels of cortisol caused by boredom, lack of movement and being forced to do things they feel hold little relevance for them. They are seriously trying to create dopamine, the feel-good neuro-chemical, because the school environment keeps drowning them in stress hormones. So, in a way it is a survival technique. I am sure from time to time you've seen a man in a workplace environment do something pretty silly possibly for the same reason.

The biological wiring to belong with friends and peers is another factor that explains much of the Neanderthal-style behaviour that happens in many classrooms. So many boys of this age call out inap-propriate things in class: 'Look who's got a stiffie!' or 'Jenny farted, Miss!' To get all your mates laughing with you is incredibly important to the tween and teen boy. It means, 'I belong and I matter.' It also makes some positive brain chemicals that help them be less aggressive and angry.

This incredible pressure on our boys to stay engaged in something they see as irrelevant and boring is simply too much for many of them so, as I have written earlier, they opt out rather than have a go and risk failing. They opt out by only using the barest amount of energy possible or through complete refusal.

> Challenging behaviour occurs when the demands and expectations placed upon the child outstrip the skills he has to respond adaptively.
> – Dr Ross Greene, *Lost at School* (2014)

Dr Ross Greene has long been a champion for children who struggle behaviourally. He believes that schools need to improve their under-standing of the factors that contribute to challenging behaviour in kids and that the way that we help these kids is by being more pro-active than reactive. Punishing boys who are struggling to navigate the landscape is unhelpful and can indeed make the problem much worse. Helping to identify the core problems underneath inappropriate behaviour and using a collaborative, creative approach to problem-solving are much better ways of helping the students.

It seems some of the unhelpful generalisations from toddlerhood are still happening in our high schools. 'He just wants attention', 'he is a lost cause', 'he's manipulating us' and 'he has a bad attitude' are phrases still commonly heard when exploring a boy's inappropriate behaviour at school. Dr Greene argues that, much like with a toddler, we need to consider that these students could be lacking the important thinking skills that are required to make different choices in the school environment.

This is exactly what I discovered in the classroom over 40 years ago. It was not that they *wouldn't* make better choices around their learning; it was more they *couldn't* make better choices. Some of the key areas I identified challenges in were transitioning from one learning opportunity to another, working out a logical sequence to do a task, maintaining focus for the duration of the task, and definitely confusion with understanding what was required of them – despite my best intentions and explanations. I found that by breaking down some of the learning requirements into predictable steps, and then scaffolding on top of that, boys started to be able to complete tasks that had previously been beyond them. I also found that building the social cohesiveness of classrooms with different fun activities certainly improved the sense of safety for the struggling boys in my classrooms.

I found that over time having no putdowns, reaffirming respectful behaviour, and gently reminding the struggling boy rather than shouting or using punitive measures diminished the common difficulties as the environment felt safer. Often these boys would ask for help when they were struggling with a task or were confused about an outcome. Mutual problem-solving was not only respectful, it was really beneficial at helping these boys find solutions to things they struggled with, rather than avoiding, escaping or just opting out or expressing their inner angst with inappropriate, often physical, expressions. These are all survival strategies driven by the amygdala in the underdeveloped brain.

Boredom, being threatened by figures of authority, lack of movement and being asked to do things that they consider have little relevance to them are serious good brain-chemical killers as I have already explained. Sadly, this is the system we have and the system your son will have to navigate. See below for tips on how to help your son at school.

TEACHING OUR BOYS ABOUT HEALTHY BOUNDARIES: THE LINE ON MOVEMENT

I like to use the metaphor of a line in the sand to teach boys healthy boundaries. Given that many boys need plenty of movement to create enough positive neurochemicals to feel good and reduce stress, it makes sense that so many boys wriggle, fidget and walk around randomly in our early childhood settings, primary schools and secondary classrooms. So many of these boys are made to feel bad and naughty when they are unable to keep their bodies still.

We need to teach our young lads about the need for healthy boundaries while acknowledging their biological need to move. Teachers need to give them options of how they can move their bodies without disrupting other students.

We can teach them that they may quietly tap their foot on the floor, or jiggle their legs or maybe they could choose to do some random doodling to help them stay seated when the teacher needs them to do so. Random walking around classrooms can be crossing the line and leaving the classroom without permission is definitely crossing the line.

Labels

I have written extensively about my concerns about how harshly many boys are spoken to as soon as they enter our schooling system. They are often shamed and spoken to much more abruptly than girls in the mistaken belief that they are somehow tougher. This creates enormous scars which they can carry very deeply inside. Not only are they called names like 'stupid' or 'idiot', they are often given less affection as well. Something else that can contribute to boys giving up on trying to make better choices is labels. Labels like 'troublemaker', 'naughty', 'the bully', 'geek', 'wimp' or 'sissy' – which often start when boys are young – definitely contribute to a mindset that can make it even harder for a boy who often makes poor choices. Some boys simply stop trying to be otherwise, because of the power of a self-fulfilling prophecy. I have worked with teen boys who wanted to stop being the bully and while their intentions were noble, it seemed that the label was stuck on pretty hard and it was others who made it difficult for them to become something more positive.

We need to keep in mind that there is still a strong conditioning that boys must hide their feelings of vulnerability or distress, especially in social settings. It's easy, then, to understand how many boys just simply get confused and lost in our school systems. Sadly, they are often disciplined harshly for such behaviour when what they really need is some help, support and guidance as explored by Dr Greene.

They are often labelled troublesome and naughty and we know the power of a self-fulfilling prophecy!

BOYS WITH ADHD AT SCHOOL

For boys who are neuro divergent with dyslexia, autism or ADHD, high school becomes a really big struggle. Navigating the unique challenges of how they see, interpret and process the world on top of the increased stresses of being a rapidly changing teen, makes it particularly difficult for these students. Unfortunately, the world is still trying to fit them into the square box of expectation of other students, rather than finding ways to tap into their unique strengths while in our school systems. Schools are under-resourced to support these special boys. Some schools run fabulous programs that enable these boys to shine, however, they are often hard to find in mainstream schooling. Even if a teen boy is non-verbal and has autism, he is still going through puberty with many of the

---

same unique hormonal, physical, psychological and brain changes. He is also awakening sexually and he can struggle even more than a boy who does not have these additional needs in his life. It would be wonderful if all schools were trained in Dr Greene's approach to understanding better ways of helping struggling students overcome their challenges and thrive. The traditional discipline and behaviourist policies have not been working for a long time.

Many boys who struggle with ADHD feel they are labelled very early in their schooling as being troublemakers. Rather than trying to punish them for behaviours that often happen as a consequence of having ADHD, it would be so much more helpful to work with these boys to help them with their distractibility, and their inability to stay focused and to self-regulate. The same goes for many neuro-divergent boys who have other challenges in group settings. ASD is unique for each child and hidden under the challenges are often incredible strengths. If found and given focus, these students could be given opportunities to fill their self-worth barometers more easily. One thing I know for sure is the safer the environment, especially the teacher, the easier it is for these boys to cope.

Supporting boys at school

Clark Wight is a passionate educator who really understands boys. In a deceptively simple way, he reminds parents of what they can do as their boy begins the journey over the bridge.

These are his top tips.

Help your sons feel:

Seen – this is not just seeing with the eyes. It means perceiving them deeply and empathically and sensing the mind behind their behaviour.

Safe – we avoid actions and responses that frighten or hurt them.

Soothed – we help them deal with difficult emotions and situations.

Secure – we help them develop an internalised sense of wellbeing.

Notice it didn't recommend that you:

Solve – fix all their issues.

Shoot the messenger – blame school, another family or other kids for telling the truth.

Smother – overprotect.

Sarcasm – laugh at or disregard their fears.

– Clark Wight, Raising Gorgeous Boys to Become
Good Men conference, Perth (2017)

Rites-of-passage programs

Many years ago, boys who were not performing academically would often leave school at 14 years of age and be made to work alongside men who would teach and guide them to learn a craft or a trade. This mentoring was a slow, very practical process that taught boys not only trade skills, but how to be responsible and accountable.

In time they would see the benefits of learning those various skills, which could also give them an income and the freedom to make choices about how to spend that hard-earned money.

Today, many of these boys are often made to stay in school until 17–18. They are frustrated, bored, feeling like failures and often disruptive and rebellious!

Boys have a tendency to need to seek self-worth or personal self-validation through an external experience or event. When their school environments are unable to provide opportunities for all boys to feel like they are achieving some success, they are effectively setting boys up to fail at a vulnerable time of their life.

There are other programs being run in our schools that are now recognising how important it is to give boys real experiences, to get to know themselves and to make some serious growth.

- **The Rite Journey** is a program created by teacher and educational consultant Andrew Lines where boys can step forward in their lives in a form of rite of passage. This program promotes exactly the challenges and meaningful education required, especially during this difficult year, that can enhance your son's maturity. If you can make the time, please check out the documentary on the ABC Compass program that follows a group of boys as they head off on their quiet wilderness challenge through this program. Christian Brothers College in Fremantle in Western Australia runs a version of this program and part of it sees the boys spending 24 hours alone in a tent with no distractions, pondering who they are, and who they want to become. When they return, they have made themselves a commitment to become someone they can be proud of.

- **Duke of Edinburgh awards program.** The award is a carefully crafted program focused on individual challenge that covers four different areas: voluntary service, skills, physical recreation and adventurous journey. Each of these is designed to stretch participants through persistence and determination so they can find their own hidden depth of character. The award is also available for your son outside of the school system, so give that some consideration as well because I believe it is a really worthwhile program that will encourage the growth and maturation of your son.

WHAT DO YOU WISH YOUR PARENTS HAD DONE DIFFERENTLY WHEN YOU WERE A TEENAGER?

- My parents were very laid back and let me run my own race. In some ways that was fantastic, but in others I wonder whether I would've benefited if they challenged me more, especially with regard to my studying routines.

- I wish they'd found a way to encourage me to study. As my parents were not educated, they didn't show me the importance. I was smarter than I was given credit for.
- I wish my parents had been more involved in my school work; they thought I was tracking OK so they didn't interfere. I was doing well but could have done better if they had pushed more or given more support.
- I wish they'd supported me more academically, and pushed me harder in school and with sports. That said, I lived in a large family and there's only so much time to go around. My parents were always there if I needed them for cuddles or whatever, but I could have achieved more at that age rather than leaving most of my academic or sporting achievements until later in life.
- I wish they'd put more pressure on me about schoolwork.
- I was told to do my homework and try harder. But I never listened, as most kids don't. I always ask myself if my parents were more forceful, would I have done TEE [end-of-secondary-school exams in Western Australia]? Would I be doing my dream job? I know it's my own fault. But when I think about what if and where I could be today, I resent them a bit for that.
- I wish my parents had helped me more in persevering with my school work.
- I wish they'd got me some help for my learning difficulties instead of allowing me to leave school.
- I wish my parents had been more strict with homework and got involved in my academic life. Support, encourage and care.

Parenting boys at school

While it is important to support boys as they go through high school, we must still remember you cannot force them to work harder or be more focused. Early in middle school, it is important that parents, particularly mums, step back from over-organising, over-reminding and even helping with their son's homework and assessment tasks.

> Stop doing homework for your son. Finishing your son's homework or helping with their assessments is actually not helping them. In actual fact, it is doing the reverse. It is making them dependent on you rather than themselves and it can make boys quite lazy.

Your son needs to experience the consequences from school of not completing his work. I have had mums gloat over a grade that their son had achieved on an assessment task that the mum had completed. If the son has not completed it, very little learning has occurred. No parent can sit in the classroom when their son is completing an examination and do it for them. The sooner you accept this reality, the more likely your son will realise that it is up to him. Obviously if he is struggling, with the help of the teacher or the year coordinator, you will need to help him identify what may be underneath those challenges and yes, you may need to get him some extra tutoring or help. Homework wars do not need to happen. Your biggest challenge will be managing healthy boundaries around his digital world rather than completing his work for him.

Teachers

Boys hunger for positive relationships with teachers (as do girls) and they tend to thrive more when they feel a teacher not only cares for them but respects them. Maybe having a positive relationship with a teacher allows a boy to feel less stressed in the classroom environment and that may be another secret as to why many of our boys are not achieving as well in our current educational climate.

Boys suffer when they feel disliked, misunderstood and disrespected by their teacher. As a parent, there is very little you can do if your son finds himself with a teacher like this. He will struggle in this class, no matter how often you might explain that one day in the workplace, he may have to work with someone similar, and that this is a life experience that can be valuable.

What to do if your son dislikes his teacher or feels they dislike him or he is going through a tough stage with school

- Be a safe listening post
- Validate his frustrations
- Still encourage him
- Keep affirming your expectations that he will do OK once the tricky stage of being an early teen passes.
- Reassure him that you believe he has what it takes to do well at school. The key is not to over-sell the idea that he HAS to do well at school – that can trigger his fear of failure and he may opt out!
- Focus on and be grateful for the fabulous teachers.

Definitely check in with him if he needs any support like a tutor or a better place to do his homework – without reminding him to do homework or pressuring him or lecturing him. He must learn from his own endeavours or lack of endeavours, or he will need his parents forever to push him!

Expectations

> **SOME THINGS THAT ANNOY TEEN BOYS ABOUT EXPECTATIONS**
>
> - The pressure I have to succeed at school because my life depends on it
> - Academic pressure (Being expected to do more than what you can handle)
> - The workload of school and the pressure and stress that has been piled onto my shoulders all over whether I will succeed and pass or not
> - Not meeting expectations

Hopefully after reading this book, you will be able to set appropriate expectations of your son as an individual and within the context of what is actually normal behaviour for a teenage boy, considering the biological, developmental and hormonal changes that he is going through and has no control over. Expectations influence behaviour and they need to be the right blend of positive and high. But when they are too high, some boys can drown and then struggle with an overwhelming sense of failure and of letting parents down.

Some expectations are passed down in families and are quite simply unhelpful for boys, and yet they can influence them invisibly and deeply.

If a well-meaning family member says something like, 'Oh, John is just like his dad and he struggled at school, so John will too,' they are expressing a low expectation and contributing to the creation of a low outcome for poor John.

Also, when I was teaching, I often spoke to parents of high-school boys at parent–teacher meetings who held similar low expectations for their sons because their dad hadn't done very well at high school. In a way, this is where boys' school disengagement can become a bigger problem when both parents and teachers support the same low expectations.

Coming from an Asian background we had high expectations of having good grades and helping out the family business (local store). I found it difficult to balance both while trying to have a social life and do the things I wanted to do. When I finally left the family business and found my own employment, there was an expectation to financially assist Mum and Dad. This was challenging as I began university and wanted to find my own place in this society.

Re-engaging reluctant boys

Helping your teen son keep a previous passion from primary school or find a new passion can be the vital catalyst that he needs to re-engage. We must help them find a spark and keep it alive even if it has nothing to do with schooling!

Choose active subjects

For many teen boys they can feel trapped in the four walls of mainstream classrooms. Encourage your son to take the core subjects, maths, English, science and social science, and then choose any other subject option to get them out of the four walls that keep them sitting! My sons eagerly did this and took options like fishing, water safety, surfing, outdoor education, mountain-bike riding, pottery, jewellery making, cooking, archery and robotics. Some lucky lads can actually find the passion of their life by sampling the smorgasbord that high school offers.

School environment

It is interesting to note the re-engagement of reluctant boys back into learning that occurs when a school creates a more adventuresome play space outside, especially for our late-primary and middle-school boys. Many high schools are putting in rock-climbing walls; high ropes; ninja courses; multimedia opportunities for creative music, film and documentary making; and setting up board game and table tennis tournaments! These are seriously positive things to help boys want to come to school. As parents, please consider joining the parent body and be an advocate for these outside curricular activities to happen.

Some high schools use therapy dogs and have noticed when they become a part of the school environment that boys become re-engaged in their schooling again. In other schools, getting boys actively involved in vegetable gardens, maintaining sporting grounds and even having sheep and chickens within the school grounds has seen a massive shift in their interest level in the school environment. These experiences trigger dopamine and an interest that breaks the boredom, and it is more fun being out of the classroom.

Strategies for motivation

Using **sporting metaphors** often works really well for many tweens and teens. Some final-year boys who I have worked with were considering giving up because they were worried they would not achieve the results they desired, or what their parents had hoped for, found some sporting analogies really helped. They would co-create their own sporting analogy and some of the boys who played football chose to use the metaphor of the last two terms of the year as being the final quarter in a grand final. They wanted to finish the game by kicking a goal on the siren. Fascinatingly, some of these boys won subject awards at their graduation – most unexpectedly! For others, it was seeing themselves in the last 10 metres of a 400-metre run, or the last kilometre in a marathon – the metaphor sets them up to seeing the end is in sight and the rest, well, that's a special kind of magic.

Another strategy that I've often used to help teen boys reach goals they strived for, whether that was sporting, academic or in the arts, was **creative visualisation**. If you cannot visualise yourself achieving your goals by imagining them, as vividly and frequently as possible, then there could be an invisible blockage or self-sabotage that is preventing you from succeeding. While I was still teaching, I created specific creative-visualisation audio tracks to help students get the best report they ever had and to reach success in whatever area they were keen to succeed in. Over the years, I have created many creative-visualisation tracks that teens and adults have used to help them realise their highest potential. When my sons were hoping something good might happen, they used to get sick of me saying, 'Have you visualised it yet?' I remember a 14-year-old boy asking me if this 'weird stuff' could help him kick more goals in soccer. I suggested why didn't he try it! The following week he came running in on the Monday morning to tell me he had kicked three goals at soccer on Saturday and his beautiful smiling face was such a joy to see.

School is not engaging – teachers don't accommodate different learning styles. Enrolled in school excellence program but I find it boring and frustrating because the learning environment is not inspiring me to achieve what I know I can.

Motivating your son at school: the deal

The deal is a very clear agreement with your son with a timeframe, and yes, there will be a much-wanted, one-off explicit reward. Boys can often get confused when parents say they want them to 'lift their grades', or 'do better' in maths or 'try harder' at school. Sorry, these phrases *lack the serious specifics* that your son needs to have. Specifying what is the target, how will I know if I've hit it and what do I get as a reward is a way of fine-tuning that vague language into something doable. I encourage parents to make the reward be less about the monetary value of the reward and more about an experiential reward that includes his friends, as that is something that can create positive memories. I have also noticed that mates often copy their striving mate and this can be really helpful. In many middle-school environments, striving to do well in your school subjects is not always something to be admired by the pack – especially the cool kids. This pressure, commonly called peer pressure, has been around since time began and so what happens at home can, with your support, make a positive difference.

THE DEAL

1. **Set the target** – lift his maths grade from an F to a C. Avoid aiming too high, too soon.

2. **Draw up the plan** – map out what afternoons he has maths homework, and his maths assessments, if possible. This way he has a clear, visual reminder of important things so they have less chance of being forgotten.

3. **Support him** – get in the habit of providing a snack, a drink, shoulder rub or a non-verbal thumbs up of encouragement to support him anchoring in his new habit.

4. **Ask for help** – normalise your son asking a teacher for help if there is something he is struggling with.

5. **Feedback** – ask your son to ask his teacher for feedback each fortnight on how he is going and what else he might do to improve.

6. **Reward** – help your son to choose a significant-enough reward so that he has something to look forward to at the end of this deal, and which includes his friends or mates. Maybe a movie night, or a night out tenpin bowling or even better a weekend camping trip.

If he doesn't achieve the specific target even though you can see that he really did try very hard, it's okay. You might be surprised how well boys can accept this – and knowing that failure can teach them something and that it doesn't define them also helps. He just needs to make another plan or goal.

Transitioning to senior high school

The transition from middle school to upper high school, particularly the increased academic pressure, can be quite a big shock for even the brightest of boys. My oldest son came home about three weeks into Year 11 and said he thought he needed to change to a vocational course. Everything inside me was screaming, *don't be ridiculous!* Thankfully, I have witnessed this with other people's sons and have talked many young lads through the same frightening transition. It gets so much harder so quickly that the fear of being a failure gives them an irrational need to change course. I gave my son a couple of weeks before we reconsidered his request and by then he had found 'he had got a grip on it' and that he was OK. He is now a highly competent and successful lawyer – and he nearly sabotaged himself at 16 years of age!

May this chapter be a poignant reminder that school is just a small part of our lives and even if our sons struggle while they are at school, there is a whole lot of life after that. Please try not to panic that they are running out of time to do well academically. *They are never defined by the grades they get at school.* Please keep reminding them of that. To be honest, most of our life's learning happens in the school of life and we must remind our boys that they are the captains of their own ship. As they gradually head into their twenties, we want them to walk with their head up high, with people they love nearby, being brave enough to take measured risks, recover from the setbacks and the disappointments, while always looking for something that matters to them and finding a way to do that, while earning an income to live in a way that allows them to be healthy and happy. Simple, eh?

WHAT ADVICE DO YOU HAVE FOR TEEN BOYS TODAY?

- Do what you are passionate about rather than what you think other people might think is a good idea. A career path should be what you look back on rather than what you plot when you set out.
- Failure is the best teacher and should be celebrated not apologised for.

16

Fragile boy friendships and what can help

Friendships matter at any age. As humans one of our fundamental primary needs is human connectedness, whether in families or outside of families. From my own childhood, through to my teaching and counselling work and as a parent raising four lads, I have learned a thing or two about boy friendships.

Boys can struggle to understand the nuances of being a good friend; indeed many find it confusing and often their attempts to show affection or a desire for connection end up in moments of public embarrassment.

Differences between boys and girls with friends

A study into friendships by the National Institute of Mental Health (NIMH) and Georgia State University using fMRIs (Functional Magnetic Resonance Imaging) was the first time scientists looked at what actually happens inside the brains of children (ages 8 to 17) in response to potential friendship opportunities.

The results showed a significant difference in the way boys and girls respond to the anticipation of making a friend. Various areas of girls' brains (areas associated with reward, hormone secretion, social learning, and subjective feelings) lit up with the prospect of a new friendship, while the boys' brains showed almost no activity and even, in some cases, decreased activity.

There are many ways to interpret this information, and scientists are reluctant to pinpoint causation, but it's safe to say that there's a lot going on for girls in the face of friendships. It may also suggest why many boys struggle in the friendship world. It also suggests that we need to support them on this journey as best we can and not just assume that it will happen in a way that is similar to girl friendships.

One of the world's leading boy experts, Dr William Pollack, author of *Real Boys: rescuing our sons from the myths of boyhood*, believes that girls communicate more, seeking attachment indirectly through activities or play. Quite differently, for boys to develop the same sense of bonding, they need to spend significant amounts of time playing with other boys – essentially in physical proximity.

Why might boys be struggling today? The play code

Pioneering play researcher Dr Stuart Brown has written and spoken extensively about the importance of children developing a 'play code', which can only be developed with hours of play with other children. The endless hours where boys play with freedom and autonomy are building the capacity to be able to read the invisible cues of friend versus foe.

This play code sets up an intuitive awareness that can be carried through into adulthood, and which can help us sense when we are in an unsafe place or when we are near unsafe people. Some think that the increased violence on our streets is a sign of a diminished play code in grown young men, especially those who have been senselessly violent – aka the coward punch.

> Without a play code, we can badly misread social situations and interpret a threat incorrectly and without the ability to defuse the situation.
> – Dr Stuart Brown, *Play: How it Shapes the Brain, Opens the Imagination, and Invigorates the Soul* (2009)

Friends as a safety net

The best thing about being a teen boy today is . . . Having some close mates to be able to help with little things you're down about.

Knowing no-one and being in an unfamiliar environment can trigger a tween or teen boy's survival instincts. Remember that his amygdala (or threat centre) is already directing his life experience, not his prefrontal cortex! Moving schools into middle school or senior school or even vocational education or university is a huge change experience that will trigger stress.

Until this environment feels familiar and predictable, a teen boy will struggle with daily anxiety and high levels of stress.

One of the best buffers for this stressful time is having friends doing the same thing. Boys who have friends with whom they are transitioning to a new situation tend to transition better than those who do not. Transitioning into a new school without friends while having the deep, almost irrational need for friends can mean they may form friendships that may not serve their best interests. This is when having a strong play code can really make an enormous difference in the friendships that boys form.

Some sage advice about the importance of friendships is also really valuable at this time. Encouraging young people to watch out for their brothers, sisters, cousins or friends at all times sounds like an easy thing to do. Family and friends are so much more important than young people realise. The village of connectedness can be such a powerful protector for our transitioning young adults because this is their safety net.

I have found that it is within these 'tribes' or 'villages' that boys have the best opportunities to form meaningful friendships as there is frequency of exposure, often in similar environments where the boys feel emotionally secure. We should understand the value of holidays in the same campsite or endless hours at a grandparent's house where cousins can play together for significant time as seriously important pathways to building deep connectedness and affection.

Unfortunately, boy friendships in real time have become less common than before the digital world arrived. While there is research that shows that playing video games can boost young people's social wellbeing and have many positive impacts (playing games with mates and friends can be a positive for boys with less confidence or who have social anxiety), the same researchers caution that 'excessive or obsessive' gaming will undo any such benefits. Neighbourhood play has declined drastically over the last 10 years and this is definitely impacting our boys in their ability to form meaningful friendships with the kids who live nearby. Indeed, most boys do not even know who their neighbours are.

The more time that they spend in proximity to other boys, the stronger the bonds of friendship form. Indeed, do everything you can to create opportunities for tween and teen boys to be able to meet the same psychological needs that gaming does. Take them camping, go for movie nights, board-game tournaments, weekend hiking trips, mountain bike riding trips, geocaching, trampolining, paintballing, local music festivals or concerts, or plan to set up a massive waterslide somewhere in your community! Setting up a fire pit in your backyard may quite simply be the best thing you've ever done to help your son connect better to his friends. Support your son's passion for music even if you have to surrender your garage to his drum kit. Opportunities to have engaged playful experiences where they have heaps of autonomy and freedom can be incredibly bonding. Encourage your high school to send your students – of either gender – on wonderful outdoor experiences that may include some risky things like rock climbing, high ropes or snorkelling! Simply prioritise time and space for boys to hang out together.

Sadly, it is not only that the play code has been weakened in the last 20 years. The pressures, often invisible, of the man code seem to still prevail strongly. These pressures encourage the need for boys to prioritise dominance, to show no pain, 'to take it like a man', and to silently suffer many experiences that are considered an acceptable part of boy culture. This causes many boys long-term, deep, shame-based wounds that can create problems as they begin the journey to manhood.

WHAT WAS YOUR MOST CHALLENGING EXPERIENCE WHEN YOU WERE A TEEN?

- Learning how to react and cope with ragging/teasing. Once I learned that process of not reacting or getting upset and developed a resistance or thicker skin, being a teenager was much easier and more enjoyable.
- Having a bad bunch of friends and trying to break away from them.
- Understanding that not everyone had to like me and it was more important to be a decent person.
- For me, it was the fear of loneliness. I constantly wanted/needed friends around me to distract me from feeling alone. I wasn't happy with who I was as a person. I wasn't comfortable just hanging out with myself.
- Finding a social group to fit in with (I didn't find one).
- Finding my place amongst friends. I always felt that I didn't fit in.
- I was overweight and had severe acne which [led] to social anxiety in my peer group at school. I was an easy target so found it hard to make core friends.

The old man-code and boys' friendships

One of the most corrosive forces on boy friendships is linked to the man-code itself. The unhealthy hierarchy of boy culture is formed early in a boy's life. In a two-year study, Judy Chu, one of the co-authors of the book *When Boys Become Boys: Development, Relationships, and Masculinity*, explored 'boys' early ability to be emotionally perceptive, articulate, and responsive in their relationships. Over time, however, these "feminine" qualities become less obvious as boys learn to prove that they are boys primarily by showing that they are not girls.' This early socialisation of little boys, combined with the unhelpful perceptions that boys are tough and deserve to be spoken to more harshly and have less need to be tenderly soothed and reassured when they are upset all create the perfect storm that allows our tween and teen boys to silently suffer from some of the traditional examples of the toxic brotherhood.

Chu found that behaviours typically viewed as 'natural' for boys reflect an unconscious following of cultures that require boys to be 'stoic, competitive, and aggressive if they are to be accepted as "real boys" otherwise they run the risk of being seen as "girls". Yet even as boys begin to reap the social benefits of aligning with norms of traditional masculine behaviour, they pay a psychological and relational price for renouncing parts of their whole humanity' that will make forming meaningful relationships with either gender much more difficult.

Needing to impress other boys by demonstrating physical prowess, verbal banter and teasing, without showing failure and vulnerability are all hidden pressures that boys struggle with every day. So often they copy what is modelled to them rather than what is spoken to them and with the constant bombardment of visual images that represent six-packed men with lots of muscles, seemingly endless videos where men dominate others, gaming where winning is the only goal and hardcore pornography where people (mainly women and often teens and children) have to submit to being treated as submissive beings all have a part to play in the formation of the code of how to be a boy in our world. This is why we must adopt the compassionate intention to teach a different, more healthy reality. When this is done with respectful language, and a tone and physiology that allows our boys to feel safe we can bring our boys to a different alignment with respect of both genders and human diversity. We need to deconstruct this pressure to conform to be one of inclusion and a focus on the greater good so that our boys do not have to shut down their hearts, before they become tweens and teens. Encouraging our boys to be whoever they really are rather than a one-size-fits-all stereotype driven by an outdated code needs to be the goal of every parent of a boy.

Teaching our boys to step forward to stop violence, to challenge the need to impress each other and to question when verbal banter and humour is used to hurt rather than help is an important step to changing these insidious pressures on our precious boys. To be honest, to do these things takes more courage than to stay silent.

> I feel like being a teen now is in some ways worse [than] it was before, social media has impacted us so much because if you want to be 'cool' you need to look a certain way have follows be popular be this and that and a lot of people lose track [of] who they really are. This can impact relationships with your family because it's no longer 'cool' to be nice to them so you start being disrespectful and pushing them away so you can maintain your status of being 'cool'. Also this can lead to mistreatment of women in general because you see them as an object for you to use as pleasure not as a real loving human being.

Hazing

Hazing is a term commonly used to cover the ways that the toxic boy culture accepts and at times encourages a group of boys to initiate a new member into their group, often by forcing him to perform or endure humiliating or dangerous actions. Some of the most extreme versions of hazing include boys having bottles or brooms forced into their anus – this is rape, not a game. Around 92 per cent of boys who have been hazed never report it, most likely because they are terrified of being completely excluded from the local boyhood. Every teen is seeking validation and acceptance and has a profound need to belong with their peers and their friends. Sadly, so many of the boys who are present when this behaviour is happening know that it is wrong and in some way wish they could stop it. However, they stand silently aside because *they have been conditioned to think this is part of the journey of life – and that there is an inevitability to it.* They also are quietly terrified of losing their friends and being alone. When boys start collectively refusing to submit to hazing, it will stop. It is not just the victim who needs to refuse; it is the silent bystanders who also must refuse. There are many ways of brotherhood bonding that do not involve anyone being hurt or shamed and we just have to hope that these things become the norm – and soon.

This blatant intentional violence towards other boys that is often still silently accepted as the norm is possibly contributing towards violence against women on some level. The imbalance of power, the need for dominance, and the projection of their own inner sense of shame could possibly all join together in a moment of heightened emotions in a boy who has been conditioned to shut down any sense of emotional vulnerability.

In an article for the *New York Times*, Michael C. Reichert wrote about a study on the link between these unhelpful norms and poor behaviour. The study found there was a strong link that showed that the young men who follow the most traditional gender identities were 'unhappier and much more prone to bullying and sexual harassment'.

This may seem quite obvious, as emotional honesty, trust and openness are emotional competences needed in genuine friendships. In a way some of our boys are in a catch-22 situation. While they crave real friendship they have been conditioned to seek power and dominance, rather than the intimacy and connection, which are important if developing authentic healthy relationships.

We must remember that boys are not born with a genetic tendency towards this behaviour of needing to dominate others or to be more aggressive. These are learned behaviours and so they can become unlearned behaviours!

Many young boys need help to be able to understand and navigate the nuances of friendships and relationships and we must prioritise this before they get to big school. Teaching our boys that it absolutely is OK to express their affection towards their best friends or mates is just one small thing that can improve their friendship dynamics in adolescence.

I once did a presentation to a large audience of girls and boys in a country high school. The presentation helped them understand many of the changes that were happening to them that made them feel sometimes confused, stressed, frightened and even dumb. At the end I had a message about being a good friend and I suggested that it would be OK if they told a friend how much they value them. To my surprise at the end of the seminar, girls started hugging their best friends and telling them they love them – and the boys were giving 'boy style' hugs, high-fives, affectionate slaps on the arm and I could hear them saying, 'Hey bro, I love you.' The room was palpable with joy and delight. Perhaps they just needed permission or a reminder, or both?

Bullying

Bullies are not born; they are formed by experiences that have happened to them and around them. In my experience with teen boys, the worst bullies are covering enormous emotional wounds and to cover their sense of insecurity, worthlessness, loneliness and shame, they often bully others. I've also found that these boys often – but not always – have poor communication skills and poor self-regulation and they have learned through the old boy-code that being verbally and physically tough will give you the acceptance and 'cred' every teen boy hungers for. I have also met the academically superior, over-entitled bully teen boy who feels that his parents' financial or professional status can give him arrogance and vast power.

We must remember that bullies are in the minority. Underneath the teen mask – often the one that says, 'I'm fine' – is not just insecurity and confusion, it is serious fear. There is a massive fear that sometimes will border on terror that a boy will not measure up to what he has been told men have to be. So many get caught in the impossible situation of run away or fight – neither things they really want! In the book *The Boy Crisis*, the authors argue that boy bullying has a lot to do with a lack of respect in the bully's life. Their research has shown that many boys in correctional institutions have experienced damage to their emotional intelligence in four different ways:

1. Father absence
2. Physical abuse by parents
3. Verbal abuse by parents
4. Parental neglect.

For many of these boys, now almost men, their method of dealing with vulnerability becomes acting out, anger and delinquency because these things distract them from the sense of feeling vulnerable.

What if my son is being bullied?

Bullying is where there is a deliberate intent to hurt another with an unacceptable use of power. It is often repeated and it threatens an individual's wellbeing. Bullies are often triggered to fight when they feel unsafe, inadequate or rejected. Random nastiness can be hurtful but technically it is not bullying. It is just being mean. Many boys are bullied mainly by shaming and by public humiliation. It can escalate into physical abuse, but not always.

I have worked with many boys who have been bullied and they tend to be desperate to hide it from parents. Some were worried that parents would make things worse, be disappointed in them or not believe them. If you discover this is happening to your son it can help if you explore what I have written about teasing, banter and aggression nurturance to see they are not misreading things. Then work out a plan to counteract the bully. Ensure your son avoids being alone as that makes him more of a target. Show him about physiology and show him how to walk with his head and shoulders up and with a confident swagger.

Next is to teach your son some simple deflectors to use towards the bully.

'Thanks for sharing.'

'Whatever you reckon!'

'Have a good day . . .'

Wink at them!

Just nod, smile and turn and walk away! It can help to choose a couple of ways and really practise them so they become automatic. If things continue to escalate please approach the school.

What if my son is the bully?

First, try not to overreact or panic. Bullying is a learned behaviour. No-one is born a bully. Often the key driver to a bully's behaviour is to make himself look more powerful and important than he does on the inside. Sometimes there is a sense of status in having others be scared of you. Discovering you have a bully as a son can be tough. I have seen adult friendships ruined forever when a son has been outed as a bully.

The first thing is to read chapter 12 on communication again. What might have started off as a bit of a boy-code tough thing may have become a habit that is now fed by the expectations of others. As a teacher I have been told that X who I will be teaching next is a bully. I have worked with a few bullies who wanted to stop being one and it was almost impossible because much of his school community had him labelled. Punishing your son for being a bully will usually make things worse and it is modelling the behaviour you want your son to stop doing to others. Underneath the bully mask is often a boy with low self-esteem and a lack of emotional intelligence.

As a parent I would work closely at building a boy's sense of self and self-worth by helping to identify the strengths he may have. I would also look for a new hobby or social activity that would allow him to start over in a different location. If you can find him a counsellor or youth worker who could become a lighthouse figure that can be really helpful. The toughest and yet most important thing to teach your son is he is not bad or unlovable. He has just learned to make poor choices that he can become accountable for and he can change, and you will support him.

Safety nets

Always remember one of the main reasons for anger
and aggression in our emerging men is many boys
find it helps to mask their vulnerability.

Without having safe grown-ups to coach, guide and reassure them about the true nature of being a tween and teen boy with all its developmental changes, emerging sexuality, additional stressors and an overactive amygdala, we will keep losing our good boys to underachievement, senseless aggression and violence, alcohol and drug addiction, mental ill-health and worst of all suicide. They need a safety net of support that is currently lacking in so many of our boys' lives. The other safety net our boys need are good friends. I believe the best way to help bullies is not with more punishment or exclusion; it is with understanding and help to learn a different map to follow that will help them develop authentic friendships.

Many teen boys suffer silently from serious bullying, especially physical bullying. I have worked with a number of boys who have worn the brunt of older boys' bullying, especially in boarding school.

As I wrote earlier, some of this is linked to hazing 'initiation' practices that are passed down year after year. I have worked with boys whose upper arms and chests are covered in serious bruising. These areas are covered by their clothes so no adult could tell! One lad even had cigarette burns that he kept silent about. Some of these 12- to 13-year-old boys had seriously contemplated ending their lives as a consequence. The non-disclosure is partly linked to the old male-code about not showing weakness and vulnerability and also the fear that it will make things worse – as it has many times. We need to shine a bright light of awareness on this practice and do everything possible to encourage connectedness among boys. We can do this through fun play activities or activities involving teamwork. Creating a lighthouse figure within our schools and boarding houses will also reduce the likelihood of this happening.

WHAT ANNOYS YOU THE MOST AS A TEEN BOY?

- Fake friends that you cannot trust.
- Other teens behaving like idiots.
- How some young boys try to hurt each other.
- Bullying and feeling I have to have a girlfriend cause other boys do.
- People who are just unkind and ill-mannered. What's the point in inconveniencing others? Don't force your opinions or views on others. Just be kind.
- The amount of talking behind your back [that] is done, then telling you to make it worse.

Teaching your son about healthy boundaries

In order to teach boys about healthy and appropriate boundaries, I like to use the metaphor of the line in the sand. **This is the metaphorical line between what is appropriate and acceptable, and what is not.**

The line on physicality

One of the things that causes a lot of confusion, particularly for mums of sons, is the incredible physicality of boys' behaviour when they are together. Some boys, but not all boys, can be quite rough when they play together. This can mean lots of slapping, jumping on each other, and wrestling, shoving and pushing. And yes, sometimes boys get hurt.

Given that the instinctual drive of males that continues from caveman days is to kill mammoths and be fearless, then this form of play is coming from a deep biological and possibly archetypal origin.

> The male approach to friendship and love is often different from female – males often emphasize challenge and the pursuit of valour together, and this kind of bonding is crucial to human survival and thriving.
>
> – Michael Gurian, *Saving Our Sons* (2017)

I have already explored the phenomenon called 'aggression nurturance' or the use of physicality to build connection. Essentially, this means that being physically aggressive with other boys is a very normal part of boys' growth and development. Michael Gurian is very careful to clarify that aggression in this instance is not violence. There are some who believe that boys have a higher tolerance of physical pain than girls and that would make sense given how rough their play can become at times!

When boys are being physically, playfully aggressive towards other boys (again we are not talking about them being physically violent), they are actually seeking connection just like most girls do through conversation and cooperative play. Boys need to learn that roughhousing or rough and tumble play is normal when they are trying to connect and have fun with other boys. Indeed, such rough play especially with their dads can help them learn to understand some of the boundaries around hurting unintentionally.

However, if a boy feels wronged or disrespected then this form of play can change from being aggressive to violent, because the underlying intention now is to hurt rather than connect. That is crossing the line.

It is important to explain to boys of all ages that this form of often physically rough play is generally only acceptable with other boys, but not all boys, and *not* with girls. Of course, there are some girls who really like this form of play and I was one of them but most will find this form of play unwanted, unwelcome and unacceptable.

It is really important not to harshly punish boys when they unintentionally hurt another boy when they are playing in a physical way. Instead, use the five-step process of what to do when a boy mucks up in chapter 10.

The line around stuff

Many little boys can struggle in early childhood settings and early primary school if they decide that something that they have created a strong attachment to (aka ownership) is used by other children. They may lash out. This is crossing the line because the item doesn't belong to them even though they have become very fond of it. Tween and teen boys can also struggle the same way. This behaviour will need some careful emotional coaching so they can see that they are unable to treat that thing as being only theirs. The same lashing out can happen when boys perceive that someone they considered a friend is chosen to play with someone else. Jealousy is a very real emotion and can feel really uncomfortable when it floods your being. Rather than just punish the boy, this should become a teachable moment where we validate the emotion and give him strategies to manage it without hurting others or himself.

For a teen, it is important they know that friends don't belong to them. Just as later in life, girlfriends/romantic partners also don't belong to them. A romantic partner may choose to be in a friendship with a boy but if the relationship ends, the other party doesn't owe the boy anything. Managing friendship rejections early in life and helping our boys understand about 'ownership' is incredibly important. For some boys it may even reduce the potential in adulthood for stalking, harassment and physical violence towards those who have chosen to end a relationship with them.

A boy needs to know there are normal human feelings around rejection and that there are things that he can do that can help process these feelings rather than needing to intentionally hurt others. Please be mindful that a lot of boys and men prefer not to talk about these big feelings but rather process them over time in their own way. Also, boys need to know that feeling lousy after we have been emotionally hurt, excluded, treated badly, misunderstood or been disrespected is *completely normal*. It is definitely not a sign of weakness and with a safe grown-up supporting a boy, these big, ugly feelings can be released rather than stuffed down into their bodies.

The line around banter and teasing

Another really important line in the sand that boys need to understand is around the verbal dynamics of male communication. Teasing, banter and nicknames are generally a part of healthy male relationships, particularly in our Australian culture. Indeed in our family my four sons still continue to do this as grown men. Nowadays, it is all light-hearted and creates a great sense of family connectedness.

Understanding the unique nuances of human communication through conversation takes time and practice to learn and this is not easy in today's screen world where many of our children and teens are simply not using as much verbal communication as previous generations.

So, name-calling and put-downs, which are technically forms of relational aggression, are often not problematic between boys who are friends when the intention beneath it is more about bonding than alienating. Of course there are times when these behaviours are problematic and when the intention is to hurt and that becomes bullying. Many boys need guidance early on to know the difference between the teasing and banter that connects, and the teasing and banter that is hurtful and often shameful.

WHAT WAS YOUR MOST CHALLENGING EXPERIENCE WHEN YOU WERE A TEEN?

- Having the self-confidence to stand up against bullying – a vicious cycle of bullying reduces self-esteem, leads to more bullying, and so on.
- Confronting bullying and being a loner.
- Bullied at school for my sexuality (I am heterosexual but was accused as gay). This went on for 2+ years and was a very lonely time.
- Being betrayed by close friends who bullied me.
- Low self-esteem – I moved to Australia at 10 years old and to a regional town. I was teased by other boys for my accent and constantly called POM. A group bullied me for the first year in Australia. Up to six boys would catch me after school and hit me. I learned to keep my mouth shut and became withdrawn.
- Being bullied/excluded so much I had to sit by my locker and hide from everyone during recess.
- Dealing with anxiety and bullying and lack of social skills.

Supporting boys' friendships

Parents can play a huge role in nurturing your son's friendships. By prioritising your tween and teen boy's social availability, being a supportive caring adult in his friends' lives, welcoming his friends in your home and always speaking well of your son's best mates, you can really help him maintain friendships.

Top tips to encourage friendships

- Always say 'hi' or wave when you see his friends around.
- Encourage boys to ride or walk home from school together.
- Offer to give rides and pick-ups to friends as well as your son.

- Have spare mattresses and swags ready for unexpected friends.
- Remind your son how to be a good friend.
- Remind your son to keep an eye out for his friend's wellbeing.
- Take your son's friend on a family holiday.
- Always have endless supplies of fruit, bread for toast and Milo.
- Have same gender 'overs' – which used to be sleepovers but there is no sleep so they are just 'overs'.
- Remind them of their friends' birthdays – I mean, he can't remember yours so he will need help here!
- Encourage him to welcome new friends who have similar interests.
- Shout the friends the occasional ice-cream.
- Model kindness and gratitude.

WHAT IS THE BEST THING ABOUT BEING A TEEN BOY TODAY?

- Being able to have a row with the boys on the river and afterwards go into the city to hang out not having to worry about what I look like because there are no girls around – it means I can just be me and have fun and enjoy myself.
- I get a bit more freedom (I'm allowed to go to the movies by myself or go out the front to my beach with just me and my friends).
- Just being with all the boys having a good time.

17

Exploring sexuality and intimate relationships

WHAT WAS YOUR MOST CHALLENGING EXPERIENCE WHEN YOU WERE A TEEN?

- Girls, trying to communicate with them, lack of self confidence.
- Talking to girls.
- Not having the confidence to ask the pretty girl out.
- Feeling awkward around girls. Not having a girlfriend until Year 11.
- Falling in love with a girl and then finding out through others that she cheated on me. Broke my heart and thought I couldn't go on. Didn't have the emotional maturity to deal with it.

To be honest, it is the most difficult time in the history of the Western world to raise boys to have a healthy sexuality and to have the knowledge and awareness of how to form relationships that are healthy, enjoyable, consensual and respectful. It is much easier to raise our sons to become creeps today because most parents, through no fault of their own, have become the last source of information for most of our teens. Both our girls and boys are being marinated in a culture of sexualisation from very early in life and no matter how hard we try, they are constantly being conditioned to look sexy and to use their bodies to gain acceptance and approval. We often see completely inappropriate messages on children's clothing that reinforce gender differences, not to mention the creep factor. In a way they are growing up in a time of disinhibition – where the norms of appropriate expectations have changed a lot.

Do everything you can to protect your children and deconstruct these messages that they see over and over again well before your son begins puberty.

We must pull off the blinkers and dig our head out of the sand and stand beside our sons (and daughters) and give them a different potential life in the world of relationships, especially intimate relationships.

> I lived on a farm and had very few opportunities to date girls other than at school socials and parties. Most of the girls around my age had boyfriends or were looking for older boys who were going to take over the family farm. Consequently, dating involved short hookups with younger girls. In my later teens I moved to the city and found it very hard to form relationships because I did not have the skills to maintain a long-term relationship with girls my age as I only had experience with immature partners. It took me many years to learn and I hurt a lot of girls along the way with my manipulations and immature attitudes to our relationships.

As parents our job is to have conversations with our co-parent and others in our boy-tribe about the uncomfortable, tricky questions. Is my son mature enough for sex? Is he aware that having sex is very much about giving pleasure as well as receiving it? Is he aware of the age of consent? Is he aware of how fake porn is? The confusion for teen boys around relationships and in particular girls is real and our boys need our support and guidance.

In early adolescence most boys will experience random erections that happen spontaneously. It can be helpful to chat about this before it happens to forewarn him. For mammas I need to caution you to largely ignore these happenings as boys can be really easily embarrassed. He has no control over these – they just happen. These erections are very different to the ones he facilitates by self-pleasuring and masturbation, and gentle guidance on the boundaries of public and private can be really helpful. I have had to have this conversation with other people's sons in my middle school classrooms when they chose to – in their words – have a 'wank' during English.

Avoiding our sons becoming creeps
Humour

In her book *Boys and Sex: Young Men on Hook Ups, Love, Porn, Consent, and Navigating the New Masculinity*, Peggy Orenstein spoke with over 100 American boys and discovered some disturbing, and culturally driven tendencies with boys and humour. Groups of teen boys and young men still have a tendency to use the demeaning of girls, commonly known as 'slut shaming', as a source of humour and a form of male bonding. Orenstein believes this may be an extension of the toilet humour of young boys, which is largely benign and harmless. Many of the boys she spoke with when questioned about the appropriateness of crude sexual harassment and blatant, disrespectful treatment of girls or females in general, argued that it was 'funny or hilarious'. Having an absence of empathy at this stage is understandable, but having such an appalling absence of human decency towards the other gender is not only worrying, it is alarming. According to Orenstein for many of the boys she spoke to who were aged 16 to 22 (notice not young adolescents, almost men) 'hilarious' is a form of group bonding, where often the boys learn to disregard other people's feelings, as well as their own.

'Hilarious' is a safe haven, a default position when something is inappropriate, confusing, upsetting, depressing, unnerving or horrifying;

when something is simultaneously sexually explicit and dehumanizing; when it defies the ethics; when it evokes any of the emotions meant to stay safely behind the wall.

– *Boys and Sex*, Peggy Orenstein (2020)

As boys leave boyhood, and step on to the bridge towards adulthood, they need to have serious guidance about a healthy sense of humour. Shed humour or paddock humour can be a little crude, and a little disrespectful, however, it is something that has happened among male-only audiences for generations. There is a clear line in the sand that boys need to learn about, before the desperate need to belong – at any cost – becomes a reality in adolescence.

The old man-code and disrespecting women

When boys and men behave in disrespectful ways towards girls and women, especially using sexism, they are being creeps. This is the word that Steve Biddulph uses and I feel it is very appropriate because they are not necessarily being bad men, rather they are acting immaturely by being thoughtless and insensitive. Especially in early adolescence when boys are desperate to belong, if left unquestioned, behaving this way can lead to ingrained attitudes. In her excellent book *Ringleaders and Sidekicks*, Rosalind Wiseman explores the power of peer pressure on teenage boys. The conditioning of the old male-code is still very strong in high schools in the Western world. Wiseman says these invisible rules about how to act like a man put pressure on boys who have been raised to be respectful. To stand up against sexism and racism and any other form of social injustice, especially if the dominant boy group thinks it is a part of being a man, could see a boy being ostracised and/or labelled as gay. As a former high school teacher, I can attest to this behaviour and no matter how many times I would have questioned the boys about it, it would still continue, especially in early adolescence.

The hunger to belong is very strong in early adolescence, and many young boys are quite prepared to sell their soul, give up their integrity and walk on their values, just so they can stay within the group.

It took me a long time to realise that the language that we use can really affect others – particularly in my peer group. At age 13, I would use the current vernacular that 'everyone' used and have what I thought were joking conversations with my peers. Some of them didn't mind and would give it straight back, some of them felt bullied and picked on. I was then in serious trouble for bullying, even though I thought that whatever I had said was what everyone was saying, so how come I was singled out? In hindsight I can understand how someone would feel if they were called 'gay' or 'homo'. I never meant it maliciously, but that was how it was perceived and it took me a long time to understand that.

Our sons need to know that the male stereotypes they see in porn and even in mainstream media and society are just that – stereotypes. Just as we've been talking about challenging the notion that boys are tough, when they are really vulnerable, we must challenge the sexual male stereotypes. So often, boys are seen as being 'up for it all the time' or sex-crazed or animalistic, unable to control themselves. We need to show boys that they don't have to buy in to those stereotypes or the old man-code. They are not hard-wired ways of being for boys. Boys are just as likely to be scared, tender, sweet, reluctant, submissive or confused about sex as girls are. We must do all we can to protect and nurture that innocent aspect and call out the unhealthy old man-code stuff wherever we see it.

There are some long-held beliefs around boys needing to be some sort of stud who needs to be promiscuous to be seen as valued. Indeed the 'hook up' culture is very different to the way parents navigated their sexual awakening. I meet many parents who tell me they are so relieved that they did not have the screen world when they were exploring sex and relationships – there are no photos that their kids will discover one day! We need to also challenge the beliefs around girls and their emerging sexuality without needing to label them 'sluts'.

SAME-SEX ATTRACTION

Around 5–10 per cent of our teen boys will not be attracted to the opposite sex. In our overly sexualised world, while there is more acceptance that relationships are more flexible than ever before, it is still a confusing time for both our girls and boys as their sexual identity emerges.

We need to avoid making assumptions about our sons' sexuality and to not label them or define them by their sexuality because the lens of parents is very different to the lens of the younger generation. Gender fluidity and the acceptance of intimate relationships with either gender are accepted by many of the millennial generation.

Caring, respectful relationships are something every human yearns for and sometimes these are platonic and sometimes they are intimate. The core message is that gay, bi, trans and intersex people need to be seen as acceptable and just as deserving of love and affection. In the past many boys with different sexual preferences lived in fear and in separation and were alone. Loneliness is a major contributing factor in mental health and suicide and men fare significantly worse, as I have already explored. See chapter 8 for more on supporting your son if you think he may be gay.

Sexting

Sexting has become widespread and this is an area where parents need to have big conversations. National statistics in Australia tell us that 49 per cent of young people (13–24) have sent a sexually suggestive image and 67 per cent of young people have received one.

It may be widespread but it is still illegal and if your son is caught sending, receiving or pressuring a girl for a nude image, he can be charged and put on the sex offenders' register. No matter that you have had this conversation, in the heat of the moment your gorgeous son could still post an image of his penis or request a naked image from a girl. He is not bad or stupid; he has poor decision-making functions, especially around social connectedness and sexual desire.

It is interesting to hear how common dick pics are today for adults as well as teens. Females seldom find them appealing or even arousing, which is probably the motive for which they are sent in the first place. Having a conversation with your son about how girls view penis pics is important. Some teen girls have said they often share penis pics and laugh about how silly they look. For the boys, it's fair to say this is not the response they were hoping for.

Even more important is the need to teach your son about not pressuring girls to send nude pics. Many girls feel pressured to send nudes, especially for a boy they like. If a girl says no that is a clear sign for a boy to stop asking. *The Hunting* is an excellent series on SBS that could be worthwhile watching for boys over 14 with a parent. There are so many good conversations to be had at so many times. It is very realistic and at times confronting, however it has some poignant messages for all of us, not just our teens.

WHAT WAS YOUR MOST CHALLENGING EXPERIENCE WHEN YOU WERE A TEEN?

- Asking girls out. I was friends with a lot of girls and could speak to them easily, but I sucked at letting myself become vulnerable and asking them out in case it ruined a friendship or I got rejected.
- The most challenging experience I had when I was a teenager was to overcome my lack of self-confidence and being able to approach and confide in girls that I was attracted to them or liked them. I had an overwhelming fear of rejection.
- Talking to girls! I'm an only child, and went to a boys' only school: women were a complete mystery. And scary.
- Talking to girls.
- Never having a girlfriend as I was one of the nerdy guys in a school full of sports gronks. It made me feel like I was missing an important part of my life at the time. Back then sports were everything and I was a thinker.

- Discovering girls and the issues with relationships.
- Not being emotionally mature enough to deal with girls and relationships.
- Getting laid.

Sexual violence

Globally the figures of family violence, especially towards women, are shockingly high. Sadly, Australia seems to be leading the world and in the last few years, while the overall rate of violence in Australia has dropped, the numbers of women hurt or killed by men has not.

The Australian Bureau of Statistics' 2016 Personal Safety Survey (PSS) reported that young women were more likely to experience intimate partner violence and/or sexual violence than older women in the 12 months before the survey:

- One in 20 or 5 per cent (or 117,000) of women aged 18–34 experienced intimate partner violence, compared with 1.5 per cent (96,000) aged 35 and over
- One in 20 or 4.3 per cent (or 125,000) of women aged 18–34 experienced sexual violence, compared with 0.7 per cent (45,000) aged 35 and over.

In terms of sexual harassment and stalking, based on the 2016 PSS:

- One in two (53 per cent or 5 million) women and one in four (25 per cent or 2.2 million) men had experienced sexual harassment in their lifetime
- One in six (17 per cent or 1.6 million) women and one in 16 (6.5 per cent or 587,000) men had experienced stalking since the age of 15.

Of the 1.2 million women who experienced stalking from a male in the 20 years before the survey:

- 31 per cent (364,000) perceived the most recent incident as a crime at the time
- 29 per cent (337,000) reported that police were contacted about the most recent incident.

– Based on Australian Institute of Health and Welfare
and Australian Bureau of Statistics material

Looking at these results, it is clear that we still have a lot of work to do in teaching boys and young men about consent, sexism, boundaries and how to behave more respectfully towards girls and women.

Given the #MeToo movement, there is an increased sensitivity and a growing awareness around how unacceptable disrespect, harassment and violence towards women are and that is a good thing. However, we need to be realistic and realise that this culture is embedded in many layers of society and that change will come gradually. It is sad to see that in some codes of football in Australia inappropriate behaviour of players, especially towards girls and women, keeps on happening regardless of the public humiliation and penalties that are given out. These are a tiny percentage of men in sport but the public exposure they get can distort the perceived reality of tween and teen boys. When these stories appear in the press it can be helpful to have a conversation with your son about the poor choices that these men made. No matter how difficult this cultural change may be, parents of sons have an important role to play. This may be a time where you consciously choose films to watch at home that show adolescent boys being respectful towards girls – and hopefully by now you would have been making helpful suggestions over many years when watching TV shows or online videos. Even though it may seem to have been a waste of time in your son's early adolescence, trust me those values that are embedded by many, many conversations over many, many years are still deep within him and they do tend to resurface as he gets older and gradually emerges from adolescence.

Sexual harassment

Sexual harassment happens to both boys and girls. In locker rooms and change rooms, boys often flick towels at each other's genitals, mostly in a harmless attempt to create light-hearted connectedness. Obviously not all boys enjoy these antics and increasingly are voicing their dislike, which is about creating healthy boundaries, however, it seems it is still considered a part of the norm. Again, this is why we must talk to our boys about respecting others' boundaries at an early age to shift this norm.

Sexual harassment towards girls from boys in high schools in the UK, Australia and US has become very problematic. Research has found that sexual harassment of girls is common in many high schools but goes largely unreported and unaddressed, with many teachers ill-equipped to tackle the problem.

One survey of UK students and teachers in co-educational secondary schools found that 37 per cent of the girls surveyed said they had been sexually harassed at school. Almost a quarter reported that they had experienced unwanted touch which was sexual in its nature. Further, 66 per cent of girls in the senior years of schooling reported being the subject of or witness to sexist language being used at school. These statistics are concerning.

We need our boys to know *there is no way it is acceptable to make rude or disrespectful comments about how a girl or woman dresses or looks – just no way*, not online, not offline, not even in private messages. It is not only a sign of immaturity, it smacks of arrogance and superiority.

The easy access to pornography and violent gaming seem to be major contributors to this culture of girls being seen as commodities. This is not only disturbing, it is extremely sad. Friendships that are formed in high school across the gender divide have long been seen as a major protective factor for boys as they separate and individuate from their parents. Common sense would suggest that these meaningful, often lifelong friendships that are formed in high school are harder to begin and to maintain given the influence of the digital world.

In her excellent book *Under Pressure*, Lisa Damour explores the verbal sexual harassment that many girls are experiencing today. Girls are being called 'sluts', 'hos', 'bitches' and 'whores', or being asked for 'nudes' or to perform sexual acts. When they push back and call boys out on this disrespectful verbal abuse, they are often told they are being 'too sensitive' or that they are overreacting. My hope is that many boys may be seeing this through the same lens as boy banter – as a form of light-hearted mocking – without realising how incredibly scary, menacing and disgusting it is for girls to be spoken to like that.

The groping, the unwanted touching, the pulling of bra straps and the forcing of male bodies against girls' bodies in stairwells and hallways is all unacceptable behaviour that is still going on. What may be OK between mates – and seriously, 14-year-old boys are continuously shoving, slapping and touching other boys in our schools – is seriously not OK when it is directed at girls.

Schools need to be very proactive in getting this message across and so working with parents to ensure these social challenges are both recognised and made to be seen as clearly unacceptable is critical if we are to change this behaviour.

The excuses 'I was just having fun' or 'I was just joking, Miss' are absolutely not acceptable either. Ignorance on the part of a boy is not an excuse to ignore this behaviour though. It needs to be nipped in the bud in our schools and in our homes. All grown-ups have got some serious work to do to ensure that boys know that there is a clear line around disrespectful verbal communication regardless of their intention – and we have plenty of badly behaving adults on the internet who are not helping this cause. One thing that has helped is when boys can listen to the voices of girls in early to mid-adolescence share their pain and fears. This can build understanding and help to re-shape these unhealthy perceptions and expectations.

Punishing boys for this behaviour will rarely change the motivation behind the behaviour. If left unchallenged in our porn-riddled world the worst thing that can happen is where boys – immature men – still feel it's OK to use girls as sources of entertainment without any consideration of how demeaning it is for girls. Girls need to be respected for being assertive and holding boys to account for this inappropriate behaviour, not threatened and harassed and insulted for speaking up. Boys also need to know it's OK to speak up against harassment and that needs to start at home with role modelling.

The case of Australian-born cricketer Alex Hepburn who was jailed for rape is a horrid example of how frightening this pattern of behaviour can become if not challenged in boyhood. This young man and some of his friends were using WhatsApp to detail their 'stats' in a sexual conquest game.

Sadly, when girls report sexually aggressive behaviour whether physical or verbal they can still find themselves in the hot seat being questioned about what they were wearing or how they were acting that may have 'invited' such abuse! Victim blaming is incredibly common especially in our media. We need to remind both our boys and our girls that sexual harassment isn't about the victim; it is about the perpetrator. They are the problem.

Thankfully there are some excellent long-term mentoring programs now going into schools that are having these conversations with our boys. The best of them are lengthy and embedded in the curriculum and they echo what traditional communities did well – having adolescent boys be mentored by older men, not necessarily punished but rather coached.

Such programs are challenging these unhelpful behaviours in respectful ways. Programs for girls are equally important to let them know that it is unacceptable to be treated in any way that makes you feel uncomfortable. They can also help girls navigate the enormous pressure of sexualisation that is being felt by girls at younger and younger ages.

Schools need to step forward and be a part of the solution because much of the awful behaviour happens on school grounds or on public transport on the way to school. Even more importantly, in changing unhealthy attitudes towards girls and women, we need to create opportunities for boys to not only hear about but be invited to become change agents through taking action. A good example is the Walk the Talk program which is delivered by Enlighten Education and Women's Community Shelters (WCS) to focus on building respectful relationships, and which also encourages students to assist WCS through practical initiatives. Schools cannot do this work alone and neither can parents. It needs to be a collective approach to transforming these unhelpful behaviours.

See also chapter 8 on confused dads for guidance for men setting a powerful example for their sons.

> **WHAT ANNOYS YOU MOST AS A TEEN BOY?**
> - Random boners.
> - The hormones that make you feel sexually active.
> - How boy crazy girls are.
> - Wanting to be in a relationship but not knowing how or if they like me.

Teaching our sons about the rape culture

Please take the time to read the *Time* magazine article by novelist Laurie Halse Anderson, herself a rape victim, who writes about the school visits she does talking to boys and girls about sexual assault. It is a real opportunity to hear the voices of boys, and some of their misunderstandings about rape. Better still read the article with your tween or teen son, and really decode the boys' misunderstandings and confusions. Challenge them, question them and explain why the rape of anyone is wrong. Without explicit and enthusiastic consent, often more than once, there is a grey area that technically is considered rape.

Unfortunately, Western culture still has a strong tendency to victim blame – what was she wearing? Hadn't she been drinking? What was she doing in the nightclub anyway? Why was she walking home by herself? There have been some well-publicised, senseless rape and murder cases in Melbourne over the last few years that have triggered much conversation and an outpouring of concern. At the vigils that were held for each of these young women, there were many men turning up to pay their respect and to stand beside the women of the city. This would not have happened 20 years ago. We are moving in the right direction, however, we still have a long way to go.

Both girls and boys need to have a real understanding of the need for enthusiastic, explicit consent. Ideally, we start by modelling this and having conversations about it. Again, one of the upsides of the internet is that there are some wonderful, very clever videos that help explain these concepts to our young people and they can be great conversation starters too (check out 'Tea and Consent' if you haven't seen it already).

Decisions made by young people who have been consuming alcohol or other drugs are decisions that can make understanding whether enthusiastic consent happened or not less clear. Indeed, in the 2016 National Drug Strategy Household Survey of Year 10, 11 and 12 students in Australia 19.8 per cent of males and 28.3 per cent of females had had unwanted sex and being under the influence of alcohol and drugs was a major contributing factor. We must make sure our boys understand that consent under the influence of alcohol may not be consent at all.

Pornography

Average age of first exposure is 11 years of age. Australian teachers and health professionals anecdotally report that the average age of first exposure is likely to be around 8 years of age. Kids and teens can access pornography on any Internet-connected device (including smartphones, tablet devices, laptops, gaming consoles and smart TVs).

– Dr Kristy Goodwin, *The Pornography Problem Plaguing
Parents In The Digital Age* free online seminar

Half of all Australian children aged 9–16 have regular exposure to sexual images, and 93 per cent of boys and over 60 per cent of girls have viewed pornography by age 18 (mostly between the ages of 14 and 17). Porn is not always something our kids seek out either – often it comes looking for them in innocent places like Minecraft, in hashtags or embedded into YouTube videos.

In a way it is pretty sad that the softening of misogynistic attitudes around men in relationships that allows men to be more emotionally available in their intimate relationships has coincided with the massive increase and ease of access to hardcore pornography. The rise of pornography is having an incredibly negative and devastating impact on our girls and our boys, but especially our adolescent boys. This is why I am urging parents to step forward and prioritise having lots of conversations about relationships and sexuality because you don't just have to give them the basic facts anymore, you have to counteract and challenge the really unhealthy information and stereotypes they are gleaning from watching online pornography.

Reports of student-on-student sexual and indecent assaults are on the rise. Statistics from NSW primary and secondary government schools show a rise from 90 incidents in 2015 to 142 in 2016. And in the first half of 2017, there were 87 allegations of such assaults involving students. This is seriously worrying.

We must step up and stop all our children from losing their innocence when they witness pornography, especially demeaning, aggressive, violent pornography. Inappropriate sexual play among pre-schoolers is increasing at frightening levels. Sadly, child-to-child molestation is happening in our primary school grounds. Another very disturbing trend has been sibling-on-sibling sexual play of a penetrative nature. These children are acting out what they see!

Disturbing pornography is easily accessible on YouTube or apps online. Of course most of our kids, especially our boys, can find endless fun watching animal videos, how to cook videos, and of course they have a fascination with watching other boys play Minecraft and Fortnite. It is so easy to accidentally touch a link that will take your son straight to a pornographic video – and often they are unable to close that page and many others pop up. The disgusting people who create and spread this horrendous material are deliberately trying to distort your child's perception of healthy, consensual sexuality. The human brain has mirror neurons which encourage us to copy human behaviour that is modelled to us. My concern is that since they aren't seeing tender lovemaking, our boys have no idea how sexually intimate behaviour can be in a different context. This is not only a problem for teen boys because increasing numbers of teen girls are watching porn too. It is shaping both boys' and girls' sexual expectations and behaviour. It is normalising some things that are not healthy or normal. Girls are appearing in emergency departments with anal tears and other injuries from physical abuse like choking!

According to experts at a 2019 New Zealand forum on the harm that misogynistic and violent internet pornography can cause, some teen boys are 'battling distressing thoughts about hurting girls, and kids are acting out sex scenes after viewing aggressive porn'.

The experts at the forum cited research that suggested young people need more support and guidance. Duh?

Pornography encourages forced female submission without explicit consent and the ease with which pornography will find our sons – without them even looking for it – is really unhelpful in raising a boy who is respectful to girls and later women. This means that a boy may struggle to form meaningful intimate relationships when he becomes an adult man. Curbing the growth of this creep culture that is often driven by male peer pressure needs both mums and dads, and our schools and our communities, to all be having the same intention to educate and redirect our boys during their formative years. One of the biggest challenges for parents today is that watching pornography online is normalising and desensitising senseless violence and inhibiting our highly impressionable, naïve tween and teen boys in their capacity to grow into healthy, happy adult men.

> . . . I have become utterly indifferent to even the most graphic sex and violence. Nothing in porn is shocking or weird to me. It's entertainment, like an action movie.

These are the disturbingly honest words of one of the young men that Peggy Orenstein interviewed in her book *Boys and Sex*. He is right that we can't just blame pornography – the same clear messages are coming from advertising, video games, movies, TV, and from the music industry. In a way it's just like a marinade that our boys are swirling around in before they step onto the bridge. The clear message that many boys get well before adolescence is that they must win and conquer as often as possible in the 'hook-up' world regardless of who gets hurt.

We need to inform ourselves about pornography and then have conversations with our sons about it, preferably before they've even seen it. There's a great video by NZ man Rob Cope on his Project Wild Dad Facebook or YouTube page called 'How to have the conversation about porn with your son'. It's great; check it out. He has one for talking to your daughters too.

Online pornography exposure is also contributing to an increase in a condition known as PIED – porn induced erectile dysfunction. Young men aged 18 to 25 are turning up at their family doctors struggling with ED. There are some studies that show that the compulsive use of porn can result in an addiction and like any addiction, that can cause serious conflict for the person concerned and their partners. Adolescents are particularly prone to developing problematic addictions due to their developing brain architecture, especially when they are rewarded as a consequence of the experience. Sexual pleasure and desire are normal human drives and when immature boys view pornography seeking a massive dopamine rush which will happen at ejaculation, it is easy to understand why they would like to do it again, and again. Let's be honest, watching porn and masturbating in your bedroom is a lot easier for teen boys than finding a sexual partner, especially when you're under the legal age of consent! It is a lot like the story of Goldilocks. Self-pleasure can be happening too much but also not be enough of the right stuff to be developmentally healthy and respectful.

> **MASTURBATION**
>
> Remember that masturbation or self-pleasuring is a completely normal experience and can help our tween and teen boys experience sexual pleasure without all the complications of being sexually active with another human being! Please be careful not to shame or embarrass your son around masturbation. Just ensure he has a large box of tissues close to his bed.

Teaching your son not to be a creep or worse

The pervasive 'hook-up' culture is impacting both boys and girls and it encourages casual, frequent sex without any sense of real intimacy. The term 'feminist fuck boy' is where a good-looking boy can become the most hunted sex partner in a school or college and girls are equally opportunistic in having sex with him!

Despite what popular culture shares about endless casual sex, there is another side that is less well known. There are many boys who choose to avoid this scene altogether. I have spoken to a number of boys who choose to avoid this overt pressure by throwing their time and energy into gaming. They tell me that rather than feel pressured in a social setting to be a part of sexual harassment, or to be a silent witness to creep behaviour driven by the hook-up or, worse still, rape culture, they choose to stay home. This shows that maybe some of our boys are more aware of the unique unhealthy pressures that exist for teen boys and rather than come out publicly, they just choose to avoid it altogether.

Raising our boys to have a healthy and respectful outlook on sexuality

So how do we raise our boys to have a healthy sexuality that is respectful of themselves and their possible partners at a time where explicit pornography finds our boys younger and younger and it is now considered more normal to find an intimate partner online than in your community?

With greater understanding and guidance, I believe if we start early in life, we can have a big impact on raising our boys to not only clearly understand healthy, appropriate boundaries but to shift attitudes and behaviours significantly.

If we have any hope of counteracting the coercion and force that is present in so much of the pornography where women's consent is not sought explicitly, we need to start young.

> Boyhood is the time when some positive words, some affection and some honour from parents and friends can make a boy brave and self-believing enough to be a good sexual partner for life.
>
> – Steve Biddulph, *Raising Boys in the 21st Century* (2018)

Resources for your son's education around sexuality

- *Secret Boys' Business* by Rose Stewart, Fay Angelo and Heather Anderson. This is a really easy-to-read book with lots of comic pictures, which are not too threatening! It is great for boys from around 9 to 13 and seriously would be great to give to any tween boy because they think they KNOW everything and sometimes they really want to check up on the facts. For everything about boys and puberty, this is your go-to book!
- *Love, Sex and No Regrets* by counsellor Elizabeth Clark. This is a bit like sex therapy for teens and it explores how sex can be special rather than demeaning or about dominance as depicted in pornography.
- *Dating and Sex: A Guide For the 21st Century Teen Boy* by Andrew P. Smiler.
- *Men of Honour: A Young Man's Guide to Exercise, Nutrition, Money, Drugs, Alcohol, Sex, Pornography and Masturbation* by Glen Gerreyn.

Resources for parents on teen sex education

The better informed you are with how to have these conversations the absolute better it is. There is nothing worse than you getting squirmy and embarrassed and being unable to speak honestly about all aspects to do with your son's emerging sexuality.

- Cath Hakanson of sexedrescue.com. Cath has an incredible ability to take the cringe factor out of sex education. (Take a listen to our chat on the ABC *Parental As Anything* podcast). Cath has an online resource that helps you know how to respond when your son (or your daughter) asks awkward questions at each age. She actually gives you the scripts to use and many parents have told me how much more confident they are now at responding to those questions or being able to have the conversations that genuinely need to be had. Cath has also written about puberty and sex education – *Boy Puberty: How to Talk About Puberty and Sex With Your Tween Boy* and *The Sex Education Answer Book*.
- *The Secret Business of Relationships, Love and Sex* by Heather Anderson, Fay Angelo and Rose Stewart.

Online resources for teens and parents

There are now more online education options that are specifically created for our adolescents. I will warn you that these may be confronting for you – however, you need to remember that teens are digital natives who have been watching naked videos, 18+ movies with high levels of violence and sexual content possibly for years. They are so much less inhibited than their parents and unless the sexual-awareness material online is not engaging, specific and transparent, they won't watch, just like they won't read a book full of great information.

- *Love and Sex in the Age of Pornography* is a documentary that follows a group of young people reflecting on the influence of pornography in their lives.
- **It's Time We Talked** is a community-based project that supports young people, parents, schools, government and the community sector to understand and address the influence of pornography on young people. Their resources page contains a range of valuable information and tools for parents, teachers, professionals and young people.
- **Love, Sex and Relationships** is a teaching resource from the Australian Research Centre in Sex, Health and Society at La Trobe University. It contains activities that explore relationships, sexual consent, equity, and sexual and reproductive health.
- **amaze.org**. They have created free videos with fabulous graphics and animations and they are seriously teen friendly. Amaze.org uses digital media to bring adolescents – wherever they live – age-appropriate, affirming and accurate sex education. The website is packed full of information for parents as well as teens and their videos are fabulous, covering everything from masturbation to erections, how to know if you're ready for sex, gender identity, condoms, sexual assault and so much more.
- The Norwegian public broadcaster NRK created a special puberty series on Newton – which is a popular science program for kids aged 8 to 12 years of age. I have to admit that when I watched it, I found it confronting as I am a child of the fifties. When I put on the lens of being a teen in the 21st century, the explicit nature with nudity makes sense. Given the highly visual nature of boys, I believe that well-researched video sex education has the best possibility of shaping our boys to have a healthy sexuality. The presenter speaks in Norwegian but there are subtitles and she does have a wonderful way of making a tricky subject light at times. Be brave and check it out. You can find it on YouTube by searching 'puberty' and 'Newton'.

- The UK documentary 'The Sex Education Show', also available on YouTube, is another entertaining way of watching something with your older teen 16+ and to stop the show at different times and have conversations. Again, I advise that you watch each episode before you decide to watch it with your teen. However, remember it is pretty tame when you think they may have already watched some hardcore porn, intentionally or by accident.
- **Ask Nurse Nettie.** An Australian state government site that answers any questions youth may have about sex. Good information on the site as well.
- **bishuk.com.** This is a great site for anyone over 14 with heaps of accurate information and explanations about pornography for teens (and you!) without having to actually watch porn!

WHAT ANNOYS YOU MOST AS A TEEN BOY?
The pressure put on you to get good marks, have a girlfriend, lose your virginity.

Teaching your son to be a good partner: emotional intelligence and competence in relationships

When we are raising our sons from boyhood to manhood it is so important for us to talk about relationships rather than just love and sex or else we miss preparing them to be capable of living in a loving, caring relationship, which they yearn for just as much as women do.

Developing an understanding of emotional competence for both girls and boys is really important. Daniel Goleman first coined the term emotional intelligence and there are many qualities that make up an emotionally mature adult.

As I mentioned in chapter 13, a person with emotional competency would, for example, have patience in queues; resolve conflict without verbal or physical abuse; be capable of loving, caring relationships; overcome setbacks quicker than others and enjoy being themselves most of the time. Building empathy is a huge part of EQ and so many teen boys do not have enough myelin to do that, however, they can learn to see the world through the eyes of others if we teach them. Emotional competence reduces the need for dominance, physical aggression and defensiveness.

When I was counselling, I was intrigued to see 16- to 18-year-old boys who on a repeat visit to see me would come with a list of written questions such as 'What does a girl mean when she giggles at you?' Or another question I was asked is, 'How do I know if they are into me or just being nice?' Without a good understanding of the emotional and social components in interpersonal relationships, it is easy to understand why so many teen boys and young men make poor choices. Without education they will continue to make the same poor choices. Knowing that building the neural connectors takes time will help parents to understand why our soon-to-be-a-man boys can take quite some time before they are able to learn how to make better choices, especially interpersonal choices.

A good place to start a conversation about intimate relationships is to talk to your son about the difference between liking someone, being sexually attracted to them and being in love with them – and how these can be easily confused. Let him know that just because he feels one way, the same feeling may not be reciprocated and that's OK. I remember working with boys who were totally infatuated and full of lust for a girl who did not have any awareness of them and who obviously did not feel the same. They experienced some serious anger issues towards the girl and one had expressed a desire to punish her for not liking him. As teens both girls and boys can struggle in this area, but boys tend to struggle alone while teen girls often talk about it.

When is the right time for a serious girlfriend/boyfriend?

Because relationships are complex, I strongly urge you to discourage your boys from having a 'girlfriend' or 'boyfriend' for as long as possible – definitely over 15 years of age. I do get deeply concerned when parents encourage intimate relationships under this age as teens lack the emotional and social maturity to make good decisions around intimacy and their emerging sexuality. By all means encourage boys to have a strong friendship – and surround them in social settings with girls and boys – just discourage them from having a one-to-one intimate relationship until they're mature enough to be respectful and responsible.

> The most challenging experience of my teen years was going through late puberty, coping with what I perceived as being behind in emotional intelligence to my peers. Also having no friends and feeling isolated and no-one to talk to about it all. In my late teens [it was] dealing with huge sex urges, no girls to have sex with therefore lots and lots of masturbation causing shame and self-disgust and fear of getting caught out.

18

Technology and the digital world

The digital world has shifted the axis of parenting and education. Unlike many of the doomsayers out there, I believe that with positive mentoring and education our boys can navigate this digital world in a healthy and constructive way. The digital world is meeting many of our boys' psychological needs, which is one of the reasons they enjoy it so much. It is also giving them opportunities to experience autonomy and freedom away from the watchful eyes of parents – something we need to give back to our boys earlier in their childhood! In our politically correct and fear-driven world, I believe in many ways we have unintentionally stolen boyhood from our boys. There are many apps and games that allow boys to experience risk and mastery, which gives them a sense of success and thus self-worth. For boys who struggle with literacy and numeracy, or who have very little athletic prowess, this can help them feel more competent and confident. Of course problematic usage of the digital world is a very real thing that I will also explore.

If you are a parent of a tween, teen or under-25-year-old son, and you have been pulling your hair out around your son's usage of his device, phone, laptop or iPad, be reassured that you are not alone. Parents everywhere in the digital trenches are having really challenging and stressful times striving to be their child's responsible adult around boys and gaming. If you have just jumped to this chapter and are looking for information around online pornography, go to chapter 17.

We need to start this chapter with a little honesty around the digital world. We adults are struggling with it as well. Much of the gaming that is aimed at kids has been created by psychologists who know exactly what is required to keep people actively engaged online. This way of staying engaged ensures that online advertisements are directed to you that have the highest chance of influencing your purchasing power. Data about every aspect of our life is collected by these large technology companies and ruthlessly sold on to third parties without our permission. The reward systems that are built into games for young children are essentially setting our kids up to be gamblers later in life. There is so much wrong with the philosophy underneath most of the large technology companies. It is based on greed with very little integrity and ethics, and sadly our children know nothing else.

Here are some statistics (from data gathered in 2016–17) to give you some perspective around today's technology.

1. 97 per cent of Australian homes with children have a device for playing games.
2. 80 per cent of Australian households have more than one device for playing games.
3. 15–24-year-old males play video games for an average of 155 minutes a day (compared to the Australian average of 89 minutes).
4. 81 per cent of kids aged between 8 and 17 have played an online game.
5. 50 per cent of 8–17-year-olds have played games with people they don't know.
6. 17 per cent of 8–17-year-olds have experienced some form of online bullying in these platforms.
7. 46 per cent of gamers are female.
8. 34 per cent of kids aged 8–17 have made in-app purchases in games.
9. Online eSport is a huge industry and some events have 454 million viewers and have generated over US$1 billion.
10. One of parents' biggest concerns raising boys is how to manage gaming activities.

– 'State of Play' report by the Office of the eSafety Commissioner; and the 'Digital Australia Report 2018' by the Interactive Games and Entertainment Association

Social media and biological drivers

Sadly, parental acceptance and love has lost some of its potential to fill the hearts of our teens. Now they need the adulation of those in the ether – the more likes, shares, comments and positive emojis they get, the better they feel! The reverse is they can feel crushed when few people give them public acknowledgement. Fame at any cost has become a powerful, irrational drive. Many parents never experienced this as teens and can feel an invisible wall has been built that keeps them away.

Just in case you haven't read chapter 14 about unmotivated sons, there are some basic biological drives that make us become self-determined individuals. They are the 3Cs as Dr Adam Price calls them: connection, competence and control. The creators of online games know this and exploit it to ensure that your son – and many girls – become incredibly motivated in the gaming platforms.

There is no question that the digital world, especially the gaming world for many of our tween and teen boys, is giving our kids these three things in bucketloads. When this also coincides with being bored at school and disengaged, especially in the 13–15 age group, gaming is certainly filling their psychological needs and making them feel great. In days gone by, boys would strive for the same three Cs while riding their bikes, swimming in a river, play fighting, extreme antics on the trampoline, chasing rabbits and generally stretching and testing themselves, in the company of other boys striving to be the best or at least good enough.

So technically we have just replaced the real world with a digital world for our biologically driven mammoth hunters and it allows our boys to do exactly the same things – with fewer trips to the emergency department! The surges of testosterone and the presence of increased levels of vasopressin also play a part in hypo-arousing our teen boys' nervous system. This is a simple explanation of what is happening in our teen boy's brain and hopefully a partial explanation of why they love technology and gaming so much.

Minecraft was one of the first online games that used the sandbox concept, where there are very few limitations placed on the gamer. They can roam, interact with and change the virtual world however they choose. This autonomy is like an incredible gift to many of our boys who feel that their freedoms are endlessly curtailed by teachers and well-meaning parents. This is the ultimate form of freedom and they don't even have to leave their bedroom or their home to experience it. Many grown-ups think that boys like gaming because it's fun. Dan Haesler, an author and educator, argues that games like Minecraft are way more than an activity for the imagination. When young people play Minecraft, they experience many life-like emotions like anger or disappointment and they are driven to succeed. So in some ways this is like a virtual reality about life.

> It's not all laughs and giggles. It turns out that humans like to struggle with things, as long as they can see the pathway to improvement. It's a concept that the late Seymour Papert called 'hard fun'. Kids rarely play games that they master easily because that's boring.
>
> – Dan Haesler, Harnessing the Minecraft Mindset for Success, in *Growing Happy, Healthy Young Minds*, Generation Next (2017)

I've shared this to give some balance to gaming because while it can cause enormous problems it is not all bad and indeed as Haesler argues it might be teaching your son some valuable life skills and resilience – it might or might not. Gaming is a form of escapism which is quite normal human behaviour. We all engage in forms of escapism: reading books, going for walks, possibly a Netflix binge or a trip to the movies. Given that many of our teens are struggling with heightened levels of stress, we need to appreciate that gaming is meeting yet another psychological need.

> For some of our boys, especially those who have a disability, are neuro divergent, have social anxiety or have experienced trauma, being connected online has often become a significantly positive thing in their lives.

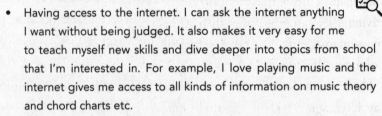

HOW DO BOYS FEEL ABOUT TECHNOLOGY?

- Having access to the internet. I can ask the internet anything I want without being judged. It also makes it very easy for me to teach myself new skills and dive deeper into topics from school that I'm interested in. For example, I love playing music and the internet gives me access to all kinds of information on music theory and chord charts etc.
- We have the opportunity to make a difference and have our voices heard in the age of social media.
- Free internet porn.
- Because we live a long way from our family, I would say technology coz I can face time, text, and call them.

How do I know if my son's gaming habits are too much or harmful?

Let's start with a common-sense statement: gaming per se is a lot less harmful than risk-taking behaviours that many teens pursue like using alcohol, illegal or legal drugs, driving like hoons, porn-driven sexual behaviour, delinquency or smoking.

May I also warn you about getting distressed when you read articles and blogs that liken gaming to being addicted to meth! Once you wonder why our boys are so keen to be gaming and are given some helpful strategies around monitoring whether their gaming has become problematic or not, you will be a much more confident parent. No, seriously, you will be.

Gaming and the brain

The sensitive window of brain changes in early to mid-adolescence up to 17 years of age means that teens are particularly susceptible to becoming addicted to anything in which they invest a lot of time and energy.

As I have already covered, this is because the brain creates an abundance of dendrites to ensure that a teen can learn fast. It is a fabulous window of opportunity because they can learn a new language quicker, pick up a musical instrument quicker and, if focused and striving, they can improve in their competence and capability in sport, any academic pursuit, or a new passion like skateboarding, singing, cooking or dancing.

However, an overuse of technology for entertainment purposes may have some serious negative impacts on that same developing brain. All of our brains are hunting dopamine – the feel-good neuro-chemical that makes us feel fabulous. In the underdeveloped teen-boy brain dopamine hunting becomes their favourite pastime. Annoyingly, dopamine has a tendency to hijack the rational part of the human brain, the very important and yet-to-be completed prefrontal cortex. This means if a boy has to choose between doing his maths assign-ment, his household chores or gaming, in his mind there is no choice to make. He's got an irrational hunger to create more dopamine and this is one of the reasons why stopping him from gaming or any other form of enjoyment online that is creating dopamine can cause such a confrontational meltdown of even the nicest of our lads.

In her excellent article for *Psychology Today*, 'Gray Matters: Too Much Screen Time Damages the Brain', Victoria L. Dunckley M.D. writes that research into video games has shown that during gaming, dopamine is released and this brain chemical is associated with reward and addiction. Because the addicted brain has been so overloaded with dopamine, it adjusts by reducing the number of dopamine recep-tors – *so the reward is no longer as satisfying, causing users to crave more and more.*

Remember, technology that is used for educational reasons is seldom used for as long a period of time or as frequently as technology used for entertainment purposes. The issues occur with what happens when the brain is doing something repeatedly, especially when it triggers our reward centre. Each time the brain will be hunting a little more dopamine and an even bigger reward which means it is even harder to stop using it, especially for our boys.

It is not just the threat of developing an addiction to gaming that is the problem. As the article outlines, studies now show a shrinking of grey matter areas, which is where we do our processing, in people with internet/gaming addiction. This can affect all sorts of things including a person's ability to organise their thoughts and themselves, to plan and to prioritise. More worrying is the possibility that this phenomenon can impact our empathy and compassion. I am deeply concerned about any further delays in the growth of the prefrontal cortex or the mature adult brain!

So from a common-sense perspective, it is important to ensure there are healthy limits to the amount of time our teen lads are gaming to ensure that they do not experience what Dunckley calls electronic screen syndrome. Some lads waste hours watching YouTube videos, ironically often about other teens playing online games. Even this activity is meeting some of their biological needs, especially of feeling they belong somewhere that is nonthreatening and safe as a form of chill-out time.

Many teen boys argue that some forms of gaming encourage problem-solving and creativity. Practicing therapist, researcher and lecturer Dr Mari Swingle argues something quite different in her updated book *i-Minds*. In her research, particularly around Alpha brainwaves, she has come to the conclusion that gaming and all excessive applications of digital media:

> . . . supplant creative process and decrease the ability to sustain focus by increasing frontal Alpha brainwaves. They decrease innovation and decrease focus on that which is not overtly stimulating. They also decrease our ability to quiet, to reach states of solace, introspection and calm.

Her book is full of real-life case studies of mainly boys with problematic behaviour as a consequence of excessive usage of technology, in some form or other. Dr Swingle tends to agree with researcher and author of *iGen*, Dr Jean M. Twenge, who believes that children who have been super-connected digitally are growing up completely unprepared for adulthood. These young people are statistically less happy, less rebellious and often paralysed with the fear of doing and the fear of failure.

Dr Swingle's modality of research and practice includes neurotherapy and electroencephalogy (EEG) and her research extends well before this army of technology inundated our homes and schools. This means she is able to compare the changes in the brain and the brain's efficiency and quantitatively explore the differences. One of the concerns that Swingle shares that can be shown with brain mapping is that *many digital children and adolescents of today are largely bored by reality*. Essentially this is because with excessive screen use these young people have rewired their brains to function on different levels of arousal, both dopamine and adrenaline. Swingle argues that rather than feeling happy, which has a particular blend of homeostasis in the human brain, many of those using gaming or eSport frequently or excessively are experiencing a high that is an artificially or purely chemical generated neurophysiological state and not an authentic emotion.

Why do teen boys like gaming so much?

There are a number of reasons why our beautiful sons can disappear down the rabbit hole of excessive gaming that can be helpful for parents to understand. It may also help you understand why you are wasting valuable time on your phone as well.

- **State of insufficiency** – which means that there is not a clear endpoint in gaming. If one game ends, there are all sorts of prompts and intermittent variable rewards that encourage them to keep going because they almost won. When you read a book, there is an ending. Online activity does not have a clear-cut ending and leaves us psychologically wanting more.

- **State of flow** – where our boys lose track of time and have absolutely no idea how long they have been gaming for, despite having given you a timeframe. This is not intentionally being disobedient; they genuinely lose all sense of time. Remember, it is better to give boys directions on how many more games they can play, rather than time because no-one will want to leave a game that is incomplete! Using external timers as a bit of a reminder can be helpful, however, one mum told me that her 14-year-old son threw the timer she gave him out the window into the swimming pool!
- **GABA** – which is a naturally occurring amino acid that works as a neurotransmitter in your brain, which means it's a kind of chemical messenger. GABA is considered an inhibitory neurotransmitter because it blocks, or inhibits, certain brain signals and decreases activity in your nervous system. GABA is turned off during the teen years and so managing potentially risky choices is impaired.
- **The fear of missing out, or FOMO** – which is a real thing for teens as well as many adults. If you are playing with your mates online and having a fabulous time, there is no way on earth that you would want to walk away and miss out on some fun. It can be helpful if groups of boys and their parents work out some regular gaming times that fit in with family boundaries. This means that they game with their mates with your blessing, which will always be much better than the opposite. This can also help protect your sons from being groomed online – which is happening.
- Elsewhere in this book, I have suggested that boys who feel that they are loved by their parents and feel secure in their friendship circles are less likely to make consistently risky and poor choices. It seems that something similar is happening underneath our boys and the need to spend hours gaming. For some boys it is an escape from other needs that are not being met in their world – like boredom, undiagnosed anxiety, being worried, feeling a failure or not feeling challenged in life.

Some boys who have lived through adverse childhood experiences can also have a stronger tendency to immerse themselves in a fantasy world because their real world has been a source of significant pain.

Other concerns to keep in mind regarding digital use and gaming

1. **Amount of time** – currently in Australia the average time that children are spending in the digital world – outside of school hours – is 32 hours a week. For teens and younger adults, it is 44 hours a week. The recommendations are for two hours a day outside school so 14 hours per week minimum. I am pretty sure weekend usage would be more than two hours a day. Obviously during the isolation caused by the coronavirus this has escalated.

2. **Avoiding myopia** – there has been a significant increase in myopia, or short-sightedness, in children and teens. We can't just blame the screen for this but the screen is displacing the valuable and essential time that children need to be outside in natural light which helps to elongate the myopic nerve.

3. **Unnecessary deafness** – our ears are sensitive things and there is significant research that is suggesting using smaller earbuds rather than noise-cancelling headphones in childhood is becoming problematic. The sound going into our ears needs to be no more than 65–75 decibels. In the midst of a battle on Fortnite, some of our boys can have the sound up to over 300 decibels. Please check on what's happening with your son's headphones.

4. **Lack of vitamin D** – vitamin D deficiency has become problematic for lots of us who spend little time in natural sunlight, however, for teen boys who are gaming excessively this is a real concern. The body needs vitamin D as part of a strong immune system. Get your son outside every day.

5. **Posture problems** – given that we are already finding four-year-olds with posture problems due to a combination of a hunched spine over a screen and a lack of physical activity that strengthens the shoulder muscles and the back, our older boys are at risk of similar concerns. There are some great suggestions online about ergonomics that can help you and your son with this. Ensure that your son is getting enough physical activity to strengthen his shoulders and back. Activities such as climbing walls, long monkey bars, zip lines, ninja warrior circuits, martial arts, certain sports and possibly some appropriate weights can help build strength.

6. **Drop in school grades** – this is another red flag that your son's digital behaviour has become problematic. If your son's grades drop, keep checking in every couple of months with your school to monitor the situation. If you leave it too long, it can be almost impossible to catch up and a boy will simply give up trying.

7. **Sleep problems** – struggling to fall asleep and stay asleep are common problems in adolescents, however, there are more and more studies showing the impact of the digital screen and the intermittent blue light and the negative impact it can have on sleep. A lack of daylight can also impact the capacity for the brain to create melatonin. Significant lack of sleep will negatively impact every area of your son's life and is a strong contributing factor to adolescent depression.

8. **School avoidance** – as a boy's usage becomes more and more excessive, and possibly addictive, he will be unable to gather enough energy or motivation to leave the house. Seek professional help immediately.

9. **Aggressive behaviour** – I have worked with boys who have absolutely trashed the family home, and even with one who attacked a locked office door with an axe. If the situation has got to this level with your son, seek professional help as soon as possible because it can escalate further really quickly.

10. **Emotional instability** – even though we know these years are confusing and stressful for our teens and that emotional angst is normal, be mindful of an increase in the irrational outbursts that may also last longer and may take a lot longer to calm down. Some of this is coming from anxiety and a sense of losing control between the real world and the digital world. Some boys are even known to begin self-harming when the pressure gets too much.

11. **Lack of physical activity** – the more everyone moves, the healthier we will be. Passivity and too much sitting down will compromise your son's healthy development throughout adolescence. Do everything you can to get them off their butt and moving their body – preferably with their mates or friends, in the fresh air while having some fun.

12. **Social withdrawal** – if your son has dropped out of his sporting teams, avoids going to family events, no longer has friends stopping by, is declining invitations to hang out and has very little movement outside his bedroom on weekends or holidays, BE WORRIED! These teen years are incredibly important in your son developing the social and emotional capacities to interact with people in the real world. It can only happen with real-world interaction. Catch this as soon as you can and turn it around. Consider getting a fire pit or taking your son and his mates camping. Do everything you can to reconnect him to real people in the real world.

13. **Increased inattentiveness, decreased capacity to concentrate, poorer metacognition, decreased creativity and problem-solving capacity** – these are signs that the brain is struggling and these attributes contribute to the rise of boys struggling, unmotivated boys stuck at home, delays in getting a licence, and boys leaving home much later in life.

14. **Increase in mental ill health, especially increase in anxiety** – many teens are stressing about small things like ordering a coffee at a coffee shop, answering a phone call and basic communication skills. Without practice from real-life human interaction, many

teens, especially boys, are floundering in the real world. Social anxiety has increased with many gamers finally stepping out of their bedroom around 18–20 to seek social connectedness. Their biological drive to find a mate will finally kick in but they lack the social and emotional awareness to know how to relate not just with girls but also with boys in real time.

Family guidelines for healthy boundaries around screen time, digital use and gaming

Rather than set the rules yourself, sit down as a family to develop guidelines for how and when digital devices can be used by the whole family. The rules will apply to you as well as your son.

Some examples of family rules:

- Strive to keep meal times screen free even if your son does not say a word or possibly grunts at you. He will know that you are fully present and that is a gift that will keep on giving.
- Stopping eating a meal to check an Instagram update, or to check on a sporting result is not OK.
- No phones or digital devices are allowed in bedrooms.
- Many families have begun removing all technology access, on phones, devices, smart speakers or smart TVs after 9 o'clock every night. This means that anything that needs to be done using technology is done before 9 pm. The families I have spoken to who have implemented this boundary have been surprised with how much happier and more connected they have become.

How to negotiate and manage gaming with your son

Dr Kristy Goodwin is a digital wellbeing expert who is constantly telling parents that they need to be the pilot of the digital plane not the passenger.

The digital world has possibly become a more predictable world for many of our tech-savvy boys. It is completely understandable that they want to escape the undue pressures of the real world and disappear down the rabbit hole of self-directed entertainment and escapism. Just as we do not let our precious children run on a highway, we must not let them run freely in the digital world. Remember that as a parent there is a huge difference between controlling and healthy monitoring.

Common sense would suggest that monitoring usage and purpose of being on a digital device is important. Fortunately, there are many parental monitoring apps and programs that can help parents do this (and often devices have built-in parental controls too). Yes, teenage boys are very good at getting around these controls – but it is a really good starting point. Even though there is a really good chance that your sons will know way more than you about technology, their ability to navigate healthy boundaries is very underdeveloped. I really appreciate Dr Goodwin's other common-sense advice that digital amputation is not the answer to managing this issue. Education and monitoring of healthy boundaries is the way to go. A wonderful, very recent book that will help with this is *The Modern Parent* by Martine Oglethorpe. Martine is an Australian mum of five boys, a former secondary school teacher and counsellor, and her book provides a very realistic, up-to-date and practical resource for anyone with tween or teen boys.

So here are my suggestions about setting up an agreement with your son, which he needs to agree to if he wants technology privileges.

The 10 agreements for tween and teen boys on gaming

It is *excessive* usage that can create serious problems and the 10 agreements can help keep everyone happy. However, you do need to keep revisiting it and negotiating changes to it!

In order to have access to the wi-fi and his PC or device your boy needs to agree to the following terms:

1. No computer or device in his bedroom without permission.
2. He needs to be actively engaged in outside of bedroom/home activity that builds emotional and social competence at least twice a week – preferably a group activity.
3. He should be engaged in some form of sport/martial arts/surfing/skating at least three times a week.
4. He needs to complete normal chores around home (create a roster if you need help to keep track).
5. His school grades need to be maintained.
6. He needs to join the family at meal times (without devices) and have an agreed bedtime (again, without devices).
7. He should have a friend/mate visit or whom he goes to visit weekly (and they have time offline together).
8. He accepts responsibility for any excessive data expenses.
9. He must not disable the parental controls that you have put in place.
10. He must avoid porn sites and limit engaging in violent content (follow age-appropriate guidelines), viewing MA 15+ or R 18+ or showing anyone else. **Please stress he is NEVER to show this material to anyone else even if they ask.**

If the terms of the agreement are all adhered to, your boy will be managing his gaming in a way that is not going to cause long-term damage. This is called healthy boundaries. In chapter 10 about helping our *boys to lose, fail and recover* I explained about the importance of consequences. Your son will be familiar with consequences that come following his choices and hopefully over time he will make choices that have pleasant consequences not painful or uncomfortable consequences.

I suggest you email your son's year coordinator every month to check that his grades are still being maintained. He will not voluntarily share this information with you especially if he has started to drop his grades. Leaving it until the end of the semester can be really problematic if he does need to catch up. Many schools now have a digital platform that staff, students and parents can access to check on academic progress. This is such a good idea.

When boundaries start slipping, I suggest your son simply lose the privilege of access for 24 hours the first time, 48 hours the second time and an extra 24 hours each time a transgression occurs. Our boys need our help to maintain this freedom to ensure they stay healthy on all levels.

Allow some flexibility if your son occasionally negotiates small changes to the terms as this encourages cooperation and fairness rather than resentment and rebellion.

What to do when problematic usage becomes worse

As parents I need you to trust your instincts around your son's usage of technology. Review the 10 steps to the agreement above and just keep your finger on the pulse. When any of the above points are compromised in a cluster, that is a red flag that things need action or an intervention of some kind.

The absolute best book available about understanding unhealthy technology usage is one called *The Tech Diet for Your Child & Teen* by Brad Marshall. This incredibly easy to read and practical book will give you the answers you are looking for.

Marshall's seven-step plan to unplug excessive digital usage does not require digital amputation (as Dr Kristy Goodwin calls it) and your son will be very happy about that. However, it is a carefully planned and managed program. I like that it is not a complicated plan, it is a written plan and your son does have some input into it.

Research is suggesting that there is a correlation between problematic gaming and existing mental-health issues like anxiety or depression, *however, it does not prove causation. If you are concerned, please seek professional help around problematic usage.*

Cyberbullying

I need to clarify a common misperception that girls may be responsible for most cyberbullying. In fact, our boys are almost equally responsible. Bullying is a learned behaviour and in many ways the anonymity of the digital world has given them more power to harass, ridicule and be cruel to others.

In the past, I have worked with teen boys who have bullied others and often they too have been a victim of bullying – no excuse, but still something to consider. If you can learn to bully, you can learn to do the opposite – be empathetic and respectful. However, the most difficult window to do this is during adolescence with an underdeveloped prefrontal cortex, heightened emotional intensity, poor impulsivity control and a strong egocentric tendency. Still no excuse for us as parents to throw our hands in the air and do nothing.

One of the accepted characteristics of bullying is a lack of empathy as a social skill. In other words, they lack the emotional maturity to understand the impact of their actions on another person. Teen boys are most at risk of lacking empathy.

> Between ages 13 and 16, boys show a temporary decline in empathy on a biological level – a decline not suffered by girls.
> – Warren Farrell and John Gray, *The Boy Crisis:*
> *Why Our Boys Are Struggling and What*
> *We Can Do About It* (2019)

Farrell and Gray explore the gap between the need for peer approval for boys and the lack of skills to get it. For some boys, bullying other boys can be a desperate attempt to gain peer approval, to give them some sense of worth and value – sadly at the cost of another boy's sense of worth and value. Underneath all of these things is a yearning for respect from others.

Let us clarify again before going any further what is not bullying. Spontaneous name-calling, occasional teasing and banter, 'aggression nurturance' and occasionally using your mates as a source of creating fun – even if not successful – is not bullying. Bullying is an intentional act that is often repeated with the purpose of disrespecting and harming another person.

One of the biggest challenges of the digital world is that bullying continues beyond the school gate. Dr Kristy Goodwin reminds parents often that at night-time *the executive functioning part of our brain goes offline*. So, for our teen boys who already have an underdeveloped prefrontal cortex, night-time behaviour online can be fraught with challenge, especially given their biological wiring to be risk-taking mammoth hunters in training.

Dr Goodwin also reminds us that one of the reasons why it is not recommended to punish your son through digital amputation, even for a short period of time, is because we want our sons to come to us if they are being cyberbullied or possibly are worried about being groomed online or are struggling with abusive and aggressive behaviour of one of the players in their online game. They will not come to you for support if there is any chance you will remove them from the device, phone or laptop.

Here are five key recommendations from the eSafety Commissioner to teach your son in the event that he has been cyberbullied.

1. Avoid taking action immediately – other than showing a parent.
2. Step away and take steps to calm yourself down.
3. Take screenshots.
4. Try to avoid revisiting or checking the offensive posts.
5. Report and block it.

These steps sound easy but they are extremely difficult for a tween or teen boy. He does not want to look weak, vulnerable, or expose the fact that he is being attacked and more often than not, he will respond by attacking back (or forward) in some way. There have been many cases where other students from school have made up malicious lies that have completely destroyed a boy's reputation and social standing beyond repair.

- In Australia the Office of the eSafety Commissioner is a wonderful first port of call if you have any concerns regarding image abuse. They have information and can support young people and their families to take action if this has happened to them. Every country will have similar sites for guidance.
- Stymie.com.au is another fantastic resource that allows students to make anonymous notifications about their peers to stop them being bystanders to cyberbullying.

WHAT'S THE BEST THING ABOUT BEING A TEEN BOY TODAY?

- The ways we can reach out for help is extensive. It allows us to have that access that other people didn't decades ago.
- If in comparison to being a youth from prior decades, my answer is probably that I have access to many things which those before me did not, such as more advanced technology in entertainment (e.g. video games, streaming platforms) and the internet in general which provides a huge wealth of sources for research on school work and many sites which are good for leisure.

Grooming and online predators

We have an enormous responsibility as parents today to make sure we are keeping all of our children safe in the real world and the digital world. Yes, it is difficult to keep up-to-date with the evolving digital landscape, however, striving to stay well informed is part of your responsibility being a parent.

Having many, many conversations about appropriate behaviour online, ways to keep ourselves safe from sexual predators, hackers and spammers needs to happen almost daily. Maybe you could suggest to your son that he keeps you up to speed with some of the new apps and the possible pluses and minuses of them. Then you can remind him with great love that he can share this vital information with his friends and mates so that he can help them stay safe as well.

Ask your son to explain to you how he knows the players he games with and what he would do if he felt he was being groomed or bullied by one of them. Remember, our teen boys can be really naïve and exploring possible scenarios can be quite helpful in building his understanding about some of the creeps and sickos that are also playing in the boy landscape.

If you are wanting a comprehensive list of dos and don'ts around the use of technology in your home may I recommend the following websites:

www.commonsensemedia.com
www.esafety.gov.au
www.drkristygoodwin.com
www.safeonsocial.com

19

How to talk about drugs, alcohol, parties, cars and going out safely

Alcohol

Alcohol has a lot to answer for in homes and communities everywhere when it is used irresponsibly and excessively. In a research study led by Wayne State University in Detroit into the relationship between sexual assault and alcohol consumption, the researchers found some common characteristics among a significant number of male perpetrators of sexual violence against women. These were that these perpetrators commonly held these attitudes and beliefs:

- traditional gender role beliefs
- acceptance of rape myth
- hostility towards women
- acceptance of force in interpersonal relationships
- alcohol expectancies regarding sexuality, aggression and disinhibition
- stereotypes about women drinking alcohol
- alcohol as a cue for consensual sex.

If you do have alcohol in your home, I seriously suggest securing the cupboard where you keep it with a padlock. Your son is unlikely to touch those bottles when you're at home with him. However, change the scenario to a time when his parents are out and the boy is at home with his friends over and one of them suggests that they drink the vodka and replace it with water in the bottle. The psychological pull to belong with his peers and friends is much stronger than his love and respect for you, especially given that he is lacking myelin and so is unable to think deeply and with insight. Chances are he will agree with his mates and he will make the poor choice that will see the vodka disappear. If you have put a padlock on the cupboard, you have helped him to avoid making this poor choice.

In 2015, males aged 15–24 experienced nearly two times the burden of disease from alcohol and drug use compared to females. What this essentially means is that problematic alcohol and drug use (use that negatively impacts physical and mental health and well-being) impacts boys at nearly twice the rate of girls. Much of the problematic usage of alcohol begins before 15 – in an incredibly vulnerable window of brain development where it is much easier to become addicted more quickly, which I explore in much more depth in chapter 4. I urge you to do everything you can to prevent your teen boy from having easy access to alcohol or developing a taste for alcohol even within your home until he is over 16 when the brain does do some serious maturation. Of course, in a perfect world we would really prefer them not to access alcohol until they are of legal age, which to be perfectly honest when exploring the statistics should be 21 at a bare minimum.

The Australian Secondary Students' Alcohol and Drug Survey (ASSAD) is conducted every three years and up to 30,000 12- to 17-year-olds are surveyed about their use of tobacco, alcohol and other substances. As this book is being finalised, their 2020 report is imminent, however the 2017 report, which analyses substance use between 1996 and 2017, reported that there had been significant *improvement* in secondary students' use of substances since the late 1990s. So, compared to 1996 and even 2008, fewer students in this age bracket are smoking, drinking alcohol and using drugs like hallucinogens, MDMA, cocaine, marijuana and others. Australia is not alone in this trend either as there's been similar downturns in New Zealand, the UK, US and Canada.

We need to be mindful to remember that the majority of our adolescents today, including our boys, are drinking much less than previous generations – especially their parents! That is not to say we dismiss alcohol abuse, particularly as it can still be problematic for teens, especially teen boys. We know that alcohol further inhibits good decision-making and, when combined with the powerful social drive of belonging, things can go bad really quickly. Many sexual assaults that happen to both teen boys and teen girls have alcohol as a contributing factor.

Drugs

Experimentation is normal for teens and the same goes for drugs, both illicit and prescription medication. Peer pressure and the biological drive to stretch boundaries and take risks are normal. Research is suggesting that drug taking levels have been stable in recent times but given that synthetic drugs can be obtained online and technically invisibly, it is difficult to know what the reality is. 'Nanging' or the use of nitrous oxide (or 'laughing gas') has reportedly been growing in popularity among Australian teens. The small canisters or bulbs (or 'nangs') containing the gas are released into balloons and then inhaled. The effect is almost immediate, lasting for about 20 seconds. The person may then take many 'hits' over a few hours.

Ecstasy or MDMA (methylenedioxymethamphetamine) is another illegal drug that has grown in popularity among teens in recent years. It is sold as a tablet, capsule (caps), powder and in crystal form.

The strength of MDMA can vary enormously, as does the content of tablets, capsules, powders and crystals sold as ecstasy. MDMA and nangs are seen as pretty safe among teens, however deaths have occurred.

Usage of marijuana has decreased among teens however the use of meth, an incredibly highly addictive drug that is reasonably cheap, has increased. Boys who have mates who use drugs are more at risk of consuming them, too.

There are many excellent websites (such as drughelp.gov.au) that you can explore that can help your son learn about the risks and legal consequences, and possible negative outcomes of using drugs. Also talk about what to do if a friend takes a dangerous amount of anything and appears distressed, incoherent or is behaving in a concerning manner. Your most important lesson around drug use is to teach your son to step up and do something immediately like call an ambulance. It's a good idea too in Australia to have the free Emergency+ app on every young person's phone – it helps anyone calling Triple Zero to provide location details to the emergency services.

Parties

Australian alcohol and drug educator Paul Dillon has often written about his concern of parents blindly trusting their teen, especially when going out to parties. Of course, your son does know your expectations and your rules, but in a group setting with lots of young people and with alcohol or other drugs clouding his judgement, he can make really bad decisions quickly.

I agree with Paul when he writes the following:

The evidence is pretty clear that if you want to do your very best to keep your child safe through the teen years, there is a simple parenting formula to follow:

- know where your child is
- know who they're with, and
- know when they'll be home.

– Paul Dillon, ' "We trusted our teen and we were terribly let down":
A Mum warns other parents about "blind trust"', Doing Drugs
with Paul Dillon blog, 7 September 2019

My additional rules when I had boys 16 plus who were going to teen parties were the following:

- Never get in a car with someone who has been drinking or using drugs.
- Watch out for your mates at all times, especially on the way home.
- Any time you feel unsafe or you need help or you need a ride home you call me and I will come, no questions asked.

Even when my sons were home from university, they could call me and I would pick them up at any time of the night or early morning to ensure they got home safely. So often there are no taxis or Ubers or simply not enough to transport a large group of young people safely home. I believe the most dangerous time of the party is the journey home afterwards. This is when teens are at the most risk of making poor choices. Model genuine unconditional love and concern. Don't just talk about it – do it.

Cars
Cars and driving

A sobering statistic shows that your chances of dying, especially for boys, increases around 300 per cent during adolescence. There are some scary statistics around teen boys and risks around driving, particularly in rural areas where four beautiful boys can be killed in a car accident after just two seconds of poor choice making. For young people, the risk of fatality increases by 50 per cent with one other young passenger in the car, and by 160 per cent with another passenger. I talked to Steve Biddulph about this, knowing that he had been a consultant in shaping the legislation about teenage driving which is being brought in to combat these terrible multiple fatalities. He told me that, 'Even though boys are legally licensed to drive, in that first year or so they are still very immature both in driving itself, and emotionally. And so if they want to attend parties, go places with friends, especially after dark, then it's still a really a good idea for you to drive them, and collect them afterwards. Of course they will chafe at this, but it's our job to really lean in at these times. A year older and wiser, the evidence is that they will be safer drivers and be out of the high-risk zone.'

Then there are hospitalisations as a result of road accidents. According to the Australian Institute of Health and Welfare: 'In nearly two-thirds of non-fatal hospitalised injury cases due to on-road crashes, the injured person was *a male*. In all but the youngest age group, males were considerably more likely than females to be hospitalised due to a road crash. The highest age-specific rate for being hospitalised as the result of a road crash was for males aged 15–24 (321 cases per 100,000 population).'

Teach your sons that cars can be lethal weapons that can kill or maim.

20

Letting go

It is an interesting irony that I have discovered over the years that often dads let go of their sons too quickly, and mums tend to let go too slowly. Essentially, parents need to gradually give the reins to their sons so these boys can develop the capacity, the confidence and the independence they need to complete the journey to being a grown adult and a mature man. Every son will need a different blend of opportunities for autonomy, encouragement, support, and life-enriching experiences full of disappointment and joy in his journey to completely individuate as a separate human being. Working *with* your son rather than *doing things to* your son will certainly enable this journey of separation to happen more effectively and compassionately.

What is called impingement during the child's infancy is often called over mothering or a mother's domination as it continues into the son's boyhood, adolescence and even adulthood. A mother must realise that if she impinges on her child too much, **not letting him find his own way**, he will not develop a true self and will risk personality disorders – **moving through life unable to achieve intimacy, unable to set appropriate boundaries for himself** and **unable to find fulfilment.**

– Michael Gurian, *Mothers, Sons and Lovers: How a man's relationship with his mother affects the rest of his life* (1993)

Sons leaving home at 18 years plus

It's a tricky window for parents of sons to understand what happens when their son becomes a legal adult – as he steps onto the launch pad to a fully adult life. Research has shown that boys tend to be a little slower than girls in their readiness for the leap into the real world of being an adult. Indeed, boys who have been raised in a screen world might find that the transition point at which they are ready to manage their own lives seems to have stretched even further into their early twenties. We need to be clear that the final growth of our mature brain – the prefrontal cortex – has been shown not to be complete for our girls until around age 22 to 24, and for our boys it is any time from 25 onwards.

Those lads who have spent endless hours in their bedrooms or on their couches gaming rather than participating in the real world with real people are arriving at this point of launch very underprepared. To avoid this happening, we need to stop doing things for our boys that they can do for themselves. It is interesting that as boys get older mums tend to do more for them than they do for their daughters. Lazy boys who know that their mum will do their washing, their chores and get their lunch will simply sit back and let it happen. Our boys need to learn they need to become equal contributors rather than occasional helpers in the parenting team of the future.

Respected paediatrician and author Meg Meeker, the late highly regarded social justice advocate and author Celia Lashlie, and I all sing from the same song sheet and believe that when mums don't make boys do things for themselves, we are disabling them on so many levels. This is why a son benefits from having a firm and loving mum – in a type of balance! If we don't expect boys to learn to do things for themselves, we are teaching them that they don't have to be responsible or accountable. We are also teaching them that house-work and chores are women's work and that is simply very unhelpful for when they are in a committed relationship later in life. How can we teach fairness if we don't ensure they play a responsible part in the family? How can he learn how to be an effective partner in an intimate relationship?

To help you ensure that you keep building skills and abilities in your sons from the age of 10, check out my life skills posters, which you can find on my website.

ADVICE FOR TEEN BOYS TODAY

Support yourself, cooking, cleaning, ironing – be independent and don't rely on mum to do everything for you.

In some situations, it is simply financially unviable for your son to leave home around 18 years of age, when he technically comes of age. Even though he may still be living in your house, he can become a boarder which means he has to contribute financially and to par-ticipate as if he was living with other housemates. This new situation needs to be negotiated well ahead of the reality happening so that your son has a chance to get used to the changes that are about to happen. If he is wanting to stay in your home while he completes further study, there still needs to be some sort of change in the arrangements that makes it different to how it was when he was attending high school. 'Let's pretend' is a great way to explore the possibilities of making living at home a different experience now that he is older. If you have a son who is wanting to stay in your home because he is saving for a deposit on a house, it can be helpful to have a timeframe and to have some way of checking that he is actually saving money – rather than freeloading off you. I know this may sound unloving but I have worked with families whose very loving care of their son had created a very needy, unconfident son who had lost all motivation to become an independent man. He was 33 years of age and had well outstayed his welcome!

I am a firm believer in gap years where young people work, travel or both – especially boys. In a way, a year to 'grow up' a little and gain some life experience can be deceptively advantageous. Hopefully, if they spend time away from the safety of home and stretch their wings, a boy can learn to make some sound choices around managing money, accommodation and living with others. Many have experiences during that gap year that change their perception of what they want to do, and experiencing mild financial challenges, or unexpected travelling setbacks all help to develop a stronger sense of character and resilience for when they are finally ready to plot the journey of the rest of their lives. To help this become a reality, speak often over the tween and teen years about the possibility of having a gap year where they can possibly visit places in the world that fascinate them. This year outside of the home, even if it does not mean overseas travel, gives boys a valuable chance at maturing at a faster rate than staying in the family home.

> High school is over really quickly, enjoy it and don't stress. No-one cares if you're popular after high school. Your twenties is where you cut your teeth. Travel early.

Many boys simply follow what their parents advise to keep the peace, and later on they can come to resent the path chosen by their parents. Figuring out what he wants to do with his life can take some time and as long as your son is actively participating in life, even if it is delivering pizza, or working as a dishwasher in a café or restaurant, every day will be taking him closer to developing the maturity to make good choices about what he wants to do with his life. Indeed, I think one of the most beneficial things for our late-teen/early twenties sons is for them to do jobs that can be a bit tough – whether boring, tiring, challenging, dirty or with other unpleasant grown-ups. Seriously, one of the best motivators for your sons to want to strive for a better career pathway is doing a job that tests them.

IF YOU HAD YOUR TEEN YEARS OVER AGAIN, WHAT WOULD YOU CHANGE?

Determining what I was passionate about and not just going with what my parents advised me to do. I am 34 and it is only now when I have determined what my passion is and where I want to head in life for my career and family.

All four of my lads ended up at university; two took gap years. When they were on university holidays, they usually worked for a local grain receiver company. What I loved about this work was that it was long hours, sometimes incredibly monotonous, always with a high need of social interaction with farmers and truck drivers as well as workmates and it was often carried out in the heat of summer. They seriously had to earn their money! Over the years, some of them have also delivered pizzas, peeled onions in a Chinese restaurant, unpacked frozen fish and done pruning in vineyards in the depths of winter. They were all challenging experiences that I believe helped my boys to be motivated to go and use the brains they had and do more study. In an interesting aside, one of my sons said he really admired some of the older men he met on the vineyard who had been doing that work for over 30 years and who took great pride in the work he did. Sometimes our young lads need to be humbled by the value of hard work, tenacity and doing what is best for one's family. I am incredibly proud of the work ethic of my four sons.

One of my sons spent the whole of his summer holidays earning money to buy his first car. Towards the end of his first year at university, he was distracted while driving (and that was before we had mobile phones) and crashed into the back of another car. Fortunately, he was not hurt but the front of his car was badly damaged. He learned a really big life lesson that year because when he came home, he had to work another whole summer holiday to be able to pay for the repairs. A tough lesson for sure but one where he learned some humility and gratitude that he had found an unskilled job that he could do to create the money he needed to help him move forward in life.

I have counselled many young men who struggled during this transition from high school to life, and who finally realised what they wanted to do when they were around 27–30 years of age. In a way, having more time to bloom at this point in life can be as helpful as having a little bit more time to bloom in the early years. In our hurry-up world, taking this time out is becoming harder to achieve.

WHAT WORRIES YOU MOST ABOUT GROWING UP?

- Having to move away from home and not knowing enough to do it.
- Not being taught what I need to know to survive in the adult world.
- . . . being able to afford a house, and supporting a family.
- . . . money, responsibility with tax bills and stuff.

Constantly reaffirming your unconditional love for your son when he has his muck-up moments in late adolescence will help him enormously when the world becomes uncertain and confusing. It can be an incredibly frustrating time.

Remember, as our boys keep stepping away from us, as they need to, unfortunately life can throw them unexpected moments of significant adversity that can tip them into a world of emotional turmoil, and they often have few tools to manage in the fallout. A teen boy can find himself dealing with the end of his parents' relationship, death, a natural disaster, serious illness or accident, a broken heart or significant bullying that is threatening his sense of safety in the world. Every child needs to have a safe grown-up that they can turn to – if not a parent then a lighthouse figure who will always hold a welcoming and safe space for them while the turmoil rages around them. The time of 18 plus can actually be more risky than the earlier years of adolescence. This is why I humbly ask all mums and dads and all those who belong in their tribe to watch out for all their son's mates and friends on this final journey to adulthood, because the more the better in creating those safe railings on that bridge. Traditionally, boys have been less forthcoming seeking help from others when they are feeling vulnerable and we need to change this so more of our beautiful boys can grow up to be healthy, happy, loving men. Every gesture of kindness and compassion will make a difference to our boys during their final stage of letting go of their mums.

For boys in the late teen years who are very sensitive to being judged, criticised and even accidentally shamed, listening to verbal communication can be really difficult. Keep checking in. With a written note, a boy has a chance to read the message several times to ensure he understands the meaning of the message, rather than jump to unintended conclusions. Keep in mind the power of the mum letter and the dad message and quiet chats while in the car, walking the dog or shooting some hoops. There are times we do need to ask our boys if they are struggling and in a way that they can hear us and know that it's OK to not be OK. Learn to trust your gut instincts around your son and keep in touch – a little, not too much! Text them funny things, tag them in funny things online and occasionally it will be OK to remind them of things – just not too often.

Letting go, even when you want to hold on tight

As I was putting together this chapter, I found this message which I wrote in my newsletter when my second son left home in 2003. I felt compelled to include it as it took me right back to that time.

When my eldest rooster confident son left to go to the city for uni, I found it hard for the first week and cried a few tears. He had been strong, often opinionated and stubborn, and he was ready to go. It is much easier to let these sons go and, honestly, when they leave you may have a huge sigh of relief.

When I had to let my second six-foot baby leave home, I thought because I had done it once, it would be easy. Not so. Number two son was more lamb-like, thoughtful, caring and so helpful. He cooked dinners, took washing off the line without being asked and knew when I needed a cuppa to soothe my frazzled nerves. He was so much harder to let go. Be prepared to experience deep grief when your sensitive tender-hearted son may leave home and know this is still the right time to let go.

Being a parent, whether biological, step or surrogate, was always going to have its moments and I am sharing this with you to remind you to be grateful for every moment in your son or daughter's lives while they are there in the family home. Don't waste time on the nagging, the growling. Let it go and love more often. Laugh with them and stand beside them as they discover who they are independent of you. Above all just know when they choose to leave – we must let them go, no matter how much you want to hang on and keep them. It may very well be the hardest and kindest thing you will ever do for them. Sometimes they may seem like a boomerang as they come back and go again and that's OK too.

Thankfully, my sons had the protection of good friendships with mates and some of their cousins. Collectively, they learned to look out for each other and to help each other when things got tough. This is how Mother Nature intended it to be. When your son will leave your family home, he will seek to create another sense of home, where he will feel he belongs with people who care for him – even if he might be really annoying at times.

The ultimate letting go is when our boys find another person to love deeply instead of us. I have joked with one of my sons who was very late in finding that woman that I needed to hand the baton over – she needed to matter more than me.

Probably the most important gift you can give your children is the right and the freedom to leave home one day, keen and full of enthusiasm to live their own lives with guts and confidence. Yes, the aim of parenting is to make yourself redundant! One day your son will leave home, not yet a man. And one day many years down the track, you'll meet your son as a man – but for this wonderful moment to happen, you have to let him go. You cannot hurry up the final stages of maturation of your son. Be patient. Be positive. Stay connected, give him the freedom and allow him to discover who he really is, and allow him to find a way to discover a meaningful purpose to make the world a better place.

A final, special message for parents

You matter.

Biological parents, step-parents, foster parents, grandparents everywhere . . . you really matter in this critical window of our boys' lives. The boys who thrive as they race or stumble across that bridge to adulthood are those who have had consistent, loving and predictable 'parents' who have ridden the tumultuous years and never given up.

We must resist the urge to hurry up these years between 12 and 25, as true life development and maturity takes time. We need to not only accept these years as important, we need to keep our eyes on the goal of raising a mature young man one day.

The more stable and committed relationships in your son's life the better. I believe teaching your son about the concept of resilience and recovery from moments of hardship as often as you can will help him have a more realistic understanding of the 'bugger-up' moments he is going to experience as a teen boy.

One of the things that I found really heartening in the messages from the more than 1600 men who lent their voices to this book was the profound wisdom they shared with the boys today. We must be careful not to give our boys any messages that they are failing, even though they will experience moments of failure, as they grow through these vital years. Life will bring moments of both success and failure – for everyone, every year of our life!

Joseph Campbell, the wise philosopher, called this journey from child to adult a hero's journey. And when our boys are on this hero's journey, they will be challenged deeply and they will change deeply. They will meet demons that have the potential to annihilate them, and they will also find allies who will walk beside them and give them the courage they are unable to find within themselves. At the end of the journey they will be transformed; they will have become someone very different – a little older, wiser, maybe with a few scars. To expect the journey of adolescence to be a smooth and predictable one is not only unrealistic, it is unhelpful.

Communities have been having babies and raising children to be adults for a very long time. The things that our boys need to become the men we hope for have not changed – however, the world around our boys has changed. As this book comes to a close, I want to remind you the basics always matter in your homes. Relationships, sometimes fantastic and sometimes pretty crappy, are the vital first component of raising boys to be healthy, happy men. They need to feel accepted exactly as they are, not just how you want them to be, and we need to be brave enough to give them the spaces of freedom to do this. They want to be valued, loved and respected – at least sometimes. They cannot traverse this journey alone. Historically our boys were surrounded by committed grown-ups to ensure they were not lost.

As parents we need to seriously prioritise the other five key things that will help our sons thrive not just survive:

1. Nutritious food – keep the rubbish and the junk food in check.
2. Sleep – ensure the boundaries around this are always maintained.

3. Physical activity – the more your boys move, the better they grow, the calmer they will be and the better they will sleep.
4. Social interaction – in the real world with friends, lighthouses and engaging in hobbies, sport or adventures in the wild.
5. Maintaining the railings on the bridge – giving your son structure and predictability and warm discipline.

Every child is born with their own unique gifts and challenges. Our world seems to have a 'deficit' focus on boys – an intent on identifying and then trying to fix up the challenges and flaws in our boys. I believe this focus weakens the strengths that each boy has. This deficit focus definitely intensifies during tween and teen years as there is an over-concentration from grown-ups about 'What's wrong with my son?' Remember the notion of positive noticing – please strive to do this and remember to celebrate them even if this will not translate into an improvement in their grades. You are raising a whole child, not a brain on a seat.

When we give our son an opportunity to grow an honest, loving heart; a creative mind; a healthy body and a strong human spirit, we give him the greatest opportunity to become the best expression of himself. All levels need to be nurtured.

My hope in writing this book was to give you – the parent – an in-depth understanding of this time of transition developmentally, culturally, emotionally and psychologically so that you are able to be an aware and conscious parent as you walk beside your son over the bridge to adulthood and a healthy manhood with confidence and swagger.

Meeting and getting to know your son on the other side is something to really look forward to and in many ways, it will be like meeting a whole new person. I believe they must leave their tribe to truly find themselves no matter how hard the letting go will be. For those of you whose sons become fathers, that moment of meeting your son's firstborn is one of the most significantly profound moments of your journey as a parent.

My last reminder is a call to gather the collective – the community – to spread their arms wide and gather every boy into the circle of support from the older men and women who have already crossed this bridge into adulthood. We need to see all the boys in our schools, our neighbourhoods and in our online communities as *our boys* – as they do in traditional kinship communities. There is no 'them' and 'us'; it is quite simply 'we'. Then we need to see them as potentially psychologically fragile rather than tough. Finally we need to give them hope that one day they will reach the other side of this often challenging bridge. Remember, every boy matters, no matter what.

Maggie Dent
Incredibly proud mum of four fabulous sons, nanny,
aunty to heaps, 'lighthouse' to even more and always
a passionate boy champion – who also likes girls.

Acknowledgements

This book has become a reality firstly thanks to some very persuasive work done by Ingrid Ohlsson who is the Director of Non-fiction Publishing at Pan Macmillan Australia. Ingrid convinced me that I had left a space at the end of my previous book, *Mothering Our Boys*, when I had apologised that I had not been able to go into as much depth about teen boys as I would have liked.

So here it is – and again I am sorry that I have written another big book because I know all parents are time-poor and incredibly busy. My intention was to give you as much quality information amidst good stories that will help you trust your own instincts about your son.

Firstly, my very competent copy editor Samantha Sainsbury – you are an amazing editor! Thank you for fine-tuning my huge manuscript, and for helping me bring the best book to the parents of our precious sons. My next thanks is to my editor at Pan Macmillan, the switched-on, totally capable young man Alex Lloyd – our master of the birthing of this book. It was so important to have a man, especially a young man, on the job on a book about boys!

I wish to thank my amazing researcher, editor and my other right hand – my dear friend Carmen Myler. Again, Carmen has tamed my apostrophes, double-checked on all my referencing and ensured I had a fantastic easy-to-use index for those who want to just dip in from time to time. You are a star, Carmen!

Team Maggie has covered my back so that I could disappear and focus on writing. My PA – my gorgeous niece Laura Browning – thank you for the endless hours of organising my conference and seminar schedule! To my amazing graphic designer/web mistress/email gate-keeper and very dear friend from when I taught her when she was 16, Katharine Middleton – thank you for keeping emails at bay so I can concentrate on writing uninterrupted. My behind-the-scenes team who also help me create the space to write – Kelly Skinner thank you for all the help with copyright permissions. Caitlin Murphy – thank you for the monitoring of my socials. To Will Ambrose – another of my behind-the-scenes team – a huge thank you for collating and sorting through all of our enormous survey material, making it easy for me to read and understand.

My growing, fabulous family are always supporting and encouraging me even from a distance. We have just welcomed another gorgeous little grandson into our family and I feel so blessed and grateful for yet another miracle coming into our big, extended, chaotic family. Thank you for all you give me especially the joy and the opportunities to steal your children from you so we can have special times together!

My good bloke and husband Steve has survived yet another birthing of a book, the seventh major book. He is a master at supporting me when I am writing very long days – by heating my wheat pack, bringing me endless cups of tea, cooking really healthy meals and allowing me to be as non-communicative as I need to be while I process the research and the writing. Again, I can only do what I do because of the unconditional love and support that my good man gives me – thanks, babe.

Within the pages of this book are so many stories and anecdotes about so many beautiful boys and men. I thank every single one of them for trusting me with their stories, their struggles and their vulnerabilities. Without their stories, there would be no book. To every single one of you, I thank you deeply and profoundly.

To every teen boy who responded to my survey – thanks a million, guys. It reminded me how much I miss teaching – especially in my middle-school classrooms.

To every man who took the time to complete the surveys, I also extend my heartfelt thanks. I was blown away with the depth of wisdom that came through many of the surveys and also the validation of the things that can make the journey over that bridge to adulthood so damn challenging.

My very last thanks goes to many of you who have read my previous books or attended my seminars. Just as I think it's time for me to step away from my parent education and advocacy work, one of you will come and share how much I have helped you to be the parent you want to be – often with tears in your eyes (and then mine!). So, your encouragement matters to me and I thank you for giving me the fuel in my tank to keep being the positive voice for the children of our world, especially the ones you love and especially our boys.

Endnotes

Introduction

xx–xxi. In Australia, there has been a huge . . .: Wood A & Crawford, S (1 November 2014). 'Kindy crisis'. *The Daily Telegraph.*

xxi. Statistically our boys are struggling right . . .: Goodsell B, Lawrence D, Ainley J, Sawyer M, Zubrick SR, Maratos J (2017). 'Child and Adolescent Mental Health and Educational Outcomes'. Graduate School of Education, The University of Western Australia.

Chapter 1

4. An Australian survey of 600 girls . . .: Plan International Australia and Our Watch report, 'Don't send me that pic'. March 2016.

5. Mission Australia's 2018 Youth Survey reports . . .: Mission Australia (2018), missionaustralia.com.au.

Chapter 2

20. Even just one hundred years ago . . .: Several studies report this including Herman-Giddens M, Steffes J, Harris D, Slora E, Hussey M, & Dowshen S et al (2012). 'Secondary Sexual Characteristics in Boys'. *Pediatrics*, 130(5), e1058-e1068.

23. It seems that the muscle layer . . .: Janssen I, Heymsfield S, Wang Z, & Ross R (2000). 'Skeletal muscle mass and distribution in 468 men and women aged 18–88 yr'. *Journal of Applied Physiology*, 89(1), 81–88.

32. Michael Gurian, author of *The Wonder . . .*: Gurian M (1996). *The Wonder of Boys.* New York: Putnam.

Chapter 3

41. More recent research suggests that rather . . .: Biddulph S (2018). *Raising Boys in the 21st Century.* Sydney: Finch.

50. Studies have been done comparing computer . . .: 'Driving Under the Influence of Friends is Risky for Teens' (2015). Association for Psychological Science.

Chapter 4

58. Teens can lose as much as 15–20 . . .: Spear, LP (2013). 'Adolescent neurodevelopment'. *The Journal of*

Adolescent Health, 52(2 Suppl 2), S7–S13.

61. Recent studies have found that as children . . .: Siegel, DJ (2014). *Brainstorm*. Melbourne: Scribe.

72. Dr Kristy Goodwin, author of *Raising . . .*: Goodwin K (14 August 2019). 'Managing attention span in the age of digital distraction'. Generation Next conference, Sydney.

Chapter 5

85. Steven Stosny, author of the excellent . . .: Stosny S (1995). *Treating Attachment Abuse*.

95. Managing our energy levels is technically . . .: Shanker S & Barker T (2016). *Self-reg*. Canada: Penguin Random House.

Chapter 6

99. In October 2018 during Mental Health . . .: Poole G (October 2018), '10 Surprising Facts About Men's Mental Health'. Australian Men's Health Forum.

100. Danny 'Spud' Frawley was an AFL . . .: McKern J (10 September 2019). 'Frawley Family Release Statement After Sudden Death of Danny'. Accessed via news.com.au.

104. Listed below are comparative numbers for . . .: World Health Organization, Mental Health Foundation of New Zealand, UK Office for National Statistics, the American Foundation for Suicide Prevention, the New Zealand Ministry of Justice and the Journal of the American Medical Association.

105. A news bulletin issued by the World . . .: WHO (9 September 2019). 'One person dies every 40 seconds'.

105. In Australia in 2017, suicide remained . . .: Australian Bureau of Statistics, 'Causes of Death 2017'.

105. The New Zealand numbers are deeply . . .: Mental Health Foundation of New Zealand. 'Annual provisional suicide statistics for deaths reported to the Coroner between 1 July 2007 and 30 June 2018'. Accessed online 13 September 2019 via mentalhealth. org.nz.

107. Professor Matthew Large from the University . . .: Carroll, L (1 February 2019). 'Suicidal thoughts not a reliable warning'. University of New South Wales Newsroom.

117. Australian researchers who investigated the barriers ...: Wilson CJ, Rickwood D, Ciarrochi JV & Deane FP (2002). 'Adolescent barriers to seeking professional psychological help for personal-emotional and suicidal problems'. Conference Proceedings of the 9th Annual Conference for Suicide Prevention Australia, June 2002, Sydney.

120. Another relatively new therapy is called . . .: Marzbani H, Marateb HR & Mansourian M (2016). 'Neurofeedback: A Comprehensive Review on System Design, Methodology and Clinical Applications'. *Basic and Clinical Neuroscience*, 7(2), 143–158.

Chapter 7

133. There was an article published on Huffington . . .: Duberman A (8 May 2015). '34 Things Women Do To Stay Safe Show The Burden Of 'Being Careful'. *Huffington Post Australia*.

Chapter 8

143. In the publication *Paediatrics* in 2017 . . .: Mitchell C, McLanahan S, Schneper L, Garfinkel I, Brooks-Gunn J & Notterman D (2017). 'Father Loss and Child Telomere Length'. *Pediatrics*, 140(2), e20163245.

162. Supporting this, we know that non-heterosexual . . .: Haas AP, Eliason M, Mays VM, et al (2011). 'Suicide and Suicide Risk in Lesbian, Gay, Bisexual, and Transgender Populations: Review and Recommendations'. *Journal of Homosexuality*, 58(1), 10–51.

Chapter 9

166. According to an article in the *Sydney . . .*: Marcus C (13 April 2008). 'Generation Z: Rich and Forgotten'. *Sydney Morning Herald*.

178. 'In the 16-to-25 age group . . .: Snow D (17 January 2020). 'Lunch with RFS boss Shane Fitzsimmons: Tears on the darkest days'. *Sydney Morning Herald*.

Chapter 10

184. Katey McPherson, an American boy advocate . . .: *On Boys* podcast (31 January 2019).

Chapter 12

210. In his research, John Gottman shows . . .: Medina J (2014). *Brain Rules* (2nd edn). Seattle, WA: Pear Press.

Chapter 13

229. Dr Matthew Lieberman has done research . . .: Lieberman M & Eisenberger N (2008). 'The pains and pleasures of social life: a social cognitive neuroscience approach'. *Neuroleadership Journal.*

Chapter 14

246. Dr Adam Price has three Cs . . .: Price, A. (2017). *He's Not Lazy.* Sterling Publishing Co.

Chapter 15

255. A good example is St Kevin's College . . .: *7.30 Report* (19 February 2020). 'St Kevin's College principal resigns after Four Corners story'. ABC.

268. If you can make the time, please check out the documentary that was done on the ABC Compass program . . .: Noel Debien (2019). *From Boys to Men.* Compass, ABC.

Chapter 16

278. A study into friendships by the National . . .: Cloud J (17 July 2009). 'Why Girls Have BFFs and Boys Hang Out in Packs'. Time.com.

281. While there is research that shows . . .: Haggman K (15 November 2013). 'Why Video Games Make Healthy Stocking Stuffers'. QUT News.

285. Around 92 per cent of boys who . . . Glenza J (14 October 2014). 'Student-athlete Hazing Victims May Number 800,000 Per Year'. *The Guardian.*

285. In an article for the *New York* . . .: Reichert MC (30 March 2019). 'It's Dangerous to Be a Boy'. *New York Times.*

Chapter 17

299. This is the word that Steve . . .: Biddulph S (2018).

301. National statistics in Australia tell us . . .: Lee M, Crofts T, McGovern A & Milivojevic S (2015). 'Sexting among young people: Perceptions and practices'. Australian Institute of Criminology.

303. Sadly Australia seems to be leading . . .: Australian Institute of Health and Welfare (11 September 2019). 'Family, domestic and sexual violence snapshot'.

303. The Australian Bureau of Statistics' 2016 . . .: *Ibid.*

305. One survey of UK students and . . .: Weale S (12 December 2017). 'Sexual Harassment "rife" in schools but largely unreported, study says'. *The Guardian.*

308. Please take the time to read . . .: Anderson LH (2019). 'I've Talked With Teenage Boys About Sexual Assault for 20 Years. This Is What They Still Don't Know.' *Time.*

309. Indeed, in the 2016 National Drug . . .: Australian Institute of Health and Welfare (2017). 'National Drug Strategy Household Survey 2016: detailed findings'. *Drug Statistics*, 31(PHE 214). Canberra.

310. Half of all Australian children aged . . .: Pratt DR (2015). 'The "porn genie" is out of the bottle: understanding and responding to the impact of pornography on young people'. *InPsych.*

311. Reports of student-on-student sexual . . .: Balogh S & Parnell S (3 July 2017). 'Early sexualisation of kids blamed for rise in student attacks'. *The Australian.*

311. Sadly, child-to-child molestation . . .: Kozaki D (2016). 'Internet pornography causing long-term public health crisis amongst Australian children, seminar hears'. ABC News.

312. Girls are appearing in emergency departments . . .: Quadara A, El-Murr A & Latham J (2017). 'The effects of pornography on children and young people: An evidence scan. (Research Report)'. Australian Institute of Family Studies. Melbourne.

312. According to experts at a 2019 . . .:
Keogh B (2019). 'Teen boys battle
'distressing' thoughts of hurting girls
after watching violent pornography'.
Stuff.co.nz.
313. Online pornography exposure is
also contributing . . .: The Reward
Foundation (21 August 2016). 'Erectile
dysfunction in 20-year olds?'
313. There are some studies that show . . .:
Weir K (2014). 'Is pornography
addictive'. *American Psychological
Association*, April (Vol 45, No. 4).
323. Here are some statistics (from data . . .:
'State of Play' report by the Office
of the eSafety Commissioner and the
'Digital Australia Report 2018' by the
Interactive Games and Entertainment
Association.
331. Amount of time – currently in
Australia . . .: Rhodes A (June
2017). 'Screen time and kids: What's
happening in our homes?'. Australian
Child Health Poll, The Royal Children's
Hospital Melbourne.
331. Avoiding myopia – there has been a
significant . . .: Wu P, Chuang M, Choi J
et al (2019). 'Update in myopia and
treatment strategy of atropine use in
myopia control'. *Eye*, 33, 3–13.
339. Dr Kristy Goodwin reminds parents
often . . .: Goodwin K (12 December
2017). '8 Simple Strategies to Prevent
Your Child's Techno-tantrums'. Guest
Blog, maggiedent.com.

Chapter 19
342. In a research study led by Wayne . . .:
Abbey A, Zawacki T, Buck P, Clinton A
& McAuslan P (2004). 'Sexual assault
and alcohol consumption: what do we
know about their relationship and what
types of research are still needed?'.
Aggression and Violent Behavior, 9(3),
271–303.
343. In 2015, males aged 15–24
experienced . . .: Australian Institute of
Health and Welfare (2015), 'Australian
Burden of Disease Study: impact and
causes of illness and death in Australia
2015'. 19(BOD 22). Canberra: AIHW.
343. The Australian Secondary Students'
Alcohol and . . .: Guerin N & White
V (2019). 'ASSAD 2017 Statistics &
Trends: Trends in Substance Use Among
Australian Secondary Students'. Cancer
Council Victoria.
346–7. For young people, the risk of
fatality . . .: Biddulph S (11 January
2007). 'Mentally, teens drive best
alone'. *Sydney Morning Herald*.
347. Then there are hospitalisations as a
result . . .: Australian Institute of Health
and Welfare (2018). 'Hospitalised
injury due to land transport crashes'.
Injury research and statistics,
115(INJCAT 195). Canberra: AIHW.
347. According to the Australian Institute
of Health . . .: *Ibid*.

Chapter 20
349. Respected paediatrician and author
Meg Meeker . . .: Meeker M (2014),
Strong Mothers, Strong Sons. Random
House USA; Lashlie C (2005) *He'll Be
OK*. HarperCollins Publishers (New
Zealand).

Reference list

Anderson H, Angelo F and Stewart R (2015). *The Secret Business of Relationships, Love and Sex*. North Balwyn, Vic: Secret Girls' Business Publishing.

Biddulph S (2018). *Raising Boys in the 21st Century*. Sydney: Finch Publishing.

Biddulph S (2013). *The New Manhood*. Warriewood, NSW: Finch Publishing.

Brown S (2009). *Play: How it Shapes the Brain, Opens the Imagination, and Invigorates the Soul*. New York: Avery.

Chu JY (2014). *When Boys Become Boys: Development, Relationships, and Masculinity*. New York: NYU Press.

Clark E (2017). *Love, Sex and No Regrets: For today's teens*. Mona Vale, NSW: Finch Publishing.

Damour L (2020). *Under Pressure: Confronting the Epidemic of Stress and Anxiety in Girls*. New York: Ballantine Books.

Dent M (2018). *Mothering Our Boys: A guide for mums of sons*. Gerringong, NSW: Pennington Publications.

Dent M (2016, Rev. Edition). *Real Kids in an Unreal World: How to build resilience and self-esteem in today's children*. Murwillumbah, NSW: Pennington Publications.

Dent M (2010). *Saving Our Adolescents: Supporting today's adolescents through the bumpy ride to adulthood*. Murwillumbah, NSW: Pennington Publications.

Dillon P (2019, 7 September). '"We trusted our teen and we were terribly let down": A Mum warns other parents about "blind trust"'. Doing Drugs with Paul Dillon blog.

Duberman A (2015, 8 May). '34 Things Women Do To Stay Safe Show The Burden Of 'Being Careful'. *The Huffington Post*.

Dunckley VL (2014, 27 February). 'Gray Matters: Too Much Screen Time Damages the Brain'. *Psychology Today.*

Farrell W and Gray J (2019). *The Boy Crisis: Why Our Boys Are Struggling and What We Can Do About It.* Dallas: BenBella Books, Inc.

Gerreyn GA (2012). *Men of Honour: A Young Man's Guide to Exercise, Nutrition, Money, Drugs and Alcohol, Sex, Pornography and Masturbation.* Sydney: Freedom House Publishing.

Gillespie D (2019). *Teen Brain: Why screens are making your teenager depressed, anxious and prone to lifelong addictive illnesses – and how to stop it now.* Sydney: Pan Macmillan Australia.

Goodsell B, Lawrence D, Ainley J, Sawyer M, Zubrick SR and Maratos J (2017). *Child and Adolescent Mental Health and Educational Outcomes: An analysis of educational outcomes from Young Minds Matter: the second Australian Child and Adolescent Survey of Mental Health and Wellbeing.* Perth: Graduate School of Education, The University of Western Australia.

Goodwin K (2016). *Raising Your Child in a Digital World.* Sydney: Finch Publishing.

Grant I (2006). *Growing Great Boys.* Auckland, N.Z.: Random House New Zealand.

Gray P (2013). *Free to Learn: Why Unleashing the Instinct to Play Will Make Our Children Happier, More Self-Reliant, and Better Students for Life.* New York: Basic Books.

Greene R (2014). *Lost at School: Why Our Kids with Behavioral Challenges Are Falling Through the Cracks and How We Can Help Them.* New York: Scribner Book Company.

Gurian M (2017). *Saving Our Sons: A New Path For Raising Healthy and Resilient Boys.* Spokane, WA: Gurian Institute Press.

Gurian M (1999). *The Good Son: Shaping the moral development of our boys and young men.* New York: Jeremy P. Tarcher.

Gurian M (1996). *The Wonder of Boys: What parents, mentors, and educators can do to shape boys into exceptional men.* New York: Putnam.

Gurian M (1993). *Mothers, Sons and Lovers: How a man's relationship with his mother affects the rest of his life.* Boston, MA: Shambhala Publications Inc.

Gurian M and Stevens K (2005). *The Minds of Boys.* San Francisco, CA: Jossey-Bass.

Haesler D (2017). 'Harnessing the Minecraft mindset for success'. In R. Manocha (Ed). *Growing Happy, Healthy Young Minds* (pp. 292–306). Sydney: Hachette.

Hakanson C (2017). *Boy Puberty: How to Talk about Puberty and Sex with your Tween Boy.* WA: Sex Ed Rescue.

Haller T (2018). *Dissolving Toxic Masculinity: Nine Lessons for Raising Sons to Become Empathetic, Compassionate Men.* Michigan: Personal Power Press.

Kessler R (2000). *The Soul of Education: Helping Students Find Connection, Compassion and Character at School.* USA: ASCD Publications.

Kohn A (2005). *Unconditional Parenting: Moving from Rewards and Punishments to Love and Reason.* New York: Atria Books.

Lashlie C (2005). *He'll Be OK: growing gorgeous boys into good men.* Auckland, NZ: Harper Collins.

Leser D (2019). *Women, Men & the Whole Damn Thing*. Sydney: Allen & Unwin.

Marshall B (2019). *The Tech Diet for Your Child & Teen: The 7-step plan to unplug and reclaim your kid's childhood (and save your family's sanity)*. Sydney: Harper Collins.

Martin A (2003). *How to Motivate Your Child for School and Beyond*. Australia: Random House.

Medina J (2014). *Brain Rules: 12 Principles for Surviving and Thriving at Work, Home, and School*. Second edition. Seattle, WA: Pear Press.

Meeker M (2014). *Strong Mothers, Strong Sons: Lessons Mothers Need to Raise Extraordinary Men*. New York: Ballantine Books.

Oglethorpe M (2020). *The Modern Parent: Raising a great kid in the digital world*. Australia: The Modern Parent.

Orenstein P (2020). *Boys and Sex: Young men on hook-ups, love, porn, consent and navigating the new masculinity*. London: Souvenir Press.

Pollack WS (1998). *Real Boys: rescuing our sons from the myths of boyhood*. New York: Random House.

Poole G (10 October 2018). '10 Surprising Facts About Men's Mental Health'. Australian Men's Health Forum.

Price A (2017). *He's Not Lazy: Empowering your son to believe in himself*. US: Sterling Publishing Co.

Rubinstein A (2013). *The Making of Men: Raising boys to be happy, healthy and successful*. Sydney: Xoum.

Shanker S and Barker T (2016). *Self-reg: How to Help Your Child (and You) Break the Stress Cycle and Successfully Engage with Life*. Canada: Penguin Random House.

Shipp J (2017). *The Grown-Ups Guide to Teenage Humans: How to decode their behaviour, develop unshakable trust, and raise a respectable adult*. New York: Harper Collins.

Siegel DJ (2013). *Brainstorm: The power and purpose of the teenage brain*. USA: Tarcher.

Smiler AP (2016). *Dating and Sex: A guide for the 21st century teen boy*. Washington, DC: Magination Press.

Stewart R, Angelo F, Anderson H and Taylor J (2011). *Secret Boys' Business*. North Balwyn, Vic: Secret Girls' Business Publishing.

Stosny S (1995). *Treating Attachment Abuse: A Compassionate Approach*. New York: Springer Publishing Company.

Swingle M (2019). *i-Minds: How and Why Constant Connectivity is Rewiring our Brains and What to Do About It* (2nd edn). Gabriola, BC: New Society Publishers.

Walker L 'Pornography Exposure And Early Sexualisation Blamed For Rise In Student Attacks', echildhood.org. 3 July.

Weale S (12 Dec 2017). 'Sexual Harassment "rife" in schools but largely unreported, study says'. *The Guardian*.

Index

abuse
- impact of 65, 200–1, 287
- of girls/women 306–7, 312
- sexual 102–3, 305–7, 342
- verbal 119, 218–9
- *see also* bullying, violence

academic ability 14, 134, 257–8, 256, 267, 276–7, 337

acceptance 32, 36, 43–4, 62, 81, 90, 163–4, 221, 285, 287, 297, 323

accountability 53, 198, 202–4, 267, 289, 350

activity *see* physical activity

addiction 66–7, 85, 89, 103, 128, 143, 162, 185, 229, 289, 313, 326–8, 332, 343

ADHD (attention deficit hyperactivity disorder) 30, 71, 101, 265–6

adolescence 1–2, 9, 82
- in the past 19–20, 167
- today 3–7, 20, 166
- *see also* biological drivers

adolescent brain development 10–11, 32, 58–70, 76–8, 136, 169, 254

adult allies *see* lighthouses

adverse childhood experiences 77, 181, 331

affection 25, 135, 154, 161, 265, 278, 286

aggression 32, 34, 48, 53–4, 75–6, 87, 117, 119, 262, 283, 286, 289, 293, 312, 332
- nurturance 95, 288, 291–2, 339

alcohol 62–3, 66–7, 206, 289, 309, 342–5

Allison, Janet 223–4

alpha
- brainwaves 328
- males 39, 149, 231

anger 23, 48, 60, 77–8, 81, 84–5, 129, 146, 157, 217, 219, 233, 319
- difference between frustration and anger 94
- masking vulnerability 287–9
- parental anger 141, 198, 203, 214

ANTs (automatic negative thoughts) 11–12, 64

MDMA 344–5
Meeker, Meg 49, 349
memory *see* forgetfulness
mental health 99–103, 162, 166, 229,
    301, 338, 343
    assessment 116, 164–5, 250
    red flags 116–17
    support services 118–21
    see also anxiety, depression, suicide
Mental Health First Aid 107, 116
mentors 20, 22, 28, 66, 108, 167–8,
    175–7, 234, 267, 307–8
#MeToo movement 304
meth 345
mindfulness 11, 79, 120, 207
mindsets 30, 65, 183, 186, 190,
    239–40, 242, 253, 259, 265
Minecraft 311, 324–5
mistakes 198–204, 226
    see also choices
mothers and mother figures 36, 81,
    125–6, 172
    cold, distant 127–8, 130
    mother wound 126–7
    mum letter 137–8
    positive mothering 132–4, 204
    smothering 127
    stepping back 23, 132, 269, 348
    see also letting go, life skills
motivation 68, 69, 183, 238–52, 274–6,
    307, 332
    see also three Cs, the deal
movement 42, 47, 214, 249, 257, 264,
    333
    see also physical activity
multitasking 72–3,
myelin 70, 198, 319, 343
myopia 331

nagging 21, 41, 60, 130, 210–11,
    224–5, 245, 250, 355
narcissism 29, 87
nature 5–6, 11, 23, 27, 93, 109–11, 206
nervous system 67, 75, 78, 82–4, 120,
    232, 234

Netflix 4, 71, 167, 325
neuro divergence 26, 30, 61, 248,
    265–6, 325
Neurofeedback Therapy (or EEG
    Biofeedback) 120
neuroplasticity 141, 229, 329
nitrous oxide 344
NLP (neurolinguistic programming) 212

Oglethorpe, Martine 335
online dating apps 159, 314–15
online world 3–5, 30, 62, 183, 323, 330
Orenstein, Peggy 298–9, 313
organisational skills
    see disorganisation
outdoor activities 233–4
overstimulation 68–9, 207

pandemic 9, 146, 193
parties 62, 206, 345–7
passion *see* 'spark'
payback/retaliation 54
penis 2, 4, 54, 159, 258, 301–2
    see also erections
pets 50, 231, 233, 249
physical activity 11, 42, 85, 93, 332–3,
    359
    see also movement
play 23, 27–30, 45, 49, 185, 241–2,
    273, 279, 290
    code 279–88
    rough housing 47, 94–5, 97, 290–2
    see also gaming, sport
Pollack, William 35, 45, 279
poor choices *see* choices
pornography 3, 4, 66, 283, 305, 310–18
    influence on sexual behaviour 160,
        312
    porn induced erectile dysfunction
        313
    see also sex
positive noticing 132, 245–6
Post-it notes 60, 93, 131, 154, 225–6
    see also reminders
posture issues 332

pragmatism 46, 81, 206
prefrontal cortex *see* brain
presence/being present 126, 148–9, 207, 334
pressures 4, 14, 29–30, 44, 47, 193–4, 262, 275, 284, 299, 314, 333, 344
Price, Adam 246, 324
pride 86–7, 90
privacy 3, 118, 132, 160
psychology, boy to man 21–22, 71, 143,
puberty 19–20, 48, 61–2, 67, 83, 266, 315–17
punishment 43, 4990–1, 96, 102, 129–30, 183, 198, 201, 258–9, 262, 289, 292, 307

rape and rape culture 55, 159, 307–9, 314, 243
Reachout 118
Redmond, Derek 164
rejection, feeling rejected 84, 88, 97, 199, 287, 293–4
relationships, intimate 291, 297, 301, 312, 318–20
    see also sex
reminders 130–1, 225, 45
    see also Post-it notes
resilience 23, 99–100, 112–13, 171, 182, 187–93, 195–6, 204, 241–2, 325, 351, 357
respect 21, 33, 36, 40, 48, 54–6, 103, 108, 113, 134, 150, 156–8, 160, 162–5, 173, 183, 186, 221, 240, 247, 263, 299, 358
    disrespect/loss of 25, 47, 97, 125, 156–7, 160, 189, 191, 212, 255, 270, 287, 292–3, 298–310
    self-respect 29, 108, 134, 168, 320
responsibility 4, 21–2, 111, 168, 199, 226, 231, 240, 336, 340–1
rewards/reward pathways 64, 67–8, 223–4, 240–4, 275–6, 313, 322, 327, 329
ridicule 37, 156, 198, 338
    see also shame

Riley, Father Chris 167
risk 10, 25, 28–9, 32, 35, 36, 50, 51, 52, 63, 66–7, 96, 113, 175, 183, 206, 241, 277, 330, 339, 344–7
rites of passage 108, 235, 267–8
rituals 149, 155
roosters *see* temperament
Royal Commission into Institutional Responses to Child Sexual Abuse 103–4
Rubinstein, Arne 21
rules 24, 31, 48, 50, 111, 155, 203–4, 259, 299, 334, 345–6
    3 rules 54–5
    see also boundaries

sadness 76, 78, 81, 84, 184, 193
safe base/safety nets 15, 78, 107, 125, 193, 218–9, 230, 280–1, 289–90
sarcasm 89–90, 214, 267
    see also shame
school
    avoidance/opting out 32, 239, 262–3, 271
    disengagement 40, 53, 69, 78, 252, 254, 256–9, 262, 272, 324
    re-engaging reluctant boys 264, 273
    selection 253–5
    trade/vocational/higher education 187, 256, 267
    transitioning to senior 259, 276–7
self-esteem 65, 103, 243, 289, 294
self-harm 82, 218, 333
self-regulation 42, 50, 72–3, 95–7, 120, 286
self-worth 32, 42, 45, 50, 54, 61, 68, 86, 93, 95, 114, 132, 134, 150, 183–92, 205, 244–5, 247, 266, 267, 289, 322
sensitive (nature of boys) 74, 88, 203, 230
separation, parental 158
SET (Simple Energy Techniques) 120

sex
creep behaviour 298–9, 303–9, 312, 314
education about healthy 159–60, 297–8, 314–18
sexism 160–1, 255, 299
sexting/image sharing 4, 301–2
sexual harassment, violence and stalking 285, 293, 303–6, 342–4
sexual orientation 161–3, 301
sexual stereotypes 160–1, 300–1
see also gender roles/stereotypes, pornography, rape and rape culture, relationships
shame 35, 49, 78, 86, 88, 103, 147, 162–3, 181–2, 184, 189–91, 198, 264, 282, 285–6
shaming boys 89, 90, 130, 150, 160–1, 200–2
shaming language 39–90, 203, 214, 236, 248
Shanker, Stuart 95–6
Shipp, Josh 202–4
shouting 89, 130, 150, 203, 211, 248
Siegel, Daniel 64, 228–9
silliness 53–4, 96
sleep 72, 117, 173, 212, 332, 358
Smith, Steve 191–2
social media 4, 9, 284, 323–4
social conditioning see male code
'spark' 12, 174, 176, 273, 281, 327
sport 5–6, 28, 30, 65, 109, 136, 188–9, 192, 235, 254, 257–8, 274, 304, 327, 336
St Kevin's College 255
stories, sharing stories 53, 134, 190–2, 231–2, 234
stress 9, 11–12, 58–9, 72, 78, 95–6, 116, 136–8, 166
easing 11, 50, 54, 80
parental 20, 54, 155
stressors 177, 195–6
see also anxiety, cortisol, emotional barometer, tipping point
Stynes, Jim 191

suicide 99, 104–8, 116–17, 148–9, 162, 184–7, 209–10, 301
support services 118–21
surfing 109–15
Swingle, Mari 260, 328–9

tapping 93, 120
teachers 20, 36–40, 53, 66, 171–2, 179, 243, 254, 260–2, 270–1
technology 322–3
and school 260–1, 270, 336–7
benefits 6, 261, 281
problematic usage 322, 327, 337–41
see also brain, digital world, gaming
telomeres 143
temperament (roosters and lambs) 38–9, 48–9, 86, 133, 231
testosterone 32, 96, 324
tests see assessments
three Cs – connection, competence, control 246–248, 250, 324
see also motivation
time out 97, 210, 353
timing 97, 136, 214–15, 219
tipping point 79–83, 85, 91–3, 102, 157, 173, 195, 209, 218
see also emotional barometer
touch 135, 227, 231, 305–6
toxic masculinity 33, 175, 199, 236–7, 283–4
see also male code
transitions 9, 93, 96–7, 108, 227, 263, 267–8, 280, 349, 353
tribe 2, 24–5, 27–8, 82, 134, 175, 250, 281, 297, 354, 359
trust 118, 168, 174, 176, 212, 237, 242, 285, 345–6

validation 43–4, 62, 84, 87, 160, 184, 190, 203, 211–12, 220–1, 233, 244
vasopressin 32, 324
violence 4, 34, 54, 103, 105, 140–1, 279–80, 285, 311–2, 316, 342
visualisation 120, 190–2, 274–5
vitamin D deficiency 331